Reading Visual Narratives

Functional Linguistics
Series Editor: Robin P. Fawcett, Cardiff University

This series publishes monographs that seek to understand the nature of language by exploring one or other of various cognitive models or in terms of the communicative use of language. It concentrates on studies that are in, or on the borders of, various functional theories of language.

Published

Functional Dimensions of Ape–Human Discourse
Edited by James D. Benson and William S. Greaves

System and Corpus: Exploring Connections
Edited by Geoff Thompson and Susan Hunston

Meaningful Arrangement: Exploring the Syntactic Description of Texts
Edward McDonald

Explorations in Stylistics
Andrew Goatly

From Language to Multimodality: New Developments in the Study of Ideational Meaning
Edited by Carys Jones and Eija Ventola

Text Type and Texture
Edited by Gail Forey and Geoff Thompson

An Introduction to the Grammar of Old English: A Systemic Functional Approach
Michael Cummings

Morphosyntactic Alternations in English: Functional and Cognitive Perspectives
Edited by Pilar Guerrero Medina

Systemic Functional Perspectives of Japanese: Descriptions and Applications
Edited by Elizabeth Thomson and William Armour

Contrastive Discourse Analysis: Functional and Corpus Perspectives
Edited by Maite Taboada, Susana Doval Suárez and Elsa González Álvarez

Choice in Language: Applications in Text Analysis
Edited by Gerard O'Grady, Lise Fontaine and Tom Bartlett

Systemic Phonology: Recent Studies in English
Edited by Wendy L. Bowcher and Bradley A. Smith

Reading Visual Narratives

Image Analysis of Children's Picture Books

Clare Painter, J. R. Martin and Len Unsworth

SHEFFIELD UK   BRISTOL CT

Published by Equinox Publishing Ltd.

UK: Unit S3, Kelham House, 3 Lancaster Street, Sheffield S3 8AF
USA: ISD, 70 Enterprise Drive, Bristol, CT 06010

www.equinoxpub.com

Paperback edition published 2014.

ISBN: 978-1-84553-198-0 (hardback)
         978-1-78179-101-1 (paperback)

British Library Cataloguing-in-Publication Data
A catalogue record for this book is available from the British Library.

Library of Congress Cataloging-in-Publication Data
Painter, Clare, 1947–
       Reading visual narratives : image analysis of children's picture books / Clare Painter,
       J. R. Martin and Len Unsworth.
           p. cm. – (Functional linguistics)
       ISBN 978-1-84553-198-0 (hardcover)
    1. Picture books for children–History and criticism. 2. Narration (Rhetoric)
    I. Martin, J. R., 1950– II. Unsworth, Len. III. Title.
       PN1009.A1P228 2012
       809'.89282–dc23
                                                                          2012000196

Typeset by JS Typesetting Ltd, Porthcawl, Mid Glamorgan
Printed and bound in Great Britain by Lightning Source UK, Milton Keynes.

For Gunther

Contents

Preface

The research we are voicing in this book was initially inspired by Talia Gill's 2002 honours thesis, entitled *Visual and Verbal Playmates: An Exploration of Visual and Verbal Modalities in Children's Picture Books* (Department of Linguistics, University of Sydney). This groundbreaking work drew on systemic functional models of language and image to analyse intermodality in Anthony Browne's *Gorilla* and Helen Cooper's *The Baby Who Wouldn't Go to Bed*. Talia's work convinced Len, Clare and Jim of the need for further research on verbiage/image relations in picture books.

In 2003 an internal University of Sydney grant allowed us to employ Talia on a part-time basis to advance the work and prepare for a large external grant. In 2004 we successfully applied for an Australian Research Council Discovery grant, which funded the project from 2005 to 2007. This grant funded Sumin Zhao to undertake her doctoral study on the pedagogic discourse of electronic primary school social science resources. It also provided further part-time funding for Talia, and in addition for Maree Stenglin and Chris Cleirigh. Chris worked closely with Len on primary school science texts, and also innovated some exciting work on Sendak's classic *Where the Wild Things Are*. During this period Ariane Welch undertook pioneering work on facial affect as part of her honours program, and this was followed up by Ping Tian in her doctoral study of evaluation in Anthony Browne's picture books.

During 2007, 2008 and 2009 Clare and Jim met weekly to adapt the analysis of images proposed by Kress and van Leeuwen (*Reading Images* 1996, 2006) to what we found in children's picture books, alongside working up a model of verbiage/image relations. Len attended these meetings on a regular basis, supporting the discussions and reporting on his science text research. Over 2010 and 2011 Clare then carefully compiled the collective research into the present volume, usually able to rely on little more than editorial support from her 'co-authors'. Len and Jim gratefully acknowledge Clare's tremendous contribution to ensuring this book has gone to press in a timely fashion.

We would like to take this opportunity to thank all in our systemic functional community who lent an ear and gave advice in support of this work during presentations in our Sydney Friday afternoon systemic-functional linguistics seminar series, regional systemic-functional linguistics meetings in Mendoza, Miraflores, Gorizia, Armidale, Brisbane and Adelaide, and international ISFC congresses in Odense, Sydney and Beijing.

Over the decades, our colleague, comrade and friend, Gunther Kress, has been a constant source of inspiration as far as our work on genre, education and social semiosis is concerned. We dedicate this work to him in honor of his ongoing initiatives opening up the field of children's interaction with words and pictures from home through school.

Acknowledgements

The authors would like to thank the following for permission to reproduce material in figures or tables in this book as noted:

Figure 2.1 from *Granpa* by John Burningham, published by Red Fox. Reprinted by permission of The Random House Group Ltd.

Figure 2.19 and Table 2.2 from *So Much* by Trish Cooke and illustrated by Helen Oxenbury. Illustrations © 1994 Helen Oxenbury. Reproduced by permission of Walker Books Australia on behalf of Walker Books Ltd.

Figures 3.14 and 3.15 from *Grandpa* by Lilith Norman and Noela Young. Text copyright © Lilith Norman, 1988. Illustrations copyright © Noela Young, 1988. First published by Margaret Hamilton Books, a division of Scholastic Australia, 1988.

Figures 2.6, 2.12 and 4.5, and Table 2.4 from *Piggybook* by Anthony Browne. Illustrations © 1986 Anthony Browne. Reproduced by permission of Walker Books Australia on behalf of Walker Books Ltd.

Figure 2.4 from *The Tinpot General and the Old Iron Woman* by Raymond Briggs (Hamish Hamilton, 1984). Copyright © Raymond Briggs, 1984. Reproduced by permission of Penguin Books Ltd.

Figure 2.4 from *Drac and the Gremlin* by Allan Baillie and Jane Tanner, published by Puffin. Reproduced with permission by Penguin Group (Australia).

Figures 2.4 and 2.11 from *Grandad's Gifts* by Paul Jennings and Peter Gouldthorpe, published by Puffin. Reproduced with permission by Penguin Group (Australia).

Figures 2.8, 3.4, 3.5, 3.20 and 3.21 from *Sunshine* by Jan Ormerod. Reproduced with permission from Frances-Lincoln Publishers.

Figures 2.9 and 2.10 from *The Great Bear* by Libby Gleeson and illustrated by Armin Greder. Reproduced with permission from Libby Gleeson and Armin Greder.

Figures 2.13 and 3.23–3.26 from *Lucy's Bay* by Gary Crew and Gregory Rogers. Reproduced with permission from the Gary Crew and Gregory Rogers.

Figure 2.14 from *Gorilla* by Anthony Browne. Illustrations © 1983 Anthony Browne. Reproduced by permission of Walker Books Australia on behalf of Walker Books Ltd.

Figures 2.16, 3.16 and 4.29 from *Not Now, Bernard* by David McKee. Illustrations © 1980 David McKee. Reproduced by permission of Andersen Press.

Figure 2.16 from *Black Dog* by Pamela Allen, published by Puffin. Reproduced with permission by Penguin Group (Australia).

Figure 2.16 from *The Baby's Catalogue* by Janet and Allen Ahlberg (Viking, 1982) Copyright © Janet and Allan Ahlberg, 1982. Reproduced by permission of Penguin Books Ltd.

Figure 2.16 from *Come Away From the Water Shirley* by John Burningham, published by Red Fox. Reprinted by permission of The Random House Group Ltd.

Figures 2.16 and 3.22 from *The Snowman* by Raymond Briggs (Hamish Hamilton, 1978). Copyright © Raymond Briggs, 1978. Reproduced by permission of Penguin Books Ltd.

Figure 2.21 from cover of *Night Of the Gargoyles* by Eve Bunting, illustrated by David Wiesner. Jacket illustration copyright © 1994 by David Weiser. Reprinted by permission of Clarion Books, an imprint of Houghton Mifflin Harcourt Publishing Company. All rights reserved.

Figure 2.22 from *Into the Forest* by Anthony Browne. Illustrations © 2004 Anthony Browne. Reproduced by permission of Walker Books Australia on behalf of Walker Books Ltd.

Figure 3.1 from *The Baby Who Wouldn't Go to Bed* by Helen Cooper, published by Picture Corgi. Reprinted by permission of The Random House Group Ltd.

Figure 3.3 and 4.14 from *Possum Magic* by Mem Fox and Julie Vivas. Text copyright © Mem Fox, 1983. Illustrations copyright © Julie Vivas, 1983. First published by Omnibus Books, a division of Scholastic Australia, 1983.

Figures 3.7 and 3.8 from *Each Peach Pear Plum* by Janet and Allen Ahlberg (Viking, 1978). Copyright © Janet and Allan Ahlberg, 1978. Reproduced by permission of Penguin Books Ltd.

Figures 3.17 and 3.18 from *Prince Cinders* by Babette Cole (Hamish Hamilton, 1987). Text and illustrations copyright © Babette Cole 1987. 1997, Puffin Books, London. Reproduced by permission of Penguin Books Ltd. and G. P. Putnam Sons, A Division of Penguin Young Readers Group. A Member of Penguin Group (USA) Inc., 345 Hudson Street, New York, NY 10014. All rights reserved.

Figure 4.1 from *Kitten's First Full Moon* by Kevin Henkes. Copyright © 2004 by Kevin Henkes. Used by permission of Harper Collins Publishers.

Figure 4.1 from *What Faust Saw* by Matt Ottley, published by Hodder and Stoughton. Reprinted with permission by Matt Ottley.

Figure 4.6 from *Rose Blanche* by C. Gallaz and R. Innocenti, published by Cape. Reprinted by permission of The Creative Company.

Figure 4.7 from *An Evening at Alfie's* by Shirley Hughes, published by Red Fox. Reprinted by permission of The Random House Group Ltd.

Figures 4.11 and 4.12 from *Don't Forget The Bacon* by Pat Hutchins, published by Red Fox. Reprinted by permission of The Random House Group Ltd. Electronic reproduction: Copyright © 1978 by Pat Hutchins. Used by permission of HarperCollins Publishers.

Figure 4.13 from *I Went Walking* by Sue Machin and Julie Vivas. Text copyright © Sue Machin, 1989. Illustrations copyright © Julie Vivas, 1989. First published by Omnibus Books, a division of Scholastic Australia, 1989.

Figures 4.15 and 4.17 from *Hyram and B* by Brian Caswell and illustrated by Matt Ottley. Reproduced with permission from Brian Caswell and Matt Ottley.

Figure 4.19 from *Voices in the Park* by Anthony Browne, published by Picture Corgi. Reprinted by permission of The Random House Group.

Figure 4.20 from *Goodnight Moon* © 1947 Harper & Row. Text © renewed 1975 by Roberta Brown Rauch. Illustrations © renewed 1975 by Edith Hurd, John Thacher Hurd and George Hellyer, as Trustees of the Edith and Clement Hurd 1982 Trust. Used by Permission of Harper Collins Publishers.

Figure 4.22 from *Olivia* by Ian Falconer. Copyright © 2000 Ian Falconer. Reprinted with the permission of Atheneum Books for Young Readers, an imprint of Simon & Schuster Children's Publishing Division.

Figures 5.3 and 5.4 from *Way Home* by Libby Hathorn and Illustrated by Greg Rogers Published in 1995. Reprinted by permission of Random House Australia and Andersen Press.

1 Reading the Visual in Children's Picture Books

1.1 Picture books as a site for multimodal discourse analysis

Children's picture book stories play a foundational role in the lives and education of young children in several ways. There is, first and foremost, the sheer delight that children take in them, whether reading or being read to, and the fact that these activities are generally regarded as an essential preparation for the child's transition into literacy and future school success. As well, picture books in narrative form arguably provide the beginning reader with an entry into the highly valued realm of literature (Meek, 1988), giving these books additional value which is capitalised on in 'literature based' reading programs in primary schools. Finally, picture books, most obviously those in narrative form, constitute a significant instrument of socialisation, as a source of both overt and covert 'ideological' messages about the world and about social values (Stephens, 1992). Perhaps for this reason, there is a growing number of contemporary picture book narratives addressed to older readers on more serious themes, such as war, history or ecology (e.g. Briggs, 1984; Jorgensen and Harrison-Lever, 2002; Wolfer and Harrison-Lever, 2005; Marsden and Tan, 1998; Van Allsburg, 1990; Baker, 1991).

Children's picture books, then, can be recognised as a key means of apprenticeship into literacy, literature and social values, which in turn means that how they are constructed to accomplish these ends is an important educational question. Since most of the space in picture books is given over to the pictures, it is reasonable to suppose that the visual component of the books, quite as much as the verbal, is crucial in this apprenticeship. But because reading, and especially reading literature, so centrally involves an engagement with written language, it has often been easy to assume that the pictures in picture books mainly serve to help children identify the meanings of the words, or function simply to make reading generally more congenial to the young. This book, on the other hand, joins a growing body of critical work arguing that picture books need to be taken seriously as a bimodal[1] form of text in which the visual modality plays just as important a role as the verbal one in creating meaning and shaping readers (see e.g. Anstey and Bull, 2000; Arizpe and Styles, 2003; Kiefer, 1995; Lewis, 2001; Nodelman, 1988, [1999] 2005; Schwarcz, 1982; Schwarcz and Schwarcz, 1991; Serafini, 2010; Unsworth and Wheeler, 2002).

The challenge arising from taking this position is that although knowledge about language – for example, about sound/letter relationships, grammar, punctuation and literary technique – are part of the toolkit of all literacy educators, relevant knowledge about how images work is less widespread. Most important here is not information about the techniques and materials of creating art, or a critical apparatus for judging images in picture books as works of art, but rather understandings about the nature of the *meanings* that can be conveyed by visual choices, and how these may relate to the structural and verbal components of the narrative text. This book develops analytical tools for understanding the visual strand of meaning in picture books that will be of use and value to literacy educators and children's literature specialists and suggests how they can be deployed alongside linguistic analysis in the interpretation of text. In addressing these goals, it will draw on and contribute to the more general field of 'multimodal' discourse analysis (O'Halloran, 2004; Jewitt, 2009).

Multimodal discourse analysis (MDA) has been a growing area of research in recent years, particularly within the field of 'social semiotics' (van Leeuwen, 2005a) – a field that has been strongly influenced by systemic-functional linguistics (hereafter SFL; Halliday, 1978, 2003; Halliday and Matthiessen 2004, 2009). SF linguists and other discourse analysts have become increasingly aware that even a rich socially and semantically based linguistic analysis of contemporary texts can provide only a partial description of how they work to create meaning. With the growing importance of the internet as a source of information and the 'incursion of the visual' (Peim, 2005: 30) into formerly language-dominated forms, such as print newspapers and textbooks, text analysts have had to face the challenge of describing textual forms which combine language with different 'modalities', such as image or sound (Baldry and Thibault, 2006; Bednarek and Martin, 2010; Djonov, 2007; Djonov *et al.*, forthcoming; Iedema, 2003; Kress and van Leeuwen, 2001; Lemke 1998, 2002; Martinec and Salway, 2005; Royce and Bowcher, 2007; Ventola *et al.*, 2004).

This enterprise requires, first, a rich description of the different modalities being brought into a relationship within any multimodal text. Contributing to this project, social semiotics has provided inaugural 'grammars' of image (Kress and van Leeuwen, 1996, 2006; O'Toole, 1994, 1995), sound (van Leeuwen, 1999), movement (Martinec, 2000, 2001), three-dimensional space (Stenglin, 2004, 2008) and film

---

1. More accurately 'bisemiotic' since both linguistic and visual meaning may occur in different modes; however in discussions of the picture book, the more familiar 'bimodal' can be accepted as referring unambiguously to the use of written language in concert with printed illustrations.

(Bateman, 2007, 2009), all drawing on and complementing the model of language provided by SFL. Second, MDA calls for a framework for understanding the synergy between the different modalities within a multimodal text. A number of suggestions have been put forward based on examination of particular kinds of multimodal texts, including documents (Bateman, 2008, 2011), science articles (Lemke, 1998), school science materials (Unsworth and Cleirigh, 2009), advertisements (Kress and van Leeuwen, 2006; O'Halloran, 2008; Royce, 1998; Thibault, 2000), television documentary (Iedema, 2003) and newsprint material (Caple, 2008, 2009; Macken-Horarik, 2003a, b), and ultimately all depend on a satisfactory description of the non-language modalities in play.

In our experience, these descriptions are ongoing projects, in need of continuing development (Martin, 2011). In particular we have found that the visual grammars currently available need expansion and refinement to be maximally useful for picture book analysis and research. Just as the elaboration of a semantically based verbal grammar by SFL (Halliday and Matthiessen, 2004) was informed by linguistic investigations of many different registers and genres, including scientific English (Halliday, 2004; Halliday and Martin, 1993), conversation (Eggins and Slade, 1997), and legal (Körner, 2000), media (Iedema *et al.*, 1994) and literary (Halliday, 2002) texts, so it can be argued that our current understandings of visual meaning need to be further developed through closer exploration of a variety of different visually based text types. While Kress and Van Leeuwen's (1996, 2006) pioneering visual grammar provides an invaluable foundation for the understanding of a broad range of images, it is insufficiently developed for addressing key aspects of picture books – for example, the nature of relations between images in a sequence, the range of possibilities for point of view in a visual narrative and the visual resources for emotional engagement with the reader in such texts.

This book therefore examines children's picture book narratives with a dual aim: on the one hand to contribute insights useful for the better understanding of how any individual picture book makes meaning, and on the other to contribute to MDA by extending the social semiotic account of the visual modality and suggesting how it can be considered in relation to verbal meaning. These aims arise from a recognition of the value of picture books as significant educational and socialising texts worthy of closer attention in their own right, and also from the expectation that developing analytical tools for such texts will push the boundaries of current descriptions of the visual modality and assist theorising of intermodal meaning relations.

To lay the groundwork for this endeavour, the rest of this chapter will briefly consider the literature on the picture book as a complex bimodal text before outlining the social semiotic model of SFL that provides the framework for the following three chapters. Each of these elaborates on one area of visual meaning and illustrates how it functions, with examples drawn from highly regarded picture book stories. The final chapter will look at correspondences and complementarities between the visual and verbal semiotics and suggest a framework for analysing a picture book as a visual–verbal unity.

1.2   The picture book and its criticism

Children's literature criticism in recent decades has recognised the unique position of picture books within the field (Sipe, 2011: 238). As Hunt (1991: 175) observes: 'Children's literature borrows from all genres. But there is one genre that it has *contributed*, that of the picture book, as opposed to the illustrated book.' Although Hunt here refers to the picture book as a 'genre', there are various different literary and textual genres encompassed by the form (Anstey and Bull, 2000: ch. 4), even when discounting alphabet books, concept books, number books and informational texts, all of which have been excluded from consideration here. For example, a picture book story may be a fairytale, a fable, a piece of historical fiction, a simple recount of contemporary daily life, a moral exemplum, a true narrative with problematic experience getting resolved by the protagonist, or it may be some hybrid or combination of these (see Martin and Rose, 2008 for a linguistically based taxonomy of story types). In terms of the bimodality of the form, there are 'wordless' books with only a visual story and comic book formats without a verbal narration at one extreme, and 'illustrated stories' at the other, with every variation in the quantity of words to image in between. All of these story forms will be relevant in the chapters to follow.

Much of the critical literature on picture books arises from an educational focus on the child reader at home or in school. One major strand examines children's responses during or following picture book readings, as a means of throwing light on their visual and general literacy. Crawford and Hade (2000), for example, survey a number of studies of children's responses to wordless picture books as well as categorising those from three children in their own study, while Lewis (1992) and Torr (2008) note differences between adults' and pre-school children's interpretations during readings of a specific bimodal text. Kiefer (1995) reports on close classroom observations of children's conversations and discussions of picture books, an approach extended by Styles and Arizpe (2001) and Arizpe and Styles (2002, 2003), who also use semi-structured interviews with children of different ages to probe their understandings of specific picture books. More recently, it has been responses to 'postmodern' picture books that have been under attention, by Pantaleo (2002, 2004, 2008) and several contributors in Sipe and Pantaleo (2008). All of this research is of great interest in terms of children's visual literacy, and much of it can support the claim by Arizpe and Styles (2003: 27) that 'picturebooks encourage intellectual growth in children'. It will not, however, be taken further in this book, where the focus will be on the text itself rather than its child or adult readers.

Other educationally oriented studies have been concerned more directly with pedagogy, whether it be explicit teaching in the classroom or implicit teaching in the home. For example, Anstey and Bull (2000: ch.10; 2006: ch. 4), Barone (2011: ch. 6), Bull and Anstey (2010), Doonan (1993: ch. 5), Michaels and Walsh (1990), Stephens and Watson (1994) and Williams (1998) all suggest, model or report on strategies for using picture books in the classroom. A related strand of educational work considers the pedagogic nature of parental 'talk around the text' in relation to the child's language and/or literacy development (e.g. Torr and Clugston, 1999; Rose, 2011), sometimes with a particular focus on the educational significance of the way joint book reading is managed differently by different social groups (Torr, 2004; Williams, 2001). While recognising the value of research into children's understandings, the importance of informed classroom teaching approaches and the fact that picture-book meanings are most often negotiated in oral contexts between adult and child, *Reading Visual Narratives* has set aside these issues in order to address itself solely to the textuality of the books themselves, particularly the images in the books. In doing this, our expectation is that a more comprehensive visual grammar and further theorising on intermodality will also be a useful base for informing future reader-oriented studies and those examining oral/aural contexts of use.

When it comes to picture books as textual objects, it is still the case that reviewers frequently include only very general, if laudatory, comments on the images, as noted by Unsworth and Wheeler (2002). This is in spite of the visual element in these books having received some serious attention within the field of children's literature criticism, most notably in Nodelman's (1988) *Words about Pictures,* which remains an authoritative classic in the field. In this book Nodelman discusses the variety of pictorial styles found in picture books, and the way that elements such as the medium, texture, colour, framing, size and shape of visuals create a particular 'tone'. The focus on the effects of different choices in the use of these elements provides valuable and generalisable insights, just as his exemplifications offer illuminating observations about classic picture book texts. In his discussions, Nodelman draws on insights from various sources, including Arnheim's (1974) *Art and Visual Perception* and Moebius's (1986) account of 'picture book codes', both of which similarly shed light on the meaning of visual *choices,* rather than focussing primarily on either art practice or the appraisal of individual master works. In this respect, Nodelman's work, like that of Bang (1991), is in harmony with the approach taken here, even though it is ultimately grounded in art theory rather than social semiotics.

In discussing the relationship between images and words in the story Nodelman emphasises the different affordances of the two modalities and the fact that they create the text together, concluding:

> Because they communicate different kinds of information, and because they work together by limiting each other's meanings, words and pictures necessarily have a combative relationship; their complementarity is a matter of opposites completing each other by virtue of their differences. As a result the relationships between pictures and texts in picturebooks tend to be ironic: each speaks about matters on which the other is silent. (Nodelman, 1988: 221)

Other writers have attempted to taxonomise the specific relationships possible between word and image, with Schwarcz (1982) offering one of the earliest analyses, suggesting 'congruency' and 'deviation' as the major types, each having a number of subcategories (cf. Golden 1990: ch. 6). More recently, picture books themselves have been classified into types according to the relations between images and words. For example, Agosto (1999) distinguishes 'parallel storytelling' (visual and verbal redundancy) from 'interdependent storytelling', suggesting eight subcategories of the latter, grouped within two main types that recall those of Schwarcz: 'augmentation' and 'contradiction'. Another alternative is Nikolajeva and Scott's (2001) five-way classification, ranging from 'symmetrical' books (visual and verbal redundancy), 'complementary' ones (visual and verbal do different work – filling each other's gaps; cf. Nodelman, 1988, above), 'expanding/enhancing' books (one modality supports the other), 'counterpointing' books (each modality tells its own story, which depends on the other for effect) and 'sylleptic' versions (containing independent narratives). While the diversity of picture books is brought into focus in these classification schemes, a general problem with them is that they allow for only one possible kind of relationship between any image and the words it accompanies and/ or propose that a single kind of relationship will hold throughout the text. Chapter 5 of this book will provide an alternative approach based on the theoretical approach outlined in Section 1.3 below.

What becomes very clear from all this analytical work is the sophistication of picture books as both visual and bimodal texts, a theme that has been taken up in other recent publications coming from a range of disciplinary standpoints. These include Doonan's (1999) explorations of Anthony Browne's books, and Lacey's (1986) and Albers's (2008) discussions of Caldecott prizewinners, all informed by a fine arts perspective; Sipe's (1998) account of text/image 'synergy', drawing on semiotic theory; and Spitz's (1999) readings of classic American picture book texts coming from a psychological perspective. A more socially oriented approach is taken by Coats (2010) in her examination of the role of postmodern picture books in identity formation and by Stephens (1992), who unpacks the ideological content of a range of children's fiction, including selected picture book texts. Social semiotics has also been drawn on in recent years in the form of the visual grammar described by Kress and van Leeuwen (1996, 2006). For example, Lewis (2001), in his general introduction to the picture book field, proposes the grammar as a valuable tool that can be utilised to deconstruct picture book images, usefully summarising Kress and van Leeuwen's (1996) analytical categories in an appendix. Similarly, Serafini (2010) advocates using Kress and van Leeuwen's (2006) account as one of three necessary approaches to analysing picture books. However, while these authors are interested in applying Kress and van Leeuwen's analytical tools to the reading of contemporary picture books, their projects do not involve developing them further in relation to such data, which is a principal goal of the current volume. To elaborate on this, the theoretical background to this work will be outlined in the next section.

1.3   Using systemic functional theory

1.3.1   The metafunctional framework of systemic-functional linguistics

As noted earlier, Kress and van Leeuwen's (1996, 2006) account of visual meaning is situated within the broad field of social semiotics, which draws inspiration from Halliday's systemic-functional theory of language. One central insight of this linguistic theory is the idea that every text realises three kinds of meanings simultaneously, since every text fulfils a threefold purpose. First, a text must be *about* something; it must represent the material and mental world. At the same time it must enable communicative interaction with others: what is represented must be able to be asserted, queried, commanded, hedged, denied, imbued with feeling, and so on. Thirdly it must make sense in being *relevant* to previous utterances or to a shared situation. These three fundamental purposes, or 'metafunctions', create three kinds of meaning that are co-present in every instance of text. Ideational meaning refers to the representation of the content or subject matter of what is expressed, while interpersonal meaning encompasses the roles and relationships between speaker and hearer or writer and reader, together with attitudes and stances incorporated into the text; finally the 'textual' aspect of meaning refers to the means by which a piece of text is organised so as to be coherent in relation to co-text and context, through devices for linking, referring, foregrounding and backgrounding.

In the adaptations of SFL to the visual modality within MDA, the three metafunctions have always been recognised by scholars working in this area – but sometimes renamed in slightly different ways, as shown in Table 1.1.

Table 1.1 Terminology for the three metafunctions.

Author	Data analysed	Metafunctions		
Halliday, 1978	Language	Ideational	Interpersonal	Textual
Kress and van Leeuwen, 1996, 2006	All image types	Ideational (representation)	Interpersonal (interaction and modality)	Textual (composition)
Lemke, 2002	Websites	Presentational	Orientational	Organisational
O'Toole, 1994	Fine art paintings	Representational	Modal	Compositional

In order to foreground metafunctional continuity across various modalities of communication, this book will maintain the original terms developed by Halliday for verbal language (ideational, interpersonal and textual). This does not, however, imply that we will impose verbal grammatical categories on the visual data.

1.3.2   System and text

Within SFL, a semiotic system is viewed as a resource for meaning – one that is organised into sets of choices within each of the three metafunctions. Following from this, a second key theoretical tool from Halliday's theory used within MDA is the formalism of the 'system network'. A 'system' is a set of meaning choices for which expressive realisations can be specified. This is exemplified in Figure 1.1, a simplified account of some basic grammatical options within the interpersonal metafunction for an English clause. These options constitute the system of MOOD,

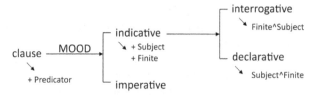

Figure 1.1 A simple system: basic options in mood.

(conventionally written in small capitals to indicate that it is the name of a system). This system consists of a choice of [indicative] as against [imperative] and, if [indicative], there is a further subsystem choice of [interrogative] or [declarative]. (A term is written in square brackets within a prose text when we wish to emphasise or clarify its status as an option or 'feature' within a system).

For each option in a system there is some expression or 'realisation' in form, which can be specified by means of a downward sloping arrow as shown in the figure. In a linguistic grammatical network such as this one, the realisation is the presence or arrangement of some element of grammatical structure. Thus, Figure 1.1 shows that the feature, [clause], is realised by the presence of an element called Predicator, while an [indicative] choice is realised by the presence of two further structural elements: Finite and Subject. An [interrogative] choice arranges the Finite before the Subject (as in *has he?*), while a [declarative] choice arranges the Subject before the Finite (Subject^Finite, as in *he has*). A system such as the one shown for MOOD can be extended in 'delicacy' to additional subsystems as finer and finer distinctions are made. For example, different types of interrogative (the *what/ where/when* type versus the *yes/no* type) could be added here for a more detailed description.

A further aspect of any semiotic system is that, even within the same metafunction, there may be more than one meaning system in play. So, for example, another significant interpersonal choice for an English clause is that of being [positive] or [negative]. Figure 1.1 can therefore be extended to become a 'system network' by the addition of the system of POLARITY as in Figure 1.2. This figure uses a curly brace to indicate that two systems are in play simultaneously. It is therefore to be read as saying that any clause is either [positive] or [negative] *and* either [indicative] or [imperative]. The formalism of the system network is designed to provide a descriptive tool for language when viewed as a 'meaning potential' rather than a set of rules. As shown in Figure 1.1, the meaning potential is described as a paradigmatic set of 'opposing' choices, each of which ultimately has some reflex in structure. Taken as a whole, the system networks developed for a particular language or other modality of communication constitute that semiotic as a system.

A discourse analyst, however, may at times be less interested in language as an abstract system and more concerned with some particular instance of language in use, such as a particular conversation, a speech, a poem, a newspaper article, a public notice or a literary narrative; in other words, the discourse analyst may be focussed on the *text* rather than the *system*. Within the SFL framework, this is

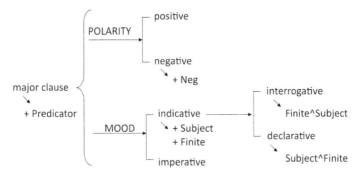

Figure 1.2 A system network showing 'simultaneous' systems.

merely a difference in perspective. For SF discourse analysis, any instance of the meaning potential (i.e. any text) needs to be described in terms of what selections in meaning have been made against the background of what selections are available in the system and thus *could* have been made.

The SFL approach to description thus maintains a dual focus on the meaning potential of the semiotic (the set of possible options and their realisations in some form of expression) and the pathway through the systems taken by any particular instance or text. In the description of the potential, it attends both to the options for meaning and how these are realised in form; in the description of the text, it attends to the particular meaning choices instantiated in the text with an awareness of the other possibilities available. With respect to language, the systems of meaning choices have been elaborated at a number of levels – as choices in genre (e.g. narrative/explanation/argument, etc.), as choices at the level of discourse-semantics (e.g. different conversational moves), as choices in grammar and lexis and as choices in phonology. (See further Halliday and Matthiessen, 2004; Martin and Rose, 2007).

As a picture book is a text that instantiates meaning from the semiotic systems of both language and image, its interpretation from a social–semiotic perspective should be based on an account of visual meaning comparable to that available for verbal language. The principal aim of this book, then, will be to make a contribution to this by laying out some of the relevant meaning systems for this visual semiotic, in order to enable more systematic description of, and reflection on, individual picture book texts. This will involve building on Kress and van Leeuwen's (2006) account of visual grammar, developing (and at times reinterpreting) their work to take better account of the picture book data. In three chapters to follow, the meaning systems proposed for each metafunction will be summarised as system networks and exemplifications of the options will be drawn from specific picture books, showing how different texts, or different points in the unfolding of a single text, make use of different options within the network to achieve particular effects. The final chapter will bring verbal and visual analyses together to address intermodal relations.

The formalism of the system network adopted in this book has already proved a useful one for describing non-linguistic semiotic systems (see e.g. Hood, 2011 on gesture; Kress and van Leeuwen, 2006 on image; Martinec, 2000, 2001 on action; van Leeuwen, 1999 on sound). However, one weakness of describing meaning in terms of categorical 'oppositions' – such as [positive] versus [negative], [interrogative] versus [declarative] – is that the description sets up very distinct 'typological' either/or categories. It has been argued that even for describing language, this typological approach may need a complementary 'topological' one that allows for fuzzy boundaries and points on a continuum rather than either/or extremes (Martin and Matthiessen, 1991). And it may well be the case that non-linguistic forms of semiosis, such as images, have even more fluid categories than does language. In this book, following Hood (2011), a convention will be adopted of tilting the square brackets of any system that is a continuum or 'cline' rather than a categorical opposition. See Figure 1.3 for a linguistic example.

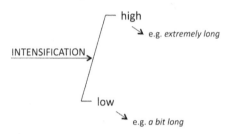

Figure 1.3 A system constituted by a continuum of choices between two extremes.

1.4   The current study

1.4.1   Data

The research underpinning this book began with a corpus of forty texts by well-respected authors and artists within the field of picture book writing. The initial selection was made so that books would be distributed along a continuum, depending on the proportion of words (henceforth 'verbiage') to images. This was seen as being a significant variable in terms of how the visuals might carry the narrative and what logical relations of time and cause, etc. might hold between the images. It also ensured that books targeting a range of ages of young reader would be included. As these books were examined metafunction by metafunction, it was necessary to repeatedly expand the corpus to embrace maximum variation along a number of other dimensions that emerged as relevant. For the interpersonal metafunction these included variation in angle and 'focalisation' of images, variation in depiction style (from cartoon-like to naturalistic) and variation in the use of colour; for the textual metafunction, variation in page layout and the use of framing and bordering devices was explored. This extended corpus of 73 books forms the data on which the descriptions in this book are based, though not all books were examined in relation to every metafunction. Although the corpus is by no means restricted to prize-winners, critically well-regarded books have been favoured for two main reasons. First, it is these texts that generally exploit the possibilities of the picture book format most fully and in ways that are reliably motivated in terms of narrative effects. Second, these are the texts that are likely to be most used in educational contexts and to be most familiar and available to interested readers, being constantly reprinted and often available in libraries. (A full list of picture book titles is provided following critical references at the end of the book).

1.4.2   The unit of analysis

As already noted, the main resource for social semiotic analysis of images within the SFL tradition is Kress and Van Leeuwen's (2006) *Reading Images: A Grammar of Visual Design*. In the chapters to follow, brief mention will be made of relevant meaning systems proposed there, but the main task here will be to extend or adapt their work into areas most relevant for analysis of picture book narratives. One such area is naturally that of describing the continuities and disjunctions in visual texts that comprise not a single image (or image/verbiage combination) but a visual or visual/verbal narrative sequence. We need to be able to analyse meanings within an image, but also across the pages of the larger text, bearing in mind that there is great variation in the number of images per page or double-page spread and also in the ways the pages or spreads are shared by words and images. The question that therefore arises immediately is whether the key visual unit should be the page, the double-page spread (also termed an 'opening'), the image, or the different components of the image.

In what follows we have taken the image as the default unit, so that where inter-image relations are discussed they may lie between images on a single page (one containing a number of panels for example, as in Figure 1.4), across the pages of a double-page spread (where each page has its own picture, as in Figure 1.5) or may be punctuated by a page-turn (where a single picture fills the double page, as in Figure 1.6) depending on how the book is arranged. The systems shown thus apply

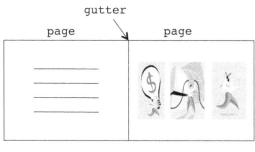

double page spread

Figure 1.4 Inter-image relations available within a single page.

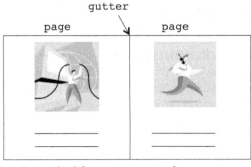

Figure 1.5 Inter-image relations available from page to page.

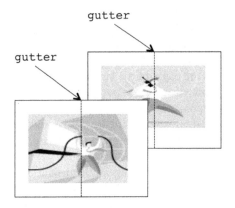

Figure 1.6 Inter-image relations available across a page-turn.

to each image in a book and systems of inter-relations are between images however they are paginated.[2]

The exception to this strategy arises when considering textual meaning. In the first place, if we wish to include the verbiage of a bimodal book as a visual component of a visual configuration, then either the page layout (as in Figure 1.5) or the double-page layout (as in Figure 1.4) becomes the relevant unit, depending on the book (See further INTERMODAL INTEGRATION in Chapter 4). Second, when considering how information is organised and attention is managed by visual

---

2. Since page numbers are not printed on picture book pages, where relevant the 'openings' have been counted and images identified as on a particular double-page spread, and (where there is more than one image) as on the verso (left page) or recto (right page) of that spread.

choices, we introduce the textual unit of 'focus group', by analogy with the linguistic tone group. An overall focus group will be constituted by the overall layout, with additional focus groups present within the image and, in some cases, the image part (see Chapter 4 for explanation and discussion). Seen in relation to Bateman's (2008, 2011) notions of text flow, page flow and image flow, we have been especially concerned with image flow; and comparable with Bateman's (2007, 2009) work on film, we propose a paradigm of options with reference to which viewers interpret inter-image relations (Chapter 3 below). Some of Bateman's concerns with page flow and image/verbiage relations are addressed in Chapter 4 with respect to our systems of INTERMODAL INTEGRATION and FRAMING.

1.4.3   Structure of the book

Chapters 2–4 of this book will each take one the three metafunctions, comment briefly on existing descriptions that are relevant for the data and then elaborate meaning systems as yet undeveloped by SF MDA theory. Within each chapter, system networks will be presented for each meaning system discussed and textual examples will be provided for illustration and clarification. Chapter 2 will examine the interpersonal metafunction, Chapter 3 the ideational and Chapter 4 the textual. Each of these chapters will conclude with a brief discussion of one complete picture book in relation to the meaning systems discussed. In the final chapter, all three metafunctions will be brought to bear and the focus will shift to image/language relations and the issues that arise in attempting to integrate descriptions of verbal and visual semiotics in order to understand the how a bimodal text of this kind 'adds up to something greater than the sum of its parts' (Sipe, 2011: 238).

2 Enacting Social Relations

2.1 Interpersonal meaning

Young children learning to become literate face a number of challenges, among the first of which is the novelty of being in a communicative relationship with a material and semiotic object rather than with a living, breathing, speaking, human being (Rose, 2011). While it is through the mediation of speaking adults that children are introduced to the verbal voice of a picture book, it is probably the visual images that are the most significant means for setting up an affective relationship between child and book, an important step in coming to terms with the print medium. The visuals achieve this partly through the depiction of characters – perhaps as objects of detached amusement, perhaps in ways inviting sympathy, judgement or the taking on of a character point of view. More generally it is also the images that can most readily establish the emotional 'tone' of the story, through the use of colour in the visual creation of settings within the stories.

These kinds of considerations all belong within the interpersonal metafunction, which is 'both interactive and personal' (Halliday and Matthiessen, 2004: 30). In a narrative text, the roles, relationships and affects realised through the interpersonal metafunction are not just those set up between reader and writer/image-maker on the one hand and those between the characters themselves on the other, but also (crucially) involve those in play between the reader and the narrative characters. This reader–character relationship has been usefully explored by Kress and van Leeuwen (2006: chs 4 and 5), who have proposed a number of visual meaning systems relevant to the relationship between the viewer and a depicted person. These are the systems of SOCIAL DISTANCE, ATTITUDE (including INVOLVEMENT and POWER), CONTACT and MODALITY. They will be given a brief consideration here before we move on to the description of additional meaning systems found particularly relevant to picture book analysis.

According to Kress and van Leeuwen (2006: 124–9), choices in SOCIAL DISTANCE are realised by the 'size of frame' – in other words by the presentation of the character in 'close up' as against 'mid shot' or 'long shot', and so on (Kress and van Leeuwen, 2006: 124; cf. Moebius, 1986 and 'the code of size'). Where only the head and shoulders of the character are viewed, a sense of intimacy between viewer and character is created, whereas a more distant 'long shot' presentation of the character has the opposite effect. Many picture books maintain a constant social distance; for example, the two characters in Burningham's ([1984] 1988) *Granpa* or the mischievous protagonist of *Where the Wild Things Are* (Sendak, 1963) are mainly presented in full-length depictions, which discourages the formation of a close personal relationship with them. Other authors vary presentations of the same character according to the narrative moment, so that the viewer is placed in a closer relationship at particular moments. This occurs, for example, in Browne's (1981) *Hansel and Gretel*, where the frightening face of the stepmother at the window and the frightening face of the witch at her door stand out as the only images where a character is presented relatively 'close-up'. (As will become clear, such a choice intersects with other interpersonal choices in the positioning of the viewer).

When we consider narrative picture books, the depicted participants are of course story-world characters who stand not only in a relationship to the viewer but are involved in social relationships with one another as well. Whether characters are shown well spaced from one another on the page, or in close proximity, or even touching, is very relevant to the way we read those relationships. We can therefore propose a system of PROXIMITY, parallel to that of SOCIAL DISTANCE, to refer to the closeness or otherwise of the characters to each other in the image at any moment in the narrative. Burningham's ([1984] 1988) *Granpa* provides a famous example of the two characters in that story abruptly and widely spaced across a double-page spread at the point where we are to infer a quarrel has taken place (see Figure 2.1). By contrast, grandparent and grandchild in *Possum Magic* (Fox and Vivas, [1983] 2004) are consistently shown in an intimate or close personal relationship, very often involving their bodies touching (as in Figure 4.14, p. 101).

Kress and van Leeuwen's systems of INVOLVEMENT and POWER (2006: 129–43) are further ways of positioning the viewer, and these depend on the use of perspective, which creates a 'subjective' position by requiring the character to be viewed from a particular angle. Greater or lesser involvement with what is depicted is

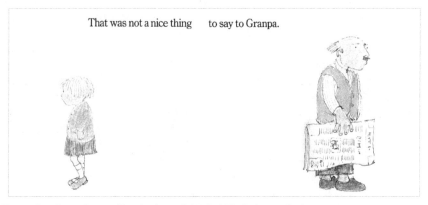

That was not a nice thing   to say to Granpa.

Figure 2.1 From *Granpa* (Burningham, [1984] 1988: sixth opening).

achieved through the horizontal angle (Kress and van Leeuwen, 2006: 133ff.). That is to say, when characters (and settings) are presented facing us 'front on', we have a maximum sense of involvement with them as part of our own world, whereas if they are depicted at an oblique angle, we are positioned to be more detached from them. We can see this system in play in *The Baby Who Wouldn't Go to Bed* (Cooper, 1996), where the recalcitrant protagonist is consistently presented so as to be viewed with detachment (i.e. from an oblique horizontal angle) until the point where he abandons his defiance and is ready for his mother's hug. In this way, the young reader is discouraged from aligning with the baby's disobedient behaviour rather than the mother's rules.

Another text that opens with an oblique horizontal angle is Browne's (1998) *Voices in the Park*, where we see the massive residence of the unpleasant narrator from an oblique angle, while she strides out in the foreground 'sideways on' to us. A number of visual choices converge in this image to alienate us from this character. She is presented in a very long shot, dwarfed by her imposing mansion, creating maximal social distance from the viewer; the horizontal angle is oblique, creating detachment, and in addition we are positioned by the low vertical angle to 'look up' to her house, making us feel somewhat oppressed by the building. Vertical angle is the realisation of POWER in the visual semiotic: what the viewer looks up to has power or authority, while what we look down on appears weak or vulnerable (Kress and van Leeuwen, 2006: 140ff.). This system is one utilised very effectively in many contemporary picture books, such as *Drac and the Gremlin* (Baillie and Tanner, [1998] 1991), where the protagonists are frequently presented as viewed from above by an unseen adult, or *Zoo* (Browne, 1992), where the overbearing father is shown looming over us from the child's perspective (i.e. from below) as he chortles over his own jokes.

Again, we must also recognise that relationships between depicted characters, as well as between the viewer and the depiction, are central in picture books. We can therefore propose a system of ORIENTATION, parallel to that of INVOLVEMENT, which takes into account the bodily orientations of the depicted characters to each other. Whatever their orientation to the viewer, two characters may face each other directly in the depiction, be placed side by side (suggesting solidarity if close), or angled away from each other, perhaps even in a back-to-back orientation, as in Figure 2.1 above. And just as a vertical angle of viewing realises the power relation between viewer and depiction, so two characters may enact a comparable relation if one is depicted looking up to or down on another character.

The other two interpersonal systems proposed by Kress and van Leeuwen, CONTACT and MODALITY, will be reinterpreted below and additional systems will be proposed that focus particularly on the affectual dimension of meaning, which Kress and van Leeuwen (2006: 267) acknowledge has 'perhaps been too thin a thread in the tapestry' of their analyses. The rest of this chapter will therefore focus on five further systems relevant to interpersonal meaning: those of FOCALISATION, AFFECT, PATHOS, AMBIENCE and GRADUATION. FOCALISATION is a reinterpretation and elaboration of Kress and van Leeuwen's system of CONTACT, and, like AFFECT and PATHOS, it is very much concerned with the depiction of characters in the stories. AMBIENCE, in part a reinterpretation of Kress and van Leeuwen's system of MODALITY, is primarily concerned with the depiction of settings and the use of colour to create a mood. GRADUATION is a term borrowed from SFL work on appraisal (Martin and White, 2005) to refer to strategies for intensifying gradable interpersonal meanings.

2.2   FOCALISATION

When considering 'point of view' in verbal texts, narrative theorists traditionally distinguish between 'who tells' and 'who sees' – that is, between the voice narrating the story and the persona whose eyes we are looking through, which may vary as the story unfolds. Two excerpts from *The Secret Garden* can illustrate this difference in 'focalisation' (Genette, 1980). The first is from the novel's first paragraph when we have the voice and point of view of a narrator who is external to the story world: 'When Mary Lennox was sent to Misselthwaite manor to live with her uncle, everybody said she was the most disagreeable-looking child ever seen. It was true, too. She had a little thin face and a little thin body ...' (Burnett, 1911: 1). Later we experience that world through the eyes and ears of the character, Mary: 'She heard something rustling on the matting, and when she looked down she saw a little snake gliding along ...' (Burnett, 1911: 2).

While the question of 'who tells' can only be relevant for verbal text, that of 'who sees' is pertinent for both verbal and visual strands of meaning. The viewer of a purely visual text can only come to know the story world by seeing it; but the viewer can be positioned to assume different viewing personas – either that of an outside observer or alternatively of a viewer 'participating' fleetingly in that world through a relationship with, or identification as, one of the characters. In a bimodal narrative, these different possibilities may harmonise with or counterpoint the focalisation provided by the verbal narration.[1]

In their visual grammar, Kress and van Leeuwen (2006) argue for a basic distinction between those images where a depicted person gazes out at the viewer and one where there is no such gaze. They interpret the former as requiring some kind of participation by the viewer, referring to it as a 'demand'. An image without such a gaze is, by contrast, an 'offer' of information for the viewer's more dispassionate perusal. In using the terminology of 'demand' and 'offer', Kress and van Leeuwen make an explicit analogy with the linguistic analysis of dialogue, in which information is demanded with 'questions' or given with 'statements', and goods and services are demanded with 'commands' or given with 'offers' (Halliday and Matthiessen, 2004). It is not obvious, however, that an image is inherently dialogic in the way a linguistic utterance is. A verbal statement, or offer of information, always entails a response from the addressee in relation to what is said, whether it be

---

1. See Yannicopoulou (2010) for a discussion of focalisation in picture books as interpreted from visual and intermodal content, rather than – as here – the interpersonal relation of the viewer to the depiction.

acknowledgement, agreement or disagreement, even if, as with a written text, such a response is not voiced aloud. A visual 'offer', on the other hand, such as a depiction of a scene or character from a picture book is not equivalent to a proposition which the viewer is called on to acknowledge, affirm or contest.[2] Indeed, images may be ideologically effective precisely because they do not engage us in overt or covert dialogic negotiation in the way that verbal language does.

When it comes to 'demands' – images of persons, animals or anthropomorphised objects gazing out to meet the viewer's gaze – Kress and van Leeuwen make two points. The first is that 'contact is established' between the depiction and the viewer, as the gaze 'creates a visual form of direct address. It acknowledges the viewers explicitly, addressing them with a visual 'you', (Kress and van Leeuwen, 2006: 117). This certainly seems to be the case, and when characters gaze out to the reader in a picture book, an effect similar to the making of eye contact between people in actuality is achieved. However, their second claim (arising from the analogy with verbal dialogue) is that the gaze 'demands something from the viewer', which is less convincing. They suggest that the nature of the demand depends on the facial and bodily stances of the depicted person, as friendly, disdainful, seductive, puzzled, and so on, enabling us to infer the social relation and hence the dialogic role demanded. Yet facial and bodily postures function primarily to signify the affect of an actual or depicted person and only in the case of certain ritualised gestures (e.g. beckoning or raising a hand for 'halt') place the viewer in a specific behavioural role. Facial and bodily postures and stances can therefore be seen as realising meanings equivalent to the attitudinal resources of verbal language rather than realising the negotiation of dialogic exchange. Moreover, our response to the affect of a depicted character is a relevant dimension in our positioning, regardless of whether we are gazed at.

For these reasons, Kress and van Leeuwen's analogy with verbal dialogue will be abandoned here. It will be proposed that 'affect' be recognised as a distinct area of visual meaning, and that the opposition between the presence and absence of gaze be construed simply as indicating whether the viewer has been positioned to engage with the character via eye contact, or just to observe the depicted participant. This then becomes the primary opposition within the system of FOCALISATION, between the two features [contact] and [observe] shown in Figure 2.2.

Many acclaimed picture books for younger readers, such as *The Baby Who Wouldn't Go to Bed* (Cooper, 1996), *Come Away from the Water, Shirley* (Burningham, 1977), *The Snowman* (Briggs, 1978) and *Possum Magic* (Fox and Vivas, [1983] 2004) in fact use only the [observe] option throughout the story, keeping the reader outside the story world to observe and learn from what goes on within it. This is also a favoured choice for many humorous stories, such as *Who Sank the Boat?* (Allen, 1982), *Rosie's Walk* (Hutchins, 1968) or *Prince Cinders* (Cole, [1987] 1997), where irony and wit are suited to an observing, rather than participating stance, by the reader. (Such a choice typically combines with relatively 'long shot' views, creating greater social distance and thus reinforcing the observer role.)

---

2. The structural elements of Subject and Finite in a verbal English proposition that render it 'arguable' (Halliday and Matthiessen, 2004) have no equivalent in a visual image.

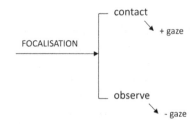

Figure 2.2 Basic FOCALISATION options.

A humorous book that does not maintain a consistency in using the [observe] option is Ahlberg and Briggs's (2001) *The Adventures of Bert*, where the metafictive nature of the framing sections of the text brings out the meaning of the different options. The book opens by introducing Bert with an instruction from the narrating voice to 'Meet Bert. This is him. Say hallo to Bert.' Accompanying this is an image of Bert looking out at us (the [contact] option) with a speech bubble that says 'Hallo!' We are then introduced to Mrs Bert in the same way. The reader is thus overtly invited to participate in the story world, both verbally and visually, which becomes a delightful joke when we are then blamed for turning the page too loudly and waking the baby! (For analysis of a more sobering deployment of a change in focalisation in Briggs, 1984, see Martin, 2006).

A focalising choice of [contact] is by no means restricted to metafictive contexts however. It may be used simply to introduce the reader to the characters in the opening image without any verbal use of second person address or overt melding of story world and viewer's world.[3] Browne, for example uses contact images on the opening page of a number of his stories (e.g. *Piggybook, Zoo, The Tunnel*), where the effect is simply to establish an initial connection with, and interest in, the story world characters. When Browne does this, the characters look straight out at us, engaging us directly, which is in contrast to the opening image of Baillie and Tanner's ([1988] 1991) *Drac and the Gremlin*, where the character's eyes are turned from the side in order to face us. The effect is to render the character somewhat mischievous or flirtatious, presenting us with an invitation to get involved. The choice of [contact] may therefore be more delicately classified as either [direct] or [invited].

Apart from its use when a character is first presented to the reader, the focalising choice of [contact] is often made to heighten identification or empathy at key moments in the story. For example, in *Way Home* (Hathorn and Rogers, 1994), a book relating the story of a homeless boy carrying a stray kitten through the city at night, there is no eye contact ever made with the main characters, but at the point where they meet a dangerous dog, we are suddenly faced with the dog, jaws slavering, staring straight out at us, in a confronting close-up image that makes us momentarily share the protagonists' terror. The verbal text at this point makes the kitten the focaliser: 'And the cat with no name sees a flash of cruel teeth, hears the angry loud bark of the monster dog, smells the blood and the hunger and danger.'

---

3. Nikolajeva and Scott (2001: 119) see this choice as that of an 'intrusive' visual narrator.

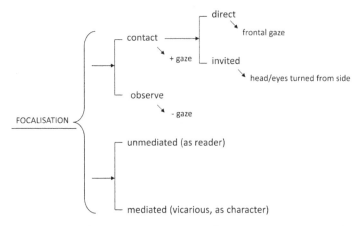

Figure 2.3 Extending the focalisation system to allow for mediated (i.e. character) focalisation.

The text therefore works intermodally to place us in the position of the kitten being threatened by the dog – we see the dog vicariously through the kitten's eyes. (See Chapter 5 for additional analysis and discussion of this text).

Even where there is *no* such verbal support, the reader can be positioned to see through the character's eyes, simply through *visual* choices. In the network shown as Figure 2.3 the visual option of viewing through the eyes of a character is termed [mediated], as opposed to the [unmediated] option when the reader observes or makes contact without being positioned as a character. The ways in which these choices are realised visually (rather than intermodally) are discussed below.

One way the reader can be positioned to see with the character's eyes is for an image to depict just the part of the body that could be seen by the focalising character (usually the hands or feet out in front of the unseen body), as in Figure 2.4 from *Drac and the Gremlin*. Because we, as readers, can see just that part of the body (the hands) that would be visible to the focalising character herself, we make vicarious contact with the children in the picture. In such a case, the reader stands temporarily in the shoes of the character to see the story world through their eyes and a choice of [mediated] rather than [unmediated] viewing has been encoded into the image. Interestingly, in this case, the adult is never mentioned in the verbal text, which is entirely concerned with the children's fantasy play and characters. Through the visual choices (including the power dimension that has us looking down at the children), however, we – as adults mediating the story – are aware that the children's imaginative world, is safely 'overseen' by the caring adult presence.

An effective alternative to depicting the focaliser's hands to signify [mediated] viewing is to show instead the shadow cast by the focaliser's body. This can be seen in Figure 2.5, where we see the shadow of the depicted boy's parents cast from the position of the reader. In this case the effect is to place us in the role of the authority figures at a point where the protagonist's failure to keep their rule has been exposed. More often it is a major character whose shoes we are momentarily invited to fill through the depiction of their shadow emerging from the bottom edge of the image.

Figure 2.4 Mediated focalisation from *Drac and the Gremlin* (Baillie and Tanner, [1988] 1991).

Figure 2.5 Mediated focalisation from *Grandad's Gifts* (Jennings and Gouldthorpe, [1992] 1994).

The tenth opening of Gleeson and Greder's (1999) *The Great Bear* provides one example, and another is shown in Figure 2.6 from Browne's *Piggybook*, at the point where the mother of the family, who departed the home earlier in the story, returns to find the males hunting around the floor for scraps of food. At this point, we take on the scene 'through her eyes'.

One night there was nothing in the house for them to cook.
"We'll just have to root around and find some scraps,"
snorted Mr Piggott.

And just then Mrs Piggott walked in.

Figure 2.6 Mediated focalisation from *Piggybook* (Browne, [1986] 1996).

When the hands or shadow of the focaliser's body can be seen emerging from the edge in the foreground of the picture, the fact that we adopt a character vantage point is made overt or inscribed in an individual picture (even if the character is not named or identified in the verbal text.) However, mediated focalisation may also be encoded across images. A picture book is a narrative sequence and it is often in the juxtaposition of successive images that character focalisation is achieved. In such a case, however, the mediated focalisation is inferred rather than being inscribed and directly perceived so the network of choices needs to be expanded to allow for this (Figure 2.7).

One technique to enable inferred character focalisation uses a two-picture sequence: first there is a [contact] image, then a depiction of what the character making eye contact with us is looking at. Since reading an image sequence of this kind as mediated focalisation is not the only interpretation available, a picture book artist may assist the child's reading by emphasising the fact that the character

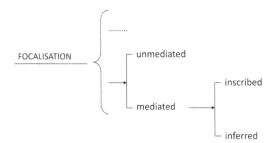

Figure 2.7 Extending the possibilities for mediated focalisation.

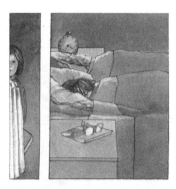

Figure 2.8 A sequence of [contact/unmediated] and [observe/mediated: inferred] from *Sunshine* (Ormerod, [1981] 1983).

making contact is indeed looking at something (other than us). Ormerod ([1981] 1983) in her wordless picture book, *Sunshine*, encourages this by using a very narrow frame to emphasise the idea of the child peeping through a doorway, so that the young viewer is clued in to interpret the following image as showing what the child character sees (see Figure 2.8). A well-crafted wordless picture book with this kind of deliberate scaffolding is well designed to apprentice young readers into this and comparable aspects of visual literacy.

An interesting example of the cueing of mediated focalisation by means of a preceding image occurs in Gleeson and Greder's (1999) *The Great Bear*, where a small line drawing of the bear occurs in the margin on the bottom left of a series of double-page spreads and large coloured images show the other characters through the bear's eyes, as in Figure 2.9. This particular spread sets us up to view the following image as also from the character's point of view even when there is no small image of the focaliser in the left margin (see Figure 2.10). The interpretation of vicarious focalisation in this second case is facilitated by the extreme emotion on the faces of the depicted people staring out at us – emotions which can only be occasioned by the positioning of the reader 'as character' (here a roaring bear).

The depiction of extreme character emotion in a contact image is itself a technique for character focalisation even where this has not been set up by previous images. This can be seen in a further example from *Grandad's Gifts*, shown as Figure 2.11. As the affective reaction of the gazing character in the picture is too extreme to be warranted by unmediated contact with the reader as reader, we must infer that a participant within the story world is being reacted to (something the verbal text makes clear). The playful use of mediated focalisation in a number of images in *Grandad's Gifts* serves in that text to create tension, since we do not know at first what role it is that we are momentarily inhabiting. The effect is to heighten the atmosphere by encouraging us not just to observe the protagonist's fear but rather to relish it by being partly responsible for it.

A third way in which character focalisation is achieved in picture books is by using the angle of viewing across two images. In Gleeson and Greder's (1992) *Uncle*

Sticks poke.
Sticks prod.
Chains yank.
Stones strike.
strike.
strike.

Figure 2.9 *The Great Bear* (Gleeson and Greder, 1999: eighth opening), showing [contact/mediated: inferred] in the large image.

Figure 2.10 *The Great Bear* (Gleeson and Greder, 1999: ninth opening), showing [contact/mediated: inferred].

Figure 2.11 Mediated focalisation from *Grandad's Gifts* (Jennings and Gouldthorpe, [1992] 1994).

David, for example, there is a picture of the child protagonist knocking on a door on one page, followed on the next by a picture of a towering adult opening the door and viewed from below. The adult gazes out, but the contact is clearly to be interpreted as between the depicted adult and (the viewer taking on the position of) the child character. The sequence this time is [observe/unmediated] followed by [contact/mediated: inferred] and it is the simultaneous deployment of viewing angle (i.e. choices within the system of POWER) that guides this interpretation.

In Browne's ([1986] 1996) *Piggybook*, as already noted, there is a significant moment when the mother in the story returns home after an absence resulting from the family's 'piggy' behaviour. In the double-page opening shown in Figure 2.12, the verso image shows a rear view of the male characters kneeling before the mother, who faces us as she looks down on them (see further discussion below). In the following picture, on the recto, we see the males facing out and looking up, placing us as readers in the mother's viewing position. In this example of [contact/mediated: inferred], it is the shift in horizontal angle along with constant choices in power that enables character focalisation at this point.

Inferred vicarious focalisation does not necessarily involve any use of a contact image, however. A subtle way of using a sequence of images to set up a vicarious viewing position is found in *Way Home* (Hathorn and Rogers, 1994). In one double-page spread we observe the boy protagonist up a tree reaching out towards a kitten that is nervously clinging to a branch. We view them from their own level high in

"P-L-E-A-S-E come back," they snuffled.

Figure 2.12 Image sequence showing [contact/ mediated: inferred] in the recto image. From *Piggybook* (Browne, [1986] 1996).

the tree. When the page is turned, we see neither boy nor kitten but simply the expanse of the city from a high vantage point. Thus even without the verbal text, which makes it explicit by saying 'The boy Shane way up in the tree, stares over the streets and lanes', it can be inferred from the high vertical angle that we are seeing what the boy sees from the tree. In this case, then, the sequence is [observe/unmediated] followed by [observe/mediated: inferred].

So far we have seen that both contact (+gaze) and observe (–gaze) images can combine with either unmediated or mediated focalisation choices. Moreover mediated focalisation may be inscribed in the image through the depiction of body parts or shadows or it may be inferred from the extreme affect depicted in a contact image and/or the particular horizontal and vertical angles deployed across a sequence of two pictures. These choices do not exhaust the focalising possibilities, however, since it is also possible for the reader to 'share' the character's vantage point by being positioned to see 'over the shoulder' of the character, as in the verso image of Figure 2.12 or in Figure 2.13, showing an image from *Lucy's Bay* (Crew and Rogers, 1992). In such a case the viewer is positioned to see as the character does, while also seeing the character from behind, thus having a dual vantage point.

A nice example of this kind of mediated focalisation is provided by the first full-page illustration in *Gorilla* (Browne, [1983] 1997), reproduced as Figure 2.14. This image depicts the lonely protagonist, Hannah, at breakfast with her father, whom she finds too busy and preoccupied to be the companion she would like. In Figure 2.14 the reader is not positioned to 'be' the child character, but maintains a perspective from outside the story world. At the same time, we are aligned to see 'with' Hannah's eyes as well as our own. This is clear when colour choices are taken into account.

Figure 2.13 [observe/ mediated: inscribed: along with character] from *Lucy's Bay* (Crew and Rogers, 1992).

Figure 2.14 [observe/ mediated: inscribed: along with character] from *Gorilla* (Browne, [1983] 1987).

The reader can see Hannah in full colour, but everything the disconsolate child sees is in washed out cool tones 'coloured' by her mood. (See further the discussion of AMBIENCE in Section 2.4 below). Thus we see what Hannah sees from her point of view, without entirely losing our own perspective. This option will be regarded as a special case of inscribed mediated focalisation, [mediated: along with character], and is only available within a single image since we must have the character in view and be positioned behind, either directly (as in Figure 2.14) or slightly to one side.[4] The way Browne has used this option at the beginning of *Gorilla* provides a subtle clue that Hannah's perspective is to be empathised with, but is not the only possible point of view. More generally the option allows for empathy without complete identification, somewhat as 'free indirect discourse' does with verbal focalisation (Toolan, 2001:121ff.).

The visual options for FOCALISATION are summarised in Figure 2.15. Realisations for mediated focalisation are summarised in Table 2.1.

Table 2.1 FOCALISATION: visual realisations.

Option			Realisation
contact			+gaze out to viewer by depicted human, animal or anthropomorphised character
contact:	direct		gazing character faces viewer front on
contact:	invited		gazing character turns head and/or eyes to face viewer
observe			no gaze out to viewer by character
unmediated			default option, no additional realisation
mediated:	inscribed:	as character	character's hands, feet or shadow (only) are depicted emerging from bottom edge of picture
mediated:	inscribed:	along with character	back view of character in foreground with what character sees beyond; i.e. viewer sees 'over shoulder' of character with closer identification where horizontal angle is shared
mediated:	inferred		1. a sequence of images with the following features: (i) first image is of character looking (usually an instance of [contact]) and subsequent image/s plausibly depict/s what character sees; (ii) first image depicts character (instantiating either [contact] or [observe]) and second image (whether [contact] or [observe]) shares spatial viewing position with that character 2. extreme affective reaction of depicted character/s in a contact image

4. If viewer and character share the same horizontal viewing angle and the focalising character is in the foreground, there is closest alignment between reader and character views. Where the horizontal angle is not exactly shared and/or the focalising character is 'deeper' into the picture, there will be less close alignment.

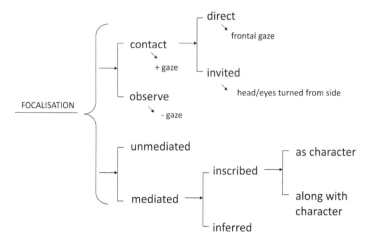

Figure 2.15 FOCALISATION: visual options.

2.3   PATHOS **and** AFFECT

Stories for children function not only as sources of pleasure and entertainment but also as a prime means for teaching the young. A simple picture book like *Rosie's Walk* (Hutchins, 1968), for example, carries not only implicit literacy lessons (see Meek, 1988), but implicit literary and social training. For example, children are introduced to a tradition of viewing the fox as a symbol of cunning and predation, (found also in older stories like Aesop's ([1484] 2002) *The Fox and the Crow*, Potter's (1908) *The Tale of Jemima Puddleduck* and in more recent ones like *Fox* (Wild and Brooks, 2000); they also learn about what counts as being funny – not only the ironic contrast between what is said (by the narrator) and what is known (by the viewer; see Meek, 1998), but also the 'slapstick' physical violence wrought on the fox; and finally, they learn the moral lesson that the world is apparently so arranged that a powerful, dangerous, lawless outsider will invariably and justly get his comeuppance.

Rosie's Walk shares with other picture books a number of stylistic features that can be regarded as having a similar function – that of a kind of social commentary. The texts are third person in verbal narration and the characters are not highly individuated. Whether or not they are named, readers are not expected to build up a personal relationship with these characters, or to feel moved or upset at the events of the story world. The appropriate reader stance is one of relative distance as the story events are observed and lessons learnt. For this reason, there is often the use of relatively long shots and frequent oblique angles, together with [observe] rather than [contact] choices from focalisation. While these choices in combination contribute to a more detached observer stance, rather than a highly empathic one, perhaps the key signifier for an appropriate orientation to the text as social commentary lies in the non-realistic 'minimalist' style of character depiction.

The way characters are depicted in picture book stories can be loosely categorised into three broad styles, here referred to as 'minimalist', 'generic' and 'naturalistic', on the basis of the degree of detail and realism of the drawing (Welch, 2005; see further below). While Kress and van Leeuwen (2006) regard the realism of a depiction as an expression of modality (and thus relating to the truth value of the image), the style of character drawing is here interpreted as realising a system of reader alignment, or PATHOS, and as affording particular ways of presenting a character's emotions or affect. In broad terms, the minimalist style for a human character is one that uses circles or ovals for people's heads, with dots or small circles for eyes, has restricted variation in head angles (perhaps only front on and side views), does not need to maintain accurate facial or body proportions and – in its extreme form – has minimal depth (Tian, 2011).

Picture books by Dick Bruna and John Burningham consistently use minimalist style, found also in Briggs's work (e.g. *The Snowman, The Bear, The Adventures of Bert*), although there is more depth and solidity in his pictures; *Not Now, Bernard* (McKee, [1980] 2004), *Prince Cinders* (Cole, [1987] 1997), *Who's Afraid of the Big Bad Book?* (Child, 2002) and *Black Dog* (Allen, 1991) are further examples of minimalist style. Since the artist is not constrained by the actual physiognomy of the human face, the depiction of emotion in this style is highly schematic, as described in unpublished work by Welch (2005), who argues that the emotional repertoire afforded by the minimalist style most strongly represents degrees of happiness or sadness. Welch's conclusions are based on a painstaking analysis of the depiction of affect in seventeen picture books in which she details the key aspects of the three styles being proposed here. Some examples of characters drawn in the minimalist style are given in Figure 2.16.

As this discussion of the minimalist style shows, the three styles of character depiction can be considered from three perspectives. First, there are the details of how 'realistic' the various aspects of the facial features are, particularly with respect to matters such as eye detail, head angle and facial proportions, pencil and/or brush style and variation in the colour palette. For example, Welch (2005: 3–4) notes that:

> Eye Detail is one of the most effective indexes of realism in texts … The Minimalist category tends to draw a pupil and an eyebrow. Occasionally

| From *Not Now Bernard* (McKee, [1980] 2004) | From *Come Away from the Water, Shirley* (Burningham, 1977) | From *Black Dog* (Allen, 1991) | From *The Snowman* (Briggs, 1978) | From *The Baby's Catalogue* (Ahlberg and Ahlberg, 1982) |

Figure 2.16   Variations on minimalist drawing style.

pupils are given more volume through the suggestion of an eye-socket, and at the most realistic end of the category, [*Where the*] *Wild Things* [*Are*], for example, we can see a pupil, eyeball, eye-socket and eyebrow. There are a few instances of under-eye shading or wrinkles. The Generic category gains an iris, as well as the potential for wrinkles around the eyes, and bags under the eyes to indicate fatigue. In the Naturalistic system individuated eyebrow hairs and eye-lashes appear, top and bottom lids appear and eyes can water.

What is interesting here is that the minimalist style is the least naturalistic and its decipherment is therefore most clearly a matter of visual literacy.

Second, there is the question of what the different styles afford in terms of depiction of affect. Welch (2005) explains that whereas the minimalist style is more iconic and stylised, focusing on un/happiness, the generic style is more detailed, with the brush or pencil stroke based on the musculature of the human face. This allows the mouth in particular to be more expressive, with corners that can be pressed, pursed, pouted or tightened towards the teeth. The emotional repertoire is therefore extended with more 'behavioural' emotions enabled; that is, those associated with watching, doing and concentrating, which draw on an increased potential for variation in 'vigour'. Compared with the other styles, the naturalistic is the most subtle, restrained and nuanced of all and the expressions are to be read much more as are those of real people. The emotional repertoire that can be suggested therefore extends to the nuanced, impressionistic, ambiguous and indefinable. As with living people, the characters' eyes are emotionally foregrounded in the naturalistic style, and in comparison with the generic style, the whole topography of the face and skin is depicted and contributes to our inferences about the character's feelings.

The depiction of affect, of course, is not carried only by the faces of the characters, although these have been used to define the three 'styles' identified. Depicted gestures and bodily stance are also key in the representation of affect as can readily be seen in Sendak's (1963) *Where the Wild Things Are,* where all three combine to suggest the gamut of emotions experienced by the protagonist, Max. Here we will not attempt to classify emotional depiction into system networks of features, but will assume that affect will be 'read' from the facial and bodily postures shown by the artists in conjunction with contextual and intermodal support, with the naturalistic style offering the potential for the greatest complexity and subtlety in depiction.[5]

Returning to a consideration of the styles in terms of their significance for the different kinds of alignment that are encouraged, it has already been suggested that the minimalist style requires us to be relatively detached observers of the characters rather than to take them to our hearts. It is a style that suits a social commentary, often one deploying humour to carry its message. By contrast, the generic style creates characters of the 'everyman' type. Many picture books using this style are

---

5. Tian's (2011) analysis of facial affect in Anthony Browne's work concludes that in all styles we can only interpret faces with certainty as positive, negative or neutral in affect, with more subtle readings dependent on contextual and intermodal guidance.

likely to be more injunctive in nature, implicitly expecting the child readers to see themselves in the protagonist role and to 'be/do like this'. Examples of the generic style are *Sunshine* (Ormerod, [1981] 1983), *Uncle David* (Gleeson and Greder, 1992), *So Much* (Cooke and Oxenbury, 1994), *An Evening at Alfie's* (Hughes, 1984) *The Baby Who Wouldn't Go to Bed* (Cooper, 1996), the Titch series (e.g. Hutchins, 1983) and many images in Browne's books, such as *Piggybook* ([1986] 1996), *Zoo* (1992 and *Into the Forest* (2004).[6] Generic texts invite an empathetic stance, where common humanity is recognised and the reader stands in the character's shoes. For example, the child reader can share the superiority of the 'generic' child protagonist of *Sunshine*, who is more capable than the parents of getting herself organised for the day, while the reader of *So Much* experiences the joy of being the loved centre of family life and the reader of *The Baby Who Wouldn't Go to Bed* will be expected to share the protagonist's learning experience and acknowledge that loving mums know best about bedtime.

The naturalistic style is found in books like *First Light* (Crew and Gouldthorpe, 1993), *Drac and the Gremlin* (Baillie and Tanner, [1988] 1991), *The Deep* (Winton and Louise, 1998), *Grandpa* (Norman and Young, 1988) or *Lucy's Bay* (Crew and Rogers, 1992). Many of these texts are for older readers, some dealing with quite serious themes; for example, a troubled relationship between father and son in *First Light* and coming to terms with a death in the family in *Grandpa* and *Lucy's Bay*. Such books will be important for leading children towards the kind of literate reading called for in secondary and higher education, where the reader's emotional response to the characters is important in creating alignments and judgements in relation to themes evoked by the story events. Here the reader engages with the characters as individuals[7] rather than as types, and through that sympathetic engagement with the other/s in the story the reader is led towards ethical discernment. For example, in *First Light*, the sensitive artistic son reluctantly accompanies his father on a dawn fishing trip, which to him is distasteful but to the father is a pleasure to be shared. Both characters are depicted in a naturalistic style and emerge as individuals capable of change and of complex and ambiguous emotions. Neither character is set up as a type or model to be emulated or avoided, but the reader can sympathetically appreciate their individual personalities and needs. The story of their rapprochement during the trip therefore invites a more mature and literary response achieved through relating to the characters as individuals. The book does not convey a simple injunctive message of 'go fishing with your dad' but invites reflection on the potential for both affection and strain in intergenerational male relationships between differing personalities, and the bonding effects of experiencing shared difficulties.

The relation between the text function, the depiction style and the form of appeal to the reader is summarised in Table 2.2. The tendency for the minimalist depiction to be favoured for younger readers and the more naturalistic for older ones

---

6. See Tian (2011) for a discussion of variation in style within a single text by Anthony Browne.

7. Cf. McCloud's ([1993] 1994: 36–7) comparison of a 'realistic' style with a 'cartoony' one, where he argues 'when you look at a photo or realistic drawing of a face, you see another', but with a cartoon style 'you see yourself' and attend more to the message than the individual depicted.

Table 2.2 Reader engagement as a function of depiction style.

Typical function	Depiction style	Reader engagement
Social commentary	Minimalist (e.g. McKee's *Not Now, Bernard* title page)	'Appreciative': some emotional distance
Injunction	Generic (e.g. Cooke and Oxenbury's *So Much* p. 33)	Empathic role identification: recognition of common humanity
Ethical inference	Naturalistic (e.g. Norman and Young's *Grandpa* p. 9)	Personalising: called on to relate and respond to depicted others as 'real' individuals

seems explicable in terms of the different kinds of reader engagement fostered even though it might be expected that a naturalistic style would be 'easiest' for the very young to interpret.

Not all styles of text illustration will fit readily into the simple taxonomy shown in Table 2.2.[8] It may be the case that caricature, as used in *The Tin Pot Foreign General and the Old Iron Woman* (Briggs, 1984), is a distinct style with its own orientation, as is the 'hyper-real' quality of a text like *The Watertower* (Crew and Woolman, 1994). This latter book makes use of hard edges and very strong contrasts of light and shade to create its own kind of eerie unreality. The effect (together with symbols, patterns of gaze within the image and filmic intertextuality) is to give apparently

---

8. More accurately to be considered a continuum between clearly differentiated poles.

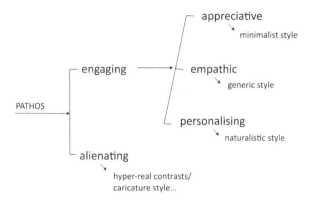

Figure 2.17 PATHOS options.

ordinary experience an edge of otherworldly science fiction (Anstey and Bull, 2000: 161–2). The pictorial style is an alienating one in which we feel the otherness of the characters without the sympathy conjured by others who are like us. This option is catered for in the PATHOS network, shown in Figure 2.17, by the feature [alienating].

2.4   AMBIENCE

While the style of character depiction provides one ready index of the nature of the book and of how the reader can be expected to engage with it, probably the most instant bonding effect created by a picture book is that established by its choices in the use of colour. Colour is a visual resource that can serve all three metafunctions (Kress and van Leeuwen, 2002; van Leeuwen, 2011). In its ideational role, colour is used to represent the appearance of things in the world, with green for grass, yellow for gold sovereigns, white for snow, red for blood, and so on. In its textual role, colour may be used contrastively to highlight or foreground some element within a composition to make it especially salient to the viewer, or repetitions of a colour may be used cohesively as a kind of visual rhyme to link different parts of a narrative.

In its interpersonal role, however, the significance of colour lies in its emotional effect on the viewer. Most people will agree that a picture book filled with bright light colours has a very different effect on our feelings from one featuring dark sombre tones and different again from one printed only in black and white. These differences do not depend on scrutiny of the content of the images or knowledge of the events of the story being told, but are a more visceral response to the colour choices. We can draw an analogy here with the use of colour within three dimensional spaces to create an 'ambience' or emotional mood (Stenglin, 2004) and regard the use of colour in picture books, especially in the depiction of the setting in which characters are placed, as functioning in a comparable way. Thus AMBIENCE in picture books will be regarded as a visual meaning system for creating an emotional

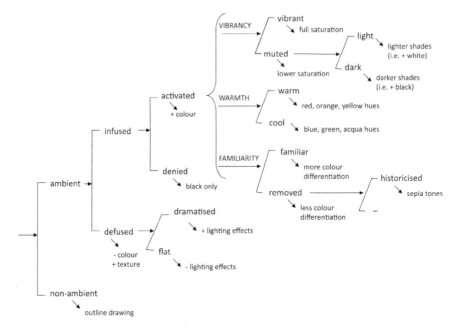

Figure 2.18 Choices in AMBIENCE.

mood or atmosphere, principally through the use of colour. The system is summarised in the network shown in Figure 2.18 (also discussed in Painter, 2008). It is important to note here that although options are presented as alternatives, most in fact represent the end point of continua, rather than starkly opposed choices with clear boundaries.

Our work on ambience is designed particularly for the register of children's picture books, rather than images in general; and we have been mindful of the need to design a system which is economical enough to be used productively by students and educators. Consequently not all of the 'parametric' systems (van Leeuwen, 2009) introduced by Kress and van Leeuwen (2002, 2006; van Leeuwen, 2011) have been developed. We have concentrated in particular on what they call value and saturation (our VIBRANCY), hue[9] (our WARMTH) and differentiation (our FAMILIARITY) – see Figure 2.18 and Section 2.4.1 below.

2.4.1   Activated ambience: VIBRANCY, WARMTH, FAMILIARITY

While the network looks quite complex in its entirety, the core systems are those named VIBRANCY, WARMTH and FAMILIARITY, all of which are available simultaneously and are realised by dimensions of colour when [activated] ambience is selected.

---

9. Van Leeuwen (2011) refers to hue as 'temperature'.

Figure 2.19 Contrasting images from *So Much* (Cooke and Oxenbury, 1994: tenth spread verso and eleventh spread recto).

The system of VIBRANCY depends on the depth of saturation to the colours used. Full or high saturation – the choice of [vibrant] from the network – creates a maximally vibrant effect: it can be used to generate a sense of excitement and vitality, while a [muted] choice within VIBRANCY creates a gentler more restrained feeling. Compare for example, the deep, bold colours of Jeannette Rowe's *Whose* series (e.g. *Whose Family?*, 2006) with the less saturated colours of Beatrix Potter's tales (see bookseller sites on the web for images of book covers). Variation in vibrancy can also be exploited for meaning within a text, as in Cooke and Oxenbury's *So Much*, where the pictures of the family sitting around waiting for visitors are in subdued, unsaturated colours, suggesting a feeling of flatness, while those depicting the entrance of guests are in bolder, more highly saturated colours, encouraging us to share the joyousness of the moment. See Figure 2.19 for the contrasting content of such images, albeit not reproduced in colour here.[10]

It is the depth of colour saturation that realises the degree of vibrancy of an image, but saturation is not an independent variable, since it is tied to a colour's 'value' – that is, to the degree of lightness or darkness of the colour. If a colour is not at full saturation (and thus maximally 'vibrant') then it must be either lighter or darker, until with total desaturation it becomes either white or black. The vibrancy

---

10. At the time of writing, the first 'muted' image in the book can be viewed at www.amazon. co.uk/So-Much-Trish-Cooke/dp/0744543967 (the toddler's clothes provide a contrasting splash of vibrancy in this image). The style of the 'vibrant' pages is used on the 1994 cover (different from the 2008 edition), viewable at http://hubpages.com/hub/So-Much-Childrens-Book-Review and elsewhere.

choice of [muted] therefore always entails a further choice of [dark] or [light], as shown in Figure 2.18. The choice made may be consistent within a complete story, as for example in Hutchins's (1968) lighthearted *Rosie's Walk*, which is appropriately [muted: light] throughout, or certain texts for older readers, such as Hathorn and Rogers's (1994) *Way Home* or Gaiman and McKean's (2003) *The Wolves in the Walls*, which favour the [muted: dark] option, in keeping with their darker social or psychological themes. These two texts contrast with the gentler, more optimistic ambience of Crew and Rogers's (1992) *Lucy's Bay*, despite the latter's theme of a young boy coming to terms with the death of his sister. Here, there is naturalistic depiction of shadows in many images, but the overall ambience is [muted: light], helping to obviate any gloomy, depressing effect and emphasising that the story is to be read as a hopeful one in which the protagonist comes to terms with his grief and guilt.

The more positive effect of the [muted: light] option is greatly enhanced in *Lucy's Bay* by the use of a second ambience system – that of WARMTH – in which the warmer colours, such as red and yellow hues are in contrast with cooler blues and greens. Choices here may depict hot and cool physical environments, but are of course also used to reflect emotional shades. In *Lucy's Bay*, the consistent choice of the [warm] option, realised here by pinkish-orange hues, plays an important part in creating a comforting, positive mood despite the tragic elements the story turns upon. As a contrast with images in this book, we can consider the opening spread of Browne's (2004) *Into the Forest*, where the option of [cool] is used. The picture shows mother and son sitting glumly at the breakfast table; both preoccupied and anxious. The absence of the father is emphasised by the length and emptiness of the table, while the subdued mood is evoked by the cool green of the background wall. Just as verbal literary technique uses description of the setting to reference characters' emotions – stormy weather for moments of crisis, and so on – so Browne uses visual ambience to facilitate reading the emotional mood of the characters. Later on, in the resolution to this story when the boy protagonist meets up with his father again, the background to the reunion picture is a warm sunny yellow, evoking in the reader the joy and light-heartedness felt by the boy.

The third of the most important ambience systems in picture books is that of FAMILIARITY, which is realised by the amount of colour differentiation in the image. The basic principle here is that the more different colours are present in the image, the greater the sense of the familiar, since we usually experience the world day to day in all its variety of colour. If, however, an image is restricted to one or two hues, or to modulations of a single colour, the meaning of being 'removed' from the normal, everyday world is created. This aspect of ambience relates to Kress and van Leeuwen's (2006) idea of the visual expression of 'modality' (or degrees of certainty), which they see as being realised by a number of visual dimensions including that of colour differentiation, with a lack of differentiation realising reduced certainty or realism in the depiction.

The use of a reduced palette to signal a literal removal from reality can be seen in *Just a Dream* (Van Allsburg, 1990), where there are [removed] monochrome 'dream' scenes in shades of all blue or all orange-pink that contrast with the [familiar] more differentiated palette of the waking environment. However, it need not be a literal

removal from reality that is at stake, something exemplified by the somewhat monochrome palette deployed to realise the [removed] option in *Lucy's Bay*, where for
example, the only colours in the original image shown as Figure 2.13 are shades of
sand and rosy peach. Here, the [removed] feature suggests rather the protagonist's
emotional withdrawal from others around him as he reflects on the past. This choice
of [removed] is in play simultaneously with the options of [soft: light] and [warm]
already discussed, all working together to create a gentle, reflective ambience for the
story (the feeling of 'saudade' as it would be expressed in Portuguese). In this book,
the [removed] option is used throughout the book, but in other stories, choices
in FAMILIARITY will vary to create narrative contrasts. For example, in Browne's
Piggybook, the [familiar] presentation of the males on the opening page contrasts
with the initial [removed] monochrome depictions of the female of the family, seg-
regated from the males emotionally and in her domain of domestic drudgery. (See
Painter, 2008 for detailed discussion of ambience choices in *Piggybook*).

Contrasts in FAMILIARITY are also important in Cooke and Oxenbury's (1994)
So Much. The two images shown in Figure 2.19 display in the coloured originals a
contrast in both VIBRANCY and FAMILIARITY. The left hand picture in the original is
not only less vibrant (in having low saturation) but also instantiates the [removed]
option in using very few different colours – only black, white, shades of pale brown
and a glimpse or two of red – suggesting the way the characters are not only feeling
flat, but are disengaged and removed into their own interior worlds, something also
indicated by their facial expressions. Contrasting pictures on many recto pages are
not only more vibrant, conveying the characters' enthusiasm and energy, but take
up the [familiar] option, realised by the use of a full range of colours – blue, green
yellow, pink, red, fawn, white and black – as the characters re-engage with each
other and their external environment when a visitor enters the scene. The entire
story is a simple recount of the gathering of guests for Dad's birthday party, the
varying use of ambience playing a significant role in conveying to the young reader
the ennui of waiting and the series of mini-climaxes created by each arrival, until
the final party is depicted in images full of movement and bright varied colour.

As shown by the examples discussed, the specific meaning of the [removed]
option can vary from story to story. It may reference a different reality (such as dream
or domestic drudgery) and/or signal an emotional or psychological withdrawal on
the part of characters. Another use is to signal temporal distancing, such as occurs
in Wolfer and Harrison-Lever's (2005) war story *Photographs in the Mud*. The drab
brown and dull green colours used in every picture emphasise the depicted soldiers'
removal from the reality and values of ordinary family life and also the distant time
period of the Second World War. The story also exemplifies a sub-option of the
[removed] feature, which is a particular monochrome effect achieved by the use of
sepia tones in the style of early photographs. This choice of [removed: historicised]
is used in this book for small portrait images inset within the larger ones, representing photographs of family members of the soldiers in the main images. The
[historicised] sub-option clarifies their status as photographs as well as referencing
the time period of the story. In another war story, *In Flanders Fields* (Jorgensen
and Harrison-Lever, 2002), all the images are painted in sepia tones to symbolise

the particular time period of the early twentieth century. As with other ambience options, the [historicised] option may be 'more or less' in that sometimes sepia tones predominate but another colour might play a minor role. This occurs in *In Flanders Fields*, for example, where glowing coals and a red-breasted robin introduce a contrast that functions symbolically in the story.

2.4.1.1   Textual distribution of ambience

While it is the setting in picture book images that chiefly creates the ambience, some have no setting, simply depicting the character on a white page background. This alerts us to the fact that even where there is no 'enveloping' ambience, a mood may be created by the 'splash' of colour created by a character or object depicted without any setting. For example, at the end of Browne's (2004) *Into the Forest*, the boy who had been anxious about his absent father returns home with him to be greeted by his mother. We see the smiling mother, arms outspread in welcome and wearing a bright red sweater, but with no circumstantial details depicted. In general, the removal of the setting draws our attention to the emotion and/or behaviour of the character, thereby evoking affect (and sometimes judgement) in us. Because the mother in this case is depicted in a vibrant red garment her enthusiasm and warmth are conveyed and equivalent feelings are invoked in the reader. Here, then, we can say that there is no enveloping ambience, but only a splash of ambience that is vibrant and warm. (Note that the subsystem of FAMILIARITY is not necessarily relevant for 'splashes' of ambience, since an entirely naturalistic representation of single element often requires a single colour).

It is not only when the background is left bare that a 'splash' of ambience may be present. Quite often in a fully contextualised picture, there will be a contrast between the enveloping ambience and some smaller element, whether a character, object, light source or part of the environment. This is the case in the original image from *Gorilla* (Browne, [1983] 1987) reproduced as Figure 2.14 and discussed already in relation to FOCALISATION. Since the enveloping ambience is [muted: cool]/[removed], while the protagonist, Hannah, constitutes a relatively [vibrant: warm]/[familiar] splash of contrast, we see her as a vibrant feeling person, but one who is emotionally isolated, projecting her subdued 'blue' mood onto the world, perhaps even finding her father's space emotionally chilling.

Another example of the use of contrastive ambient splashes can be seen in *First Light* (Crew and Gouldthorpe, 1993). The first part of the story – about a fishing trip taken by a father and son – takes place in the dark of pre-dawn and the gloom of a difficult relationship between the two characters. While the overall ambience is dark, the glow of lamp or torch and the orange lifejacket worn by the boy repeatedly provide a lighter splash, prefiguring the positive outcome of the trip. Later as the dawn approaches, symbolising the dawn of better understanding between the two, the warm splashes of the lifejacket and other objects in the boat contrast with the cool of the surrounding blue sea feared by the boy, again foreshadowing the positive resolution with which the story closes. (See Martin, 2008b and Painter, 2008 for discussion of further examples of the way splashes may contrast with the enveloping ambience in a picture book image.)

Finally, in relation to the textual distribution of ambience, we need to consider not only the possibility of smaller splashes that contrast with an enveloping ambience, but also other potential contrasts. For example, a picture may have a coloured frame or margin whose chief function is to carry an overarching ambience. In the image from *Lucy's Bay* (Crew and Rogers, 1992) reproduced as Figure 2.13, the coloured margin matches and reinforces the [warm: light] choice of the enveloping ambience, while in other cases there may be a margin choice that counters it. A more frequent contrastive distribution, however, occurs when the image itself has a composition that divides it into sections with different ambience choices in the different parts. For example, one half of a scene may be in shadow, creating a dark ambience, while the other half is in light. A split image of this kind, shown as Figure 5.3 in the final chapter of this book, provides a very effective opening to *Way Home* (Hathorn and Rogers, 1994). Here, the illuminated wall on the far left contrasts with the rest of the image in being more vibrant and a warm orangey colour, while the rest of the image is more muted and much darker. This split, together with smaller splashes of light within the generally dark ambience, reflect the thematic content of the story of a homeless boy's journey home with a stray kitten, where the dark aspects of his life – the aggression, exclusion and insecurity he faces – are balanced by the gentleness and affection he displays or encounters and the eventual security of the 'home' he finds.

2.4.2   Black and white

While a white margin to the page is arguably neutral and does not contribute background ambience (whether that page be printed words or an image), a black margin or indeed a black setting does have an effect. We cannot discern colour when desaturation is complete, so the choices of WARMTH, VIBRANCY and FAMILIARITY do not apply to either black or white, yet our response to black margins and pages is not simply neutral as with a white page. Rather our inclination to relate emotionally to the setting is frustrated by a choice of black. For this reason, the systems of WARMTH, VIBRANCY and FAMILIARITY are only available when ambience is [activated] by a realisation in colour, rather than [denied] by a realisation of black – see Figure 2.18.

This raises the question of whether black and white drawings simply by-pass the potential for ambience. This would indeed seem to be the case for simple line drawings on a white page, such as the diagram of Figure 2.18 or the drawing that is Figure 2.20, both of which take up the option of [non-ambient].

There are a minority of children's picture books, however, that are entirely in black and white, in which ambience is downplayed rather than entirely absent. In effect there is a continuum between bare line drawings with no ambience, drawings that include shading, hatching or dotting to create some texture and solidity with minimal ambience, and finally those that emphasise lighting effects to create a greater sense of atmosphere. Where simple line drawings have no ambience at all, the other black and white options can be considered as having [defused] rather than [infused] ambience. Drawings that create texture and minimal lighting effects are

Figure 2.20 [non-ambient] image.

[defused: flat] in comparison with those that dramatise lighting effects to create atmosphere, such as Van Allsburg's (1981) *Jumanji* or Bunting and Wiesner's (1994) *Night of the Gargoyles,* as seen in Figure 2.21. These take up the option of [defused: dramatised].

Black and white is an atypical choice in a picture book, so it is instructive to consider the effects achieved when it is taken up. In *Granpa*, Burningham ([1984] 1988) uses largely non-ambient line drawings (together with verbal text) on the left-hand pages opposite large, delicately coloured pictures on the right hand pages. The coloured pictures on the right depict scenes from the life of Granpa and grand-daughter, while scenes on the left appear to depict Granpa's memories or imaginings and never show the protagonists together. Rather than an immediate emotional response, these drawings, which require considerable interpretation, invite a more ideational scrutiny. The reader has to work out the puzzle of how they fit in to the episodic 'story' shown in the coloured pictures and it is with the relationship shown in the latter that we remain emotionally involved.

Inviting closer attention to the ideational content of the image is also an effect of those black and white images that do contain [defused] ambience. Browne plays with different ambient effects in his *Into the Forest*, shifting from colour to black and white for the setting at the point where the protagonist enters 'the woods' of a fairytale world where he encounters characters from rhymes and tales. Browne incorporates many 'hidden' characters and objects in the shapes of the environment in these pictures (see Figure 2.22), and the reader explores them in a different way from the emotionally compelling coloured pictures that open and close the story.

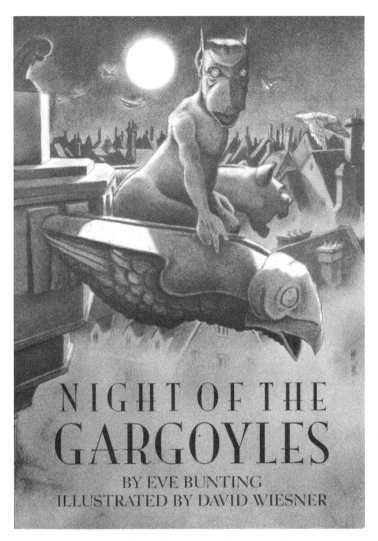

Figure 2.21 [defused: dramatised] from (Bunting and Wiesner, 1994).

While Browne's drawings depict textures and some light and shade effects, a more emotionally compelling atmospheric effect is created in *Night of the Gargoyles* (Bunting and Wiesner, 1994), where the ambience is much more clearly [defused: dramatised]. The exaggerated lighting effects here create an eerie, sinister atmosphere appropriate to the topic (see Figure 2.21). While the lighting effects themselves create an atmospheric mood, the absence of colour again encourages the reader to scrutinise the 'content' of the image and take note of the weirdness and sinister nature of the creatures being depicted. In general then, picture book artists will only ignore the rich meaning potential of colour choices and their capacity to work on the reader's emotions when they wish either to avoid that emotional

Figure 2.22 [defused] enveloping ambience from *Into the Forest* (Browne, 2004).

engagement or else to invoke our feelings, particularly a sense of the uncanny or sinister, specifically by drawing attention to the ideational content of the images.

2.5 GRADUATION

We are all familiar with the ways in which we can ramp up or play down attitudinal meanings in language, as exemplifed in expressions such as ***utterly*** *wonderful* or ***reasonably*** *successful, a long **long long** time ago,* ***tons of*** *good ideas,* and so on. These linguistic resources for 'upscaling' or 'downscaling' evaluative meanings are detailed in Martin and White (2005) as the system of GRADUATION. Recent work by Economou (2009) on the evaluative meaning of news photographs has built on this to propose corresponding systems of VISUAL GRADUATION. While these have been established from a very different kind of visual data from picture book illustrations, some of the key choices identified for news photos in the subsystem of FORCE appear to have considerable relevance for picture books as ways of increasing the attitudinal impact of visual elements. In Figure 2.23 and Table 2.3, Economou's

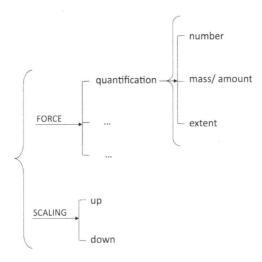

Figure 2.23 Quantification choices from the system of FORCE within VISUAL GRADUATION (adapted from Economou, 2009).

Table 2.3 Example realisations of VISUAL GRADUATION.

Force feature	Upscaled	Downscaled
quantification: number	High number of same item	Low number of same item
quantification: mass/amount	Large scale relative to other comparable elements	Small scale relative to other comparable elements
quantification: extent	Ideational item takes up large amount of available space	Ideational item takes up small amount of available space

subsystem of 'quantification' is displayed, and in Table 2.4 (overleaf) some exemplification is provided, with further examples from *The Tin Pot Foreign General and the Old Iron Woman* to be discussed in Section 2.6. Note that as quantification features may be in play singly or in combination, they are displayed in Figure 2.23 (following Economou, 2009) both as alternatives and as simultaneous options.

Quantification choices can play an important role in ensuring an attitudinal response in the reader, often working together with other interpersonal choices. In Figure 2.9, shown again as the top image in Table 2.4, even if only one person had been depicted, the mediated focalisation would encourage the viewer to react emotionally to the aggressive behaviour shown, but by using upscaled quantification – a crowd rather than one or two people – our negative reaction is more strongly invoked. It is also possible for upscaled quantification to provoke an attitudinal response even when the ideational content is relatively neutral. Eating a dinner of sausages is not an action that is likely to attract negative evaluation from most people, but in the depiction shown in Table 2.4, we may well judge Mr Piggott

Table 2.4 Example instances of upscaled force for picture book characters.

Force	Example of upscaling		Realisation
quantification: number	From *The Great Bear* (Gleeson and Greder,1999)		High number of persons watching bear
quantification: mass/amount	From *The Tin Pot Foreign General and the Old Iron Woman* (Briggs, 1994)		Unrealistically large size of general in comparison with ships
quantification: extent	From *Piggybook* (Browne, [1986] 1996)		Mr Piggott more than fills the picture frame, taking up 'too much' space

negatively because of the excessive amount of picture space he occupies – a graduation choice of upscaled [quantification: extent]. While VISUAL GRADUATION has not yet been systematically explored in relation to picture book illustrations, the fact that the small set of quantification choices proves readily applicable suggests that this is an area that is likely to prove fruitful for further investigation.

2.6   Visual interpersonal meaning in *The Tinpot Foreign General and the Old Iron Woman*

The visual systems discussed in this chapter function to depict the emotions of characters and interpersonal relations between them, as well as to position readers with respect to the characters and the story as a whole (which in turn involves constructing our point of view and working on our emotions). The richness of the possibilities simultaneously available from multiple systems and the skill with which picture book artists deploy them mean that brief and 'simple' stories can have very powerful effects. One celebrated text that illustrates this well is the political satire, *The Tinpot Foreign General and the Old Iron Woman* (Briggs, 1994), which relates the story of the Faulklands war between Britain and Argentina in the 1980s – a war that was costly in human life though the disputed territory had only symbolic value for either side (discussed in Martin, 2006). There are three different styles of depiction in the book, each associated with a different ambience in relation to a different set of participants. In this final section to this chapter, a commentary will be given on some of the interpersonal options deployed in this text (see Table 2.5 on pp. 50–52), particularly contrasts in ambience.

The book opens verbally with 'Once upon a time …' and visually with a distant observing view of the disputed 'sad little island' dwarfed by the empty ocean and gathering stormclouds. The ambience is muted, dark, cool and removed, the latter suiting both the fairytale distance invoked by the verbiage and the geographical remoteness of the actual island. On the succeeding spread, we meet the shepherds on an island shown as barely thirty paces wide, but are kept at a distance by the long shot and by the minimalist drawing style, which makes it difficult to discern any eye contact that may be being made by the shepherds. The exaggeratedly tiny size of the island (in comparison with its inhabitants) is a downscaling choice of quantification (mass/amount), emphasising the absurdity of the dispute over such territory. Equally striking once again is the ambience, which is again cool, dark and removed in the use of only dull shades of green and blue.

All these interpersonal choices are transformed when the page is turned. Instead of fuzzy, distant, outlined characters surrounded on all sides by the natural environment of sea and rain, we are presented with the sharply drawn 'wicked foreign general' made of tin pots, who gazes down at us powerfully from a high angle in a medium to close shot. Instead of being diminished by the environment, he fills the entire page – an upscaling choice of extent; instead of a blurred minimalist style there is sharp-edged and detailed caricature, alienating and humorous in effect. Instead of a soft, removed ambience there is one that is comparatively vibrant and more familiar, with the cool blue of the sky above countered by the red rocks of the general's kingdom below and the vibrant splashes of blood on his dagger and gold on his uniform. The Tin Pot General's eyes glare down at us in a disturbing choice of contact and the energy of the ambience is menacing, given his size and stance.

Over three more spreads, an upscaled graduation choice of mass/amount (i.e. excessive size) for the general emphasises his power as he perches on a ship that is toylike in comparison (see Table 2.4), or bestrides the island in boots large enough to contain its entire population or yells at the shepherds in a hurricane of bossiness. The image of his colossal boots creates a possible visual allusion to the Colossus of Rhodes, which, given the graduation choices of upscaled number (of accompanying soldiers), extent and mass/amount (of general's legs) helps provoke an additional negative reaction in the reader. And it is at this point that we are aligned with the shepherds through shared focalisation as both we and they face the innumerable invaders. Again the prevailing ambience is cool and removed until, after four spreads with the general, 'an old woman' made of iron is introduced on the next page turn. The caricature drawing style and exaggerated size of depiction used for the Tinpot General resumes here, and as with the general, her symbolic attributes (guns, money and red hair) create vibrant, warm splashes on the white page in contrast to the cool muted ambience of the shepherds' world. Her guns and money also instantiate upscaled force in terms of number, amount and extent. Multiple high force choices continue in the wickedly funny caricature-style depictions of the iron woman as a grotesque and demented dominatrix that take up the three succeeding spreads, culminating in a double-page spread in which the Tin Pot Foreign General and the Old Iron Woman face each other in hostility from the edges of the two pages with the intervening space filled with cannonballs and red, yellow and pink explosions, as we read below: 'BANG! BANG! BANG! went the guns of the Tin-Pot Foreign General. BANG! BANG! BANG! went the guns of the Old Iron Woman.' This page, like the whole section, is vibrant in ambience, alienating in style and uses upscaled force to create satirical effect.

When the page is turned again, there is a shocking contrast as the cartoon-like hilarity and energy of the previous pages is unexpectedly replaced by an indistinct black and white image of a single fallen figure on the recto page. The left page contains only the words 'Some men were shot.' The next five spreads similarly separate verbal and visual on facing pages. Each contains a short sentence describing a form of death facing a black and white image indistinctly depicting that death, concluding with a single image across the two pages, where a group of men look out at us, illustrating the proposition 'Some men were only half blown to bits and came home with parts of their bodies missing'. The effect of this section of the book is extraordinarily moving. The pictures themselves make the choice of defused flat ambience and thus do not impact on the viewer in any visceral way. But they do force attention onto the 'fact' of what is being shown (the ideational content) and onto the spare verbal accompaniment, which states in succession, 'drowned', 'burned alive' and 'blown to bits'.[11] In this way, Briggs brings us back to the reality of war without in fact opting for a particularly realistic visual style. Instead he makes visual ambience choices that leave us no choice but to attend to the ideational and to the verbal. And it is by these means that our feelings are engaged in a more sober and reflective way.

After this section, the text reintroduces in quick succession each of the three different visual styles: the bold bright high force cartoon style, the 'island' style with its cool, removed and now darker ambience and then the defused flat ambience of black and white drawing. This occurs in three spreads presenting the culmination of the war in relation to the three sets of participants. There is high glee ('I won, I won') from the Old Iron Woman, a sad continuation of life for the shepherds and a 'big iron box full of dead bodies' of the soldiers. After these three double pages, Briggs again makes unexpected and highly effective ambience choices in relation to the ideational content. First there is a double page that depicts only a single medal on the large expanse of the white background. The splash of red, white and blue created by the medal ribbon reminds us textually of the colour choices for the general's first appearance, perhaps hinting in this way that the winner is linked to the loser in terms of imperial pretensions and aggression. At any event, the total absence of enveloping ambience not only makes the medal and its coloured ribbon highly salient, but invites us to read it with appraisal, as does the switch to low

---

11. The images show that within the [defused: flat] option there can be a further choice of [higher energy] versus [lower energy] depending on the amount of black/white contrast created. Briggs creates greater contrast for images accompanying 'burned alive' and 'blown to bits' to suit the greater violence of these meanings.

force choices of number and extent. Coming immediately after the mention of the box of dead bodies, it is overwhelmingly likely that negative judgement will be our response. This means that when we turn the page again to meet the vibrancy of a double page spread of innumerable fluttering union jack flags and raised bayonets filling the entire spread, we are likely to feel more appalled than celebratory in our response. Following the 'excess' of upscaled force and vibrant ambience here, invoking negative judgement, the final pages again shift to defused ambience. The book concludes on the verso page with a black and white sketch of a single family tending a grave, with their backs to the viewer. This restrained picture has a powerful effect in directing our attention to the ideational content at hand in both image and verbiage. By this point we can be left to form a moral response without the image using interpersonal choices to position us in any obvious way.

Briggs thus uses three visual styles within the text, making telling use of choices in focalisation, pathos, graduation and ambience in conjunction with verbal language and the ideational depictions. The book enables readers to enjoy both the humour of the satire and the pathos of the history, but above all to be emotionally worked over through the interpersonal choices so as to be aligned with Briggs's ethical stance on the war. Even such a brief discussion of a single text indicates the huge contribution to meaning made by visual interpersonal meanings, but also shows that it is not possible to discuss these meanings in isolation from a consideration of the ideational content of the pictures (and of course the verbal co-text). The next chapter will therefore address directly some of the ideational meaning systems drawn upon by picture book illustrators both within individual images and across narrative sequences.

Table 2.5 Summary interpersonal analysis of *The Tin Pot Foreign General and the Old Iron Woman* (Briggs, 1984).

Page opening	Ideation	FOCALISATION	SOCIAL DISTANCE	PROXIMITY	PATHOS	AFFECT (INFERRED)	GRADUATION (FORCE: QUANTIFICATION)	INVOLVEMENT	ORIENTATION	POWER	AMBIENCE
1	Seascape	observe	very far	–	–	–	downscaled mass/ amount and extent (island)	–	–	–	muted: dark, cool, removed
2	Island	unclear	far	v. close (sheep; shepherds)	appreciative	placid (shepherds)	downscaled mass/ amount (island); number (building, shepherds)	involved	side-by-side (shepherds)	equality	muted: less dark, cool, removed
3	Tin Pot General (TPG)	contact	medium	–	alienating	aggressive, manic (TPG)	upscaled extent (TPG)	involved	–	TPG power	more vibrant, cool with v. warm splashes
4	TPG's fleet	observe	far	v. close (soldiers)	alienating	menacing (TPG)	upscaled mass/ amount and extent (TPG); number (soldiers)	detached	side-by-side (soldiers)	equality	less vibrant, cool with warm splashes
5	Arrival	observe	close (TPG); far (others)	v. close (soldiers; shepherds)	appreciative	–	upscaled mass/ amount and extent (tp g); number (soldiers)	involved	side-by-side (soldiers; shepherds)	TPG power	muted, cool, removed
6	TPG bossing	observe	close (TPG); far shepherds	close (shepherds); quite far (TPG and shepherds)	appreciative	aggressive, angry	upscaled mass/ amount and extent (TPG)	detached	face-to-face (TPG & shepherds)	TPG power over shepherds	muted, cool, removed
7	Old Iron Woman (OIW)	observe	far	–	alienating	hateful	upscaled mass/ amount and extent (OIW); number (money, guns)	detached	–	OIW power	vibrant warm splashes only; removed
8	OIW shoots	observe	medium	–	alienating	enraged	upscaled mass/ amount and extent	involved	–	OIW power	vibrant warm splashes only; removed

#											
9	OIW with coins	observe	closer	–	alienating	gleeful	upscaled mass/amount and extent (OIW); number (coins)	less involved	-	OIW power	vibrant warm splashes only; removed
10	OIW's fleet	observe	far	v. close (soldiers)	alienating	positive, encouraging	upscaled mass/amount and extent (OIW); number (soldiers, guns)	detached	side-by-side (soldiers)	OIW power	vibrant warm and cool splashes
11	BANG!	observe	close	separated (TPG and OIW)	alienating	aggressive	upscaled number (explosions, balls)	detached	face-to-face	TPG, OIW power	vibrant and warm
12	some ... shot	observe	far	–	–	–	–	detached	–	–	defused: flat
13	some ... drowned	observe	v. far	–	–	–	–	involved	–	–	defused: flat
14	some ... burnt alive	observe	far	–	–	–	–	involved	–	–	defused: flat
15	some men ... blown to bits	observe	far	–	–	–	–	detached	–	–	defused flat
16	Maimed soldiers	unclear	far	v. close	appreciative	sombre	–	involved	–	equal	defused: flat
17	Crosses	observe	far	–	–	–	upscaled number	involved	–	–	defused: flat
18	TPG defeated by OIW	observe	medium	separated	alienating	negative (TPG) triumphant (OIW)	downscaled mass/amount & extent (TPG); upscaled mass/amount & extent (OIW)	detached	face-to-face	OIW power	vibrant, warm, removed
19	Destroyed island	observe	far	close	appreciative	unclear (grim?)	as for second opening	detached	side-by-side (shepherds); back-to-back/face-to-face (soldiers & shepherds)	–	muted: dark, cool, removed,

Table 2.5 (*Continued*)

Page opening	Ideation	FOCALISATION	SOCIAL DISTANCE	PROXIMITY	PATHOS	AFFECT (INFERRED)	GRADUATION (FORCE: QUANTIFICATION)	INVOLVEMENT	ORIENTATION	POWER	AMBIENCE
20	Box	observe	far	–	–	–	–	detached	–	–	defused: flat
21	Medal	observe	–	–	–	–	–	involved	–	–	splash only (union flag colours)
22	Flags on parade	observe	–	–	–	–	upscaled extent and involved number	involved	–	flag power	vibrant; cool with hot splashes
23	Family watches TV	observe	far	close (family members)	appreciative	–	–	detached	side-by-side (family); face-to-face (family and TV image of OIW)	family lack of power	defused: flat, vibrant, warm splash of TV
24	Family at grave	observe	far	quite close but separate	appreciative	dejected	–	detached	aligned alongside grave	equality	defused: flat

3 Construing Representations

3.1 Ideational meaning

Children are offered picture books as their first reading experience partly because a visual semiotic representation is so much more accessible than a linguistic one. This is because a picture of a scene or object in a picture book uses the same forms and shapes as are familiar to us from our experience of that scene or object in the material world. A red balloon is perceived as red in hue and round in shape whether we see the material balloon or a picture of it. And using a semiotic device such as perspective to represent depth and three-dimensionality enables the content of an image to be perceived in a way that mimics the perception of the material reality it depicts. Not surprisingly, then, one kind of simple picture book (the 'concept' book) uses drawn or photographic images chiefly as a means of teaching the child to recognise the written forms that name the object or event that is represented. At the same time, many of the depictions in children's first stories are far from naturalistic: Dr Seuss's famous cat in a hat bears very little resemblance to anyone's family feline, the Mr Men characters are not much like actual people in shape or proportions, while the bright yellow, sharply pointed stars of pictorial convention are a far cry from the tiny dots of light we see in the night sky. It takes repeated juxtapositions of spoken word and visual image to gradually familiarise children with conventional and more abstracted forms of visual representation in their reading material.

The fact that children can have difficulty in interpreting meaning even where depictions are generic or naturalistic in style becomes clear from the following excerpt from an unscripted conversation between a four-year-old boy and his mother. They are looking at the verso (left) page of the second opening of Cooper's (1996) prize-winning book, *The Baby Who Wouldn't Go to Bed*, shown as Figure 3.1. The conversation proceeds as follows:

> *Child:* Hey that's – that's boy (pointing at the depicted mother); that's –
> *Mother:* That's a girl; that's the mother.
> *Child:* That's – that doesn't look like –

Figure 3.1 *The Baby Who Wouldn't Go to Bed* (Cooper, 1996: second opening).

Mother: That's the baby (pointing to the boy in car).
Child: Oh, how come it doesn't look like a mother?
Mother: Well it is; that's the mother, and the baby's there.
Child: Is that the real mother?
Mother: The real mother in the story, yes.
Child: Well, it doesn't look very big does it?
Mother: Do you think she's too small to be a mother, do you?
Child: Yeah. Do you?
Mother: She looks big enough to me; especially with the baby so small.
Child: Yeah well; you're bigger than her aren't you?
Mother: I am bigger than her.
Child: How come?
Mother: I just am. She just didn't grow very big, that's all.
Child: Oh, does mothers sometimes be small?[1]

Notwithstanding the greater 'transparency' of experiential visual meaning, then, children still have to do interpretive work and their inexperience either with material phenomena (such as the body types and range of clothing worn by young women) and/or with visual ones (such as the foreshortening effect of a high angle of vision) may initially contribute to minor confusions.

By way of exploring the semiosis of visual ideational representation, it is useful to draw on some of Kress and van Leeuwen's (2006) observations on visual 'representational' meaning, which will provide a framework for elaborating on those aspects particularly relevant for picture book stories. As a basis for their discussions, Kress and van Leeuwen draw analogies between visual and verbal experiential

---

1. Data here and below courtesy of Jane Torr (see Torr, 2008 for details).

Table 3.1 Participants, processes and circumstances in clause structures.

Participant	Process	Participant	Circumstance
The young woman	ran	–	quickly
A small boy	is pulling	a cart	along the street
That baby	cries	–	every night
The baby	is looking at	the ball	–
The old man	is	our teacher	–

structures.[2] They argue that images, like verbal clauses, may usefully be seen as potentially involving three aspects of experience: participants (who or what is depicted), processes (depicted actions or relations) and circumstances (where, when, how, with what) – elements that together make up what Halliday and Matthiessen (2004) refer to as ideational 'figures'. Some verbal examples of these elements are shown in Table 3.1.

Turning to visual images, Kress and van Leeuwen (2006) suggest that the categories of participants, processes and circumstances can also be identified here. They argue that the enclosed shapes, masses or 'volumes' (Arnheim, 1982) in an image constitute the participants, while oblique lines or 'vectors' created by their limbs or other elements create a sense of dynamism, process or action. Thus in Figure 3.1, the mother and the baby in the car (or the baby and the car) in the verso image are the depicted participants, while the sense of action is created not only by our extra-semiotic knowledge of cars, but by the diagonal line formed by the edge of the car (see Figure 3.2). The depiction of the house interior constitutes the spatial circumstance of 'setting'. Note that this image is typical in that the participant and the action are not discrete visual elements. The car is both a participant and, through the vector it forms, the 'process' of driving.

The rest of this chapter will consider picture book images in

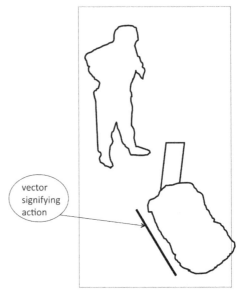

Figure 3.2 Motion vector in verso image shown in Figure 3.1.

2. The term 'ideational' encompasses two kinds of meanings: the 'experiential' (processes, participants and circumstances) and the 'logical' (recursive links between different structures). Kress and van Leeuwen's (2006) analysis of representational meaning is concerned with the former.

terms of these three categories of meaning – participants, processes and circumstances – with most attention paid to aspects of their representation in a narrative
sequence.

3.2   Participants

3.2.1   Depicted participants: character attribution

The previous chapter considered semiotic choices relevant to the way that readers
relate to picture book characters and the way that those characters exhibit feelings and social interactions within the story world. When it comes to ideational
meaning, we are concerned instead with the identity and attributes of the character – both in a single image and in relation to the story sequence. While the only
experiential aspect of a character that can be explicitly inscribed into an image is
his or her physical appearance, the viewer can, as in life, infer from this (and the
depicted context) other categories, such as age, class, ethnicity, role and place in
the family.

While picture book characters are usually shown engaged in some kind of activity, in what Kress and van Leeuwen (2006) term 'narrative' processes, they may
also be presented to the reader in a more static image of the type that they refer to
as 'conceptual' in nature. Lacking vectors, such images invite slower scrutiny and
interpretation of the participant's attributes. They may occur at the very beginning
of the story, initiating the Orientation stage,[3] where one or more portraits can be
used to introduce the character/s, as in *Hyram and B* (Caswell and Ottley, 2003)
or the opening of several of Anthony Browne's stories, such as *Piggybook* ([1986]
1996) and *Little Beauty* (2008). Static images, including pictures of participants, also
occur at moments within a story where the rhythm of the text calls for a pause or
a reflective moment rather than a depiction or evocation of action and movement.
The double-page spread showing only a medal in *The Tin Pot Foreign General and
the Old Iron Woman* (Briggs, 1984) would be an example (see discussion in Chapter
2, Section 2.5). Another is shown as Figure 3.3 from *Possum Magic* (Fox and Vivas,
[1983] 2004), showing the page following the little possum's statement 'I don't mind.'
In this example, the verbal text reads 'But in her heart of hearts she did', while the
conceptual image of the possum invites the reader to pause on this evaluation of the
narrative complication.

Another role for conceptual images in picture books is to guide the child in
reading for significance rather than simply recognition of the character in action.
Anthony Browne's (1992) *Zoo* is an example of a book that is not primarily concerned with specific actions, being a moral exemplum about animal freedom, and it
includes a number of head-and-shoulders portraits of different characters. Among
these is one showing the overbearing father in the story set against the background

---

3. For discussion of story structures see Martin and Rose (2008).

Figure 3.3 A 'conceptual' image from *Possum Magic* (Fox and Vivas, [1983] 2004).

of blue sky as he glares down at us irascibly. Behind him, the clouds form the shape of horns which appear to grow from his head, functioning as what Kress and van Leeuwen (2006: 105) call 'symbolic attributes'. Later in the story, we are faced with the child narrator and his brother gazing out at us, each wearing a monkey-face hat, these also functioning as symbolic attributes suggesting the likeness between human and animal. Perhaps most striking of all is the close-up of the long-suffering gorilla's face, bisected vertically and horizontally by cage bars which form a cross, again inviting a symbolic reading (see Styles and Arizpe, 2001 for children's responses to this picture). Images like these help apprentice their readers into a literary approach to text in which the meaning of a story is not found in the series of events *per se*, but in their symbolic value in constructing a narrative 'theme' (see Hasan, 1985 for this use of the term 'theme' in relation to underlying message symbolised by the story; cf Martin, 1996a).

Symbolic attributes may also be incorporated into more dynamic images containing vectors, since all such 'narrative' images (Kress and van Leeuwen, 2006) also afford relations of attribution. Examples of this are the wolf suit worn by Max in all the pictures of *Where the Wild Things are* (Sendak, 1963) or the spectacles and apron worn by Grandma Poss in *Possum Magic* (Fox and Vivas, [1983] 2004) – symbolising her erudition and her caregiving role. Symbolic attributes are less pointedly drawn to our attention in such narrative images, whereas their presence in essentially static pictures encourages contemplation and probably facilitates the young reader's recognition of their symbolic role.

Finally, with respect to the creation of visual symbols, we can note that over the course of a book, some depicted element/s may accrue symbolic and interpersonal force by an accumulation of choices within the text that gradually discharge the ideational meaning and re-charge the object with attitudinal meaning (as outlined in Martin, 2010). See Martin, 2008b for exemplification of this process of 'iconisation' in the picture book *Photographs in the Mud* (Wolfer and Harrison-Lever, 2005)

3.2.2   Recognising and tracking characters: MANIFESTATION and APPEARANCE

The point has already been made that the ideational content of pictures is not always as obvious to the young child as it may appear to adults. In particular, since any individual image can only depict one moment of a single action – its inception, final result or some midpoint – a picture book narrative may compensate for this limitation by using a sequence of images to depict stages of the action. This can result in a strong contrast with the material reality being depicted when a double-page spread like that shown as Figure 3.1 shows the same character at different moments of the action. The facing pages allow us to perceive the two representations simultaneously, quite unlike the perception of a person in reality, who can only be perceived twice at two different moments. The viewer thus has to infer that multiple depictions of a character or object signify a single constant identity, something not self-evident simply from experience with the material world. The following fragment of a transcript of a conversation between a four-year-old child and his teacher reading *The Baby Who Wouldn't Go to Bed* (Cooper, 1996) illustrates this issue:

> *Child [looking at recto of second spread, shown in Figure 3.1]:* Oh, wow look, he's got two engines.
> *Teacher:* He does have two engines doesn't he? I think this one is the same one and he's driving up the hill.

Such moments of conversation with children remind us that even with respect to ideational meaning, pictures are a form of semiosis, albeit one we come to understand (in its non-abstract manifestations) without formal tuition. In particular, the issue of how participants are presented and tracked over the course of the story is worth discussing in more detail.

A visual narrative differs markedly from a verbal one in the lack of anything equivalent to the explicit system of 'REFERENCE' (Halliday and Hasan, 1976) or 'IDENTIFICATION' (Martin, 1992), whereby a presuming pronoun like *she* is used to avoid constantly reintroducing a character by name or description. In a purely visual story, a character is inferred to have the same identity when salient features of his/her appearance are repeated in subsequent images. Usually this means that at least the head is redepicted so that facial features and hair can aid recognition; and often clothing will be a clue as well, such as in the second image of Hannah in *Gorilla* (Browne, [1983] 1987), where she is shown from the rear (see Figure 2.14). More experienced readers can also recognise a character simply from a depiction of a body part and/or shadow/silhouette. Figures 2.4–2.6 from the previous chapter exemplify these possibilities. And while it is most common for a complete manifestation (i.e. one including the head) to precede a metonymic one, this is not always the case: the mother in *The Tunnel* (Browne, 1989), for example, only ever appears as a pointing arm directing the children out of the house.

A 'training' text in this regard is the wordless book *Sunshine* (Ormerod, [1981] 1983), which generally has several image panels on each double page. One such spread, shown as Figure 3.4, holds six images, the first featuring father in the kitchen, the next four depicting both father and daughter (he having moved to stand behind her) and the last showing father and just the pointing forearm of the daughter (he having moved back to his original position). In this case, after four images of the girl's head and torso in distinctive clothing, the young reader is primed to recognise her continuing presence in the final picture just from the arm, even though the father's activity is now centre stage again. With this priming, a little later the opposite occurs: the father is shown again but initially just as a hand holding a newspaper and then in a following image the whole person is revealed. (Conversely the mother is shown and subsequently must be inferred from the bump in the bedclothes created by her knees). See Figure 3.5.

In her discussion of filmic techniques for identification of participants, Tseng (2009) argues that both explicit visual repetition of a character (as of the father in

Figure 3.4 Character reappearance in *Sunshine* (Ormerod, [1981] 1983) as whole then part.

Figure 3.5 Character reappearance in *Sunshine* (Ormerod, [1981] 1983) as part then whole.

every frame following the first in Figure 3.4) and 'implicit reappearance' through depiction of a body part (as of the daughter's arm in the final picture of Figure 3.4) are visual textual systems for 'presuming' identity. In other words, these techniques are claimed to be deictic in nature, pointing the viewer elsewhere for identity retrieval. Thus, in Tseng's analysis, the girl's arm in the final picture of Figure 3.4 'refers' backwards to the previous depiction in a way analogous to a pronoun. Where a character is first seen as a body part and later has his/her identity revealed by a shot of the face, as in Figure 3.5, Tseng speaks of the body part as a 'prelude' that refers forward to the later shot (cataphoric reference in cohesion theory). By interpreting explicit and implicit reappearance (among other visual and multimodal techniques) as a deictic means for participant identification, Tseng locates these choices within the textual rather than ideational metafunction.

While there is an argument for seeing a metonymic manifestation as functioning deictically in a way similar to a linguistic pronoun, the difference between the two semiotics should not be underplayed. Visually there is no real equivalent to a pronoun and the principal means of 'tracking' a character within a visual picture book narrative is by inferring identity from the reappearance of the face or salient features of the depicted participant. In other words, it is necessary to construe character identity from the ideational representation rather than from a system of deixis: it is through ideation rather than phoricity that we recognise the characters.

Another relevant factor in identifying a participant as the story progresses is whether the character reappears in the very next image or at some later point in the story. This is something that may well be significant for the theme of the story – for example the absence of the mother during the episodes of the baby's (failed) escape in *The Baby Who Wouldn't Go to Bed* (Cooper, 1996) is important, as is the shifting between appearances of males and female in *Piggybook*, again with the mother's absence in the central portion pivotal to the story. In terms of character recognition of course, a reappearance that occurs immediately strengthens the inference of 'same identity' compared with a later reappearance that may rely much more strongly on mediation by the verbal text.

We can sum up the discussion of character depiction to this point in terms of the small set of choices shown as Figure 3.6. An interesting apprenticing text in regard to these choices is the rhyming book *Each Peach Pear Plum* (Ahlberg and Ahlberg,

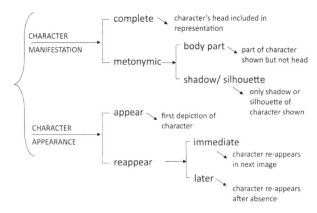

Figure 3.6 Basic character depiction options.

[1978] 1989), where new characters are often first shown as a body part – such as an arm, legs or bottom – before being shown in full (and named) on the following page turn. On repeated readings the child viewer becomes familiar with this pattern and delights in recognising the character from the metonymic manifestation before he or she is fully revealed.

3.2.2.1   Character reappearance: variation in status

An additional or alternative strategy used in *Each Peach Pear Plum* is first to show a new character (either complete or metonymically) as just a small element in the background or off to the side, and then on the page-turn to depict them in full, and centre stage (see Figures 3.7 and 3.8). This has the effect of moving the character from being embedded in the circumstantial setting to being a fully fledged participant, inviting the reader to have fun attending to apparently insignificant elements in the image. Cultivating this kind of attention has value not only for visual literacy,[4] but also for reading purely verbal stories where apparently inconsequential details may well prove significant in terms of thematic meaning.

Each Peach Pear Plum is, strictly speaking, not a narrative text, but this strategy of shifting the status of a character into or out circumstantiation also occurs in narrative picture books and is identified as the option of [reappear: varied: status] in Figure 3.9 below. A narrative example can be found in *Hyram and B* (Caswell and Ottley, 2003), where it underlines the status of the teddy bear protagonists, changing from loved toys to discarded rubbish and back again. During their time as disregarded unwanted objects, the teddies are on occasion on the periphery of the image, or hard to distinguish or locate. In this respect there is a similarity with another text involving teddy bears where there is ambiguity between setting and participant – McKee's (1982) humorous story, *I Hate My Teddy Bear* – although the

---

4. See Tseng (2009) on the possibility of 'gradual' as well as 'immediate' establishment of salience to endow a depicted object or person with participant status in film.

Figure 3.7 Cinderella's first appearance as an arm in background (Ahlberg and Ahlberg, [1978] 1989: third opening, verso).

Figure 3.8 Cinderella emerging on second appearance (Ahlberg and Ahlberg, [1978] 1989: fourth opening, verso).

function of the ambiguity in this latter book is rather different. In McKee's story there are two child characters, each with a teddy bear, whose competitive dialogic exchanges form much of the sparse verbal text, making them central protagonists. But the children and their teddies are sometimes partly hidden or less prominent than the numerous unknown 'peripheral' characters who fleetingly take up more space and attention in the image. In this way the text subverts, and thus alerts us to, our taken-for-granted expectations about the nature of narratives as singular stories consistently focussed on key protagonists. The choice of [reappear: varied: status] thus serves the book's metafictive purpose rather than being what the story is about.

A metafictive intent also appears to lie behind another narrative exhibiting variation in participant status. This is Crew and Scott's (2000) *In My Father's Room*, which features a first-person narration about 'Dad', voiced by a child who is shown in almost every picture. We hear about all of Dad's varied and short-lived hobbies (and Mum's indulgent comments) but not a word of the child's own depicted activity, which is the creation of a life-sized papier mâché head. In the first image, where the child is shown constructing it, the head is very prominent and has the status of a depicted participant, but in the next it is just a very small item in the far background as we view the child sorting through Dad's discarded stamps in the foreground. Subsequently the head reappears in close-up a number of times, as well as again peripherally. On the final page we see the completed bust, labelled 'Dad' and smiling out at us. We realise that all along the child has been creating a representation of Dad not only through the language of the narration, but also manually through materials (which symbolically comprise detritus from Dad's discarded hobbies). The text thus cleverly exploits its bimodality to invite reflection on the process of character creation – something emphasised at the end when the child discovers that Dad's latest hobby is to write a fictional story about the narrator. The emergence and receding of the model head during the course of the story is deployed as a strategy allowing us to take in visually one creative endeavour (the building of the head) while consciously attending to another (the verbal picture of Dad), which in turn includes the secret of a third (Dad writing about the child).

Another function of variation in participant status towards or away from circumstantiation is to suggest the imaginative life of the child. In *The Baby Who Wouldn't Go to Bed* (Cooper, 1996), the defiant toddler drives into the landscape and has conversations with a tiger, a troop of soldiers, a train and even the moon, all of which recede on the final page to be revealed as toys forming part of his bedroom setting, confirming that the child has been engaged in an imaginative journey. Similarly in *The Tunnel* (Browne, 1989), a wolf depicted within a small picture in the girl's bedroom early on, reappears later emerging from a tree in the forest as she runs in terror, suggesting her projected fears. Thus the option of [varied: status] can be used to symbolise both a character's changing status as a protagonist, and the depicted character's creative imagination.

As already noted, the possibility of a character's reappearance involving a change in status towards or away from participant-hood is catered for in Figure 3.9 by the features [varied: status], with moving into salience being the [emerge] suboption and moving into the setting being the [recede] suboption.

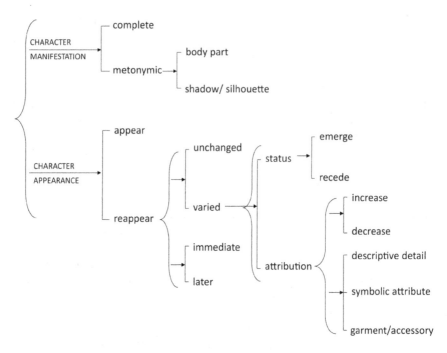

Figure 3.9 CHARACTER MANIFESTATION and APPEARANCE options (see Table 3.2 for realisations).

3.2.2.2   *Character reappearance: variation in attribution*

The receding of a participant into an aspect of the setting is just one kind of change in the depiction of a character that can take place over the course of a picture book. Other changes enabled by the reappearance of the same character from page to page may be either more or less dramatic. Minor changes in attribution, such as in clothing or accessories, do not confuse recognition and may have symbolic significance in the story, as in the case of Peter Rabbit's loss of clothing (Potter, 1902), which has been noted as playing a complex role in his shifts between more human and more animal identities (Scott, 1994; Mullins, 2009). The young protagonist of *Sunshine* is another whose loss of clothing is to be read metaphorically as well as literally. She sheds her night-clothes over a series of images in order to don her schoolwear and schoolbag, with the change in attire clearly representing her independence and competence. Another possible variation in attribution relates to descriptive detail. In Browne's ([1986] 1996) *Piggybook*, the increased detail in the depiction of the mother, who is virtually faceless on first appearance, signifies her assertion of herself as a person by the end, while in *The Tunnel* (Browne, 1989) the increase in descriptive detail of the 'petrified' boy symbolises his restoration to life and vigour through the love of his sister.

Finally, the temporary acquisition of symbolic attributes, as already described for *Zoo* (Browne, 1992) in Section 3.2.1, is another possible variation in attribution over the course of a story. These various possibilities are indicated by the suboptions

Table 3.2 Realisations of CHARACTER MANIFESTATION and APPEARANCE.

MANIFESTATION feature/s				Realisation
complete				Depiction of character including face or head
metonymic:	body part			Part of body depicted, excluding head
	shadow/silhouette			Depiction of shadow/outline only of all or part of body

APPEARANCE feature/s				
appear				Depiction of first appearance in story
reappear:	unchanged			Character depicted as recognisably the same in participant status and appearance as previous depiction
	varied:	status:	emerge	character has moved (further) from background setting (relative to previous depiction)
			recede	character has moved (further) into background setting (relative to previous depiction)
reappear:	varied:	attribution ...		Character depicted with increase or decrease in clothes/accessories, symbolic attributes or descriptive detail relative to previous depiction

dependent on [varied: attribution] in Figure 3.9. (Note that variation in attribution may be an alternative to or additional to variation in status, indicated by double bracketing of these options.) Realisations of all options are listed in Table 3.2.

More extreme changes in appearance occur when a character transforms into a participant of a different kind. This happens in *Piggybook* (Browne, [1986] 1996), when the male family members morph into pigs as Browne's images invest the ideational meaning in the metaphor involved in the mother calling them 'pigs'. As they give up their piggish, male chauvinist ways, the characters transform back into humans. Another book of Browne's, entitled *Changes* (1990), makes participant transformation a key feature of the text in order to address the theme of the young child's anxiety about the impending change in his family occasioned by a new sibling. Here it is not the human character whose essence changes, but all the participant objects in his environment – a slipper morphing into a bird, a chair into an animal, a ball into a potato, etc., shown either as a hybrid object in mid-transformation in a single image or changing over the course of two or three pictures. This possibility of radical transformation of a participant has not been built into the network, as it may prove to be a feature peculiar to Browne's surrealistic style rather than a more generalisable option. In Browne's work it helps to teach the young reader how to read what is literally going on as metaphorical, a necessary ability for recovering the themes symbolised by what is going on in thematic narratives (Rothery, 1996: 112–14). For example, in *Piggybook*, the visual re-semiosis of the insult *pig* underscores the word's negative metaphorical meaning, while in *Changes*, the representation of transforming participants as a projection of the child's mental state similarly literalises the meaning of the wording used in the story: 'everything was going to change', showing by the end that this literal visual representation isn't the interpretation of the statement that matters for this story's theme.

3.2.3   Relations between characters

Being spatial and compositional in nature, the visual semiotic is especially well adapted to enabling comparison and contrast. We are all familiar with this in 'spot the difference' quizzes in magazines and 'before and after' advertising shots. In a picture book, this facility can be exploited in many ways, which include linking characters to one another. In their visual grammar, Kress and van Leeuwen (2006) point out that a symmetrical presentation of comparable images on the page is a way of 'covertly' constructing them as members of the same class. An example of this co-classification relation is found on the first page of *Zoo* (Browne, 1992), where the four family members are shown as four portraits of identical size and orientation (see Figure 3.10; in this case, the superordinate category is available in the verbal text above the pictures, which says 'My Family'). Within a single image, even where a narrative action is being depicted, the co-classificational relation is also found, often when characters are lined up in a row, for example linking the Wild Things

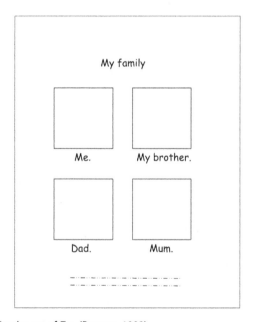

Figure 3.10 Opening layout of *Zoo* (Browne, 1992).

in some of the images in *Where the Wild Things are* (Sendak, 1963) or the camp inmates in *Let the Celebrations Begin* (Wild and Vivas, 1991).

As well as these co-classificational relations between characters, it is common for pairs of participants to be compared and contrasted.[5] *The Tunnel* (Browne, 1989) is a text that strongly foregrounds this relation. It opens with adjacent portraits of the two protagonists, a sister and a brother, she set against a 'feminine' flowery background and he a 'masculine' brick wall. We can see simultaneously the great family likeness in their facial features and the contrast not only in their settings, but in her soft muted clothing and his vibrant sweater in bold primary colours.

Another text by Browne invites comparison of characters through the configurational shape of the participants. In *Gorilla* ([1983] 1987), this occurs within a single image, between adjacent images and across different parts of the book. Comparison and contrast through configurational shape within one image is found on the recto of the sixth opening when we see the gorilla in hat and coat framing one side of the picture, while the father's hanging hat and coat above his standing boots forms a shape framing the other side. Before this point, though, comparison of characters has already been set up through adjacent images, this time featuring Hannah and her father. The very first spread shows Hannah facing us absorbed in reading her book and on the facing page (shown earlier as Figure 2.14) her father facing us absorbed in reading his newspaper. This juxtaposition hints at a likeness between the two that is nowhere available in the verbal narrative presented from Hannah's point of view. It works with the ambience choices discussed in the previous chapter to allow a more complex assessment of the characters. Finally, the book concludes with a silhouette of Hannah and her father walking away hand in hand, which links retrospectively to a very similar picture of Hannah and the gorilla at the start of their 'perfect outing' together, again pointing to the role of the gorilla in Hannah's mind as the perfect father.

This discussion of how characters relate within the narrative sequence references the options shown in Figure 3.11, with realisations detailed in Table 3.3.

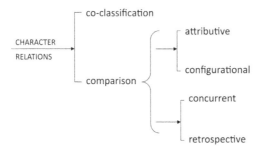

Figure 3.11 Relations between characters.

---

5. While verbal language discriminates between comparison (likeness against a backdrop of difference) and contrast (difference against a backdrop of likeness), a visual text has non-directional affordance, making both relations equally and immediately available.

Table 3.3 Realisations of CHARACTER RELATIONS options.

CHARACTER RELATIONS FEATURE		Realisation
co-classification		Symmetrical display of equal size participants with same spatial orientation
comparison/contrast:	attributive	Comparison/contrast in attributes/accessories of two characters comparably displayed
	configurational	Comparison/contrast invited by similar shape and contours of two characters/groups
comparison/contrast:	concurrent	Comparison/contrast available in single or adjacent images
	retrospective	Comparison/contrast with character from previous point in story

3.3 Processes

3.3.1 Depicted actions

As the picture books under discussion here are those telling stories, we can expect the majority of their images to constitute what Kress and van Leeuwen (2006) refer to as narrative processes; or in other words to depict some kind of event or action and thus to contain oblique lines or vectors. Table 3.4 shows some of the different types of narrative action identified by Kress and van Leeuwen (2006), indicating the kind of vector that is relevant. It should be noted that although only one type of process has been named for each example, both action and perception ('reaction' in Kress and van Leeuwen's terminology) are construed in a number of cases.

While Kress and van Leeuwen (2006) argue that the depiction of physical, verbal or mental action will always involve vectors (including 'invisible' lines of gaze), we do of course interpret ideational meaning in an image using our real-world knowledge as well as the depicted context, so that we may still interpret participants in a visual story as 'doing something' whether or not there are prominent vectors. For example, given the visual context, we will probably interpret the woman in Figure 3.12 as speaking as well as looking even though there is no vector provided by a speech bubble. Similarly, in the unfolding story of *Where the Wild Things Are* (Sendak, 1963) we may interpret Max's facial expression and bodily stance in the third picture as signifying that he is thinking even though there is no vector leading to a thought bubble. More generally, in the context of a narrative, an image of a child sleeping – as in the opening of *The Snowman* (Briggs, 1978) or *Sunshine* (Ormerod, 1983) – or a dog waiting – as in *John Brown, Rose and the Midnight Cat* (Wagner and Brooks, 1977) – will still be seen as part of the narrative event sequence. Lacking vectors, however, such images will not create a sense of motion and dynamism.

Table 3.4 Visual processes with vectors.

Principal type of action depicted	Example picture
1. Action (single participant: intransitive, or 'non-transactional', structure) vectors created by limbs	
2. Action (two participants: transitive, or 'transactional', structure) vector created by arm, spout, water drops	
3. Verbal vector leading to speech bubble.	
4. Mental: cognition vector leading to thought bubble	
5. Mental: perception ('transactional reaction' structure) vector created by line of gaze from cat to fish	

Figure 3.12 Implied verbal process.

3.3.2   Relations between actions: INTER-EVENT options

The reader of a picture book narrative must interpret not only the actions being depicted in a single image, as in Table 3.3, but the way one event relates to another in successive images. Within a verbal text, links between clauses are created through 'logico-semantic' relations of 'expansion' or 'projection' (Halliday and Matthiessen, 2004). Expansion relations, such as those of addition, time, cause, purpose, comparison, etc., can be explicitly inscribed in language with conjunctions like *and, then, because, so that, as if,* and so on, while projection relations are those of direct and reported speech and thought (e.g. *Jill said 'the baby is hungry'; Jill thought the baby was hungry*) and also of mental perceptions (*Jill noticed the baby was hungry*).

In a visual text, which does not have the same potential for explicitly specifying relations between events, the reader is called on to compare adjacent or successive images and draw inferences from likenesses and differences between them. As part of the reading process, then, comparison/contrast is a semantic strategy necessarily deployed by the reader in making sense of relations between any two depicted events. Also brought to bear, of course, is cultural knowledge relevant to the type of text, which in the case of picture book stories involves the understanding that events in a story unfold through time. Drawing on these understandings, the INTER-EVENT network shown as Figure 3.13 displays the visual options available in our corpus of picture books for relating the actions depicted in successive images.[6] It shows that

---

6. Or where there is more than one focus group in the image (see Chapter 4), the relations may obtain between actions depicted within a single image

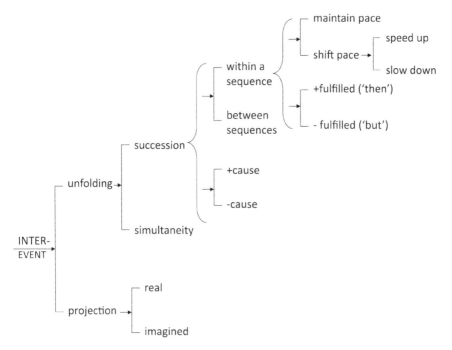

Figure 3.13 INTER-EVENT relations.

both expansion and projection relations are found, though with far fewer subcategories available than for language and fewer resources for making relations explicit.
The nature of the options and their realisations will be discussed in what follows and
are summarised in Table 3.5 on p. 77. For comparable work on conjunctive relations
in film, see Bateman, 2007, 2009 and van Leeuwen, 1991. Like Bateman we consider
the options in Figure 3.13 as options for interpreting unfolding sequences of images
– as a 'defeasible' discourse semantics in his terms. They delimit, in other words, the
kinds of relation we have to infer to make sense of the sequence.

3.3.2.1 Unfolding of narrative events

The main possibility for linking two actions within a story is the option of [unfold-
ing], which concerns the articulation of time in the narrative. The two main options
here are of temporal [succession] or alternatively of [simultaneity] being inferred
between different actions.

The default reading of a narrative image sequence is that when the same character or characters appear in successive images, either within a single page, across a
double-page spread or across a page turn, the reader is to infer a temporal relation
of succession between the actions depicted. Wherever this is not in fact the case, a
greater burden of interpretation is placed on the reader, as will be discussed below.
In some cases the succession will be between different moments of the same 'activity
sequence' (see below); for example different moments of the girl having breakfast
depicted in successive pictures in Figure 3.4. In other cases the temporal succession

is between actions that belong to different activity sequences; for example the two successive images from *Grandpa* (Norman and Young, 1988) shown as Figures 3.14 and 3.15, where the first depicts Grandpa smoking and talking while his grandson uses crayons and the second depicts the child carrying a box of toys while his mother makes a bed and his father fixes a shelf. The relation between these images is one of [unfolding: succession: between sequences].

Figure 3.14 From *Grandpa* (Norman and Young, 1988: fifth spread image).

Figure 3.15 From *Grandpa* (Norman and Young, 1988: sixth spread).

Martin (1992: 537–8) draws on Barthes' work to explain the concept of 'activity sequence', saying:

> Barthes's sequence, which is equivalent to the notion of activity sequence used here is defined as follows: 'A sequence is a logical succession of nuclei bound together by a relation of solidarity (in the Hjelmslevian sense of double implication: two terms presuppose one another): the sequence opens when one of its terms has no solidary antecedent and closes when another of its terms has no consequent. To take another deliberately trivial example, the different functions *order a drink, obtain it, drink it, pay for it* constitute an obviously closed sequence, it being impossible to put anything before the order or after the payment without moving out of the homogenous group "*Having a drink*"' (Barthes 1977: 101).

Activity sequences can be of different 'sizes', whether construed verbally or visually. That is, an activity sequence like 'having breakfast' can be construed either as a series of successive images (as in Figure 3.4 above), or a single image, perhaps depicting eating breakfast as a single action within a larger sequence such as 'getting ready for school'. Clearly four or five images depicting the component actions of a 'small-scale' sequence like 'having breakfast' requires less inference and cultural knowledge – and/or less verbal mediation – than does the same number of images depicting a 'larger-scale' sequence like 'buying a house' or 'having a holiday'.

Whatever the scale of the activity sequence, a narrative can take more or less text time to relate particular sequences, depending on their significance for the narrative theme. Each picture book will tend to establish some kind of baseline 'norm' for the number of images per activity sequence such that any variations gain significance. While many stories offer little variation, simply choosing repeatedly the option [maintain pace], longer or more complex stories may select [shift pace] at particular moments. The pace will slow down when a story that has not set this up as its norm shifts to spread a single action over a sequence of images, while conversely a shift from using several images per sequence to only one has the effect of speeding up the action. See Painter (2007: 52–3) for a discussion of the visual shifting of pace in *The Bear* (Briggs, 1994) and how this relates to the work done by the verbal co-text.

While the essence of any story lies in its temporal sequence, a narrative text also involves the notion of counter-expectation. Indeed, as Barthes observed, the very notion of (activity) sequences involves both expectancy and risk. That is, we have an expectancy about the next action to come in a sequence, and thus there is always the risk of that expectancy not being fulfilled. This means that counter-expectation is crucial in the creation of a narrative problematic. *Rosie's Walk* (Hutchins, 1968) is a text that apprentices young learners into this feature of narrative by making it highly salient. This is done by the repeated depiction of 'unfulfilled' sequences over two images; for example, the fox in mid-air leaping above the hen to pounce on her, followed (after turning the page) by the fox coming to grief and failing to get his prey.

Figure 3.16 [–fulfilled/+cause] relation between adjacent images from *Not Now, Bernard* (McKee, [1980] 2004: first spread).

In David McKee's ([1980] 2004) *Not Now, Bernard*, the facing images on the first spread set up a pattern whereby the parent's activity sequence is unfulfilled, creating a 'but' relation between the two pages (see Figure 3.16). At the same time, the visuals present another fundamental feature of narrative by depicting an interplay between the activity sequences of different characters. In doing so, the visual sequence allows for a relation of causality to be inferred (at least by the adult reader!) between the actions of the two. That is, the distraction of Bernard's speech might be inferred as causing Dad to hammer his finger instead of the nail. Reading a causal relation between two depicted events will always be a matter of inference, dependent on our understandings of how actions relate to one another and on our ability to interpret the reactions of depicted characters.

Figure 3.17 [–fulfilled/+cause] relation between adjacent images in *Prince Cinders* (Cole, [1987] 1997: fourth spread).

Figure 3.18 [unfolding: simultaneity] relation between adjacent images in *Prince Cinders* (Cole, [1987] 1997: second spread).

On this basis it is not difficult to read causality between the processes depicted in Figure 3.17, showing facing images from *Prince Cinders* (Cole, [1987] 1997). On the left, the fairy acts on the drink can with her wand, while on the right we zoom in to see the result. The cause + effect relation will be obvious not only to anyone familiar with the *Cinderella* story being spoofed here, but to anyone familiar enough with the function of a fairy's wand to be able to interpret the action of the first image. The expression on the cat's face and the 'embarrassed' posture of the fairy's legs clue us in to the failure of the spell – 'unfulfilled' in terms of producing a means of transport for Prince Cinders.

So far all the [unfolding] options we have discussed involve temporal succession between the actions depicted, realised by the repetition of characters from image to image. The alternative temporal relation between two images is that of [simultaneity]. This relation depends on our being able to see the actions of different characters at the same time, either in two panels on a single page or two images on facing pages. So while a simultaneous view of the *same* character across two images (as in Figure 3.17) signals temporal succession, simultaneously visible actions of *different* characters implies temporal simultaneity, as in Figure 3.18. Inferring simultaneity involves comparing and contrasting the adjacent images and the inference is assisted in this case by the shift in ambience as well as in character and setting.

3.3.2.2   Projection

A further logico-semantic relation shared by language and image is that of projection. In language, this involves mental and verbal processes like *he thought, he noticed*, or *he said*, which can 'project' another clause, as in *he thought (that) Jill had brought her dog, he noticed (that) Jill had brought her dog, he said 'Jill has brought her dog'*, and so on. This is the realm of indirect and direct thought and speech that often plays an important role in storytelling.

Where the projection of speech is concerned, a visual image can only form part of a bimodal (visual-verbal) figure, since speech itself can only be construed explicitly by language. Cartoon-style picture books like *The Bear* (Briggs, 1994) make frequent use of such figures within a single image, where a speech bubble from a depicted character encloses verbiage. Without the words, an image can depict talking (see Figure 3.12 or Figure 3.16 verso image) but cannot construe what is said.

The situation is a little different with the representation of thoughts and perceptions. For one thing a single image can show projected thought explicitly by depicting the content of thought as an image within a thought bubble. This occurs in *An Evening at Alfie's* (Hughes, 1984) when we see young Alfie being read the story of Noah's ark and an image of the ark tossing in the flood is shown in a large thought bubble leading from Alfie's head. Another example can be found in the final image of Kitamura's (1997) *Lily Takes a Walk*, where the protagonist's anxious dog is shown with a number of thought bubbles containing images of his memories of their walk. More commonly, though, picture books give us access to the mental life of characters in less overt ways. One possibility is to show a character looking at something not depicted in one image and then in the next image to depict what that character sees – a type of sequence already discussed in terms of focalisation in Chapter 2 (see Figure 2.8). From the ideational point of view, the relation between the two pictures is one of [projection: real] since the second image is a depiction of the material reality perceived by the character.

The alternative projection option is for a set of two images to depict a character thinking about something in one picture and the content of what is being thought in the other – a relation of [projection: imagined]. In such a case there will be no thought bubble to signal a mental process of cognition and a heavy burden of inference is placed on the reader. This is true of Burningham's ([1984] 1988) *Granpa*, an ambiguous and powerful text in which the words give us fragments of the characters' speech, while the images show both their current actions and their thoughts. The book consists chiefly of a series of double pages where each right-hand (recto) page comprises a coloured depiction of grandfather and grandchild and each left-hand (verso) page has a small line drawing, most plausibly interpreted as depicting something remembered by Granpa or currently imagined by him or his granddaughter – a choice of [projection: imagined]. We are helped to understand the different status of the two images in each pair by a contrast in ambience, with the present and actual depicted in full colour and the remembered or imagined in a smaller non-ambient line drawing. Even so, the text is a demanding one, whose patterns emerge only on successive readings.

The Australian text *Hyram and B* (Caswell and Ottley, 2003) is another complex story offering visual projection of cognition, this time with the thoughts appearing in full colour. Here the visual clue to the projection relation is provided by the placement of one image of the character in the margin of the main image. In this 'marginal' representation the character appears pained or upset. The main image shows the character again but in a traumatic situation being remembered from the past. (See Figure 4.17 in Chapter 4 of this book). Unlike *Granpa*, the verbal text in this case assists the interpretation through narrative phrases using mental processes: *he remembers, I remember, she understands*. Given that picture books are mainly targeted at the very young child, purely visual mental projection is not a common choice. And where it occurs, most young readers will need some experience or guidance to interpret the relation. They need, in other words, to be apprenticed into the kind of relation that can be most appropriately 'abduced' in relation to the image sequence in question (Bateman, 2007, 2009). Table 3.5 summarises this discussion of options and realisations of inter-event relations.

Table 3.5 Realisations of INTER-EVENT options.

INTER-EVENT feature/s				Realisation
unfolding: succession:				Successive images depict actions of same participant
	within a sequence:			Successive events form part of single activity sequence
		maintain pace		Each action in sequence takes up similar number of images
		shift pace:	speed up	Actions in sequence are elided, or action is depicted with fewer images than usual (for this text)
			slow down	'Single' action spread over more images than usual (for this text)
	between sequences:			Successive images depict different activity sequences
		+fulfilled		Second of two images depicts expected next action/state
		−fulfilled		Second of two images depicts unexpected next action or state
	+cause			Second of two images depicts action inferrable as result of previous action
	−cause			No causal relation implied between actions in sequence
	simultaneity			Two facing images show actions involving different participants
projection: real				First of two images shows a character looking. Second image shows what is (inferrable as) being looked at.
	imagined			First of two images shows a character who may be thinking. Second image depicts what is (inferrable as) being thought or imagined.

3.4   Circumstances

Any picture book image may include a background context or not. This is a choice with interpersonal significance (ambience is afforded by the colour choices of the background) and textual significance (see Chapter 4), but most obviously a depiction of the setting functions ideationally to provide details of the physical environment in which the characters act. Here we will be concerned with the background context in this ideational function, which means predominately its role in providing a visual location for the depicted process. It is notable that while language affords the explicit construal of an array of different kinds of circumstances, including Location, Manner, Cause, Condition, Extent, Role and Matter (see Halliday and Matthiessen, 2004), most of these either cannot be inscribed visually at all or are simply incorporated into the process itself, as for example with Manner. (An exception to this incorporation of Manner would be distinct lines used to indicate 'speed' or 'shakiness' of movement). Circumstantial meaning in an image is predominately concerned with specifying the details of spatial location, although the depiction of clocks, lighting, the moon, and so on, may also be used to show location in time.[7]

Where a fully realised background setting is provided, as is the case with books like *Where the Wild Things Are* (Sendak, 1963), *Drac and the Gremlin* (Baillie and Tanner, [1988] 1991), *First Light* (Crew and Gouldthorpe, 1993) or *Just a Dream* (Van Allsburg, 1990), the details of the fictional world are available to the reader much more readily than they would be through verbal description. On the other hand where circumstantiation is absent, the focus is necessarily simply on the character and/or the process depicted. This is the default choice, for example, in *Olivia* (Falconer, 2000), where it is not the details of the setting that matter, but Olivia's dizzying series of behaviours, with just a few circumstantial elements indicated here and there – a mirror and basin for cleaning her teeth, a few waves as she builds a sandcastle, an artwork on a wall as she looks intently, a set of stairs for her to sit on when 'cooling off'. The point is not to create her material world, but to build a picture of her energy and activity.

3.4.1   Relations between circumstances: INTER-CIRCUMSTANCE options

In a picture book narrative, it is necessary to consider not only the individual image and what, if any, circumstantiation is depicted, but what relations there are between successive images, when we consider them from the point of view of the circumstances depicted. Not surprisingly, when comparison/contrast relations are set up between characters, as in the adjacent portraits of the brother and sister at

---

7. Kress and van Leeuwen (2006: 72) refer to spatial location as 'Setting' and also regard 'Accompaniment' and 'Means' as distinct visual circumstances. The former can be treated as a minor participant or character in a picture book image and as they themselves note, a 'circumstance of Means' may in fact take the form of vectors that realise the process.

the beginning of *The Tunnel* (Browne, 1989), our attention is likely to be drawn also to similarities and differences in the depiction of the setting, noting in that case the floral wallpaper behind the girl in the first picture and the brick wall behind the boy in the second.

More generally, when comparing the depiction of circumstances in the narrative sequence, it is consistency or change in the degree of circumstantial detail and consistency or change in the location itself that are important. These are the principal options presented in Figure 3.19 (overleaf), which provides the network for INTER-CIRCUMSTANCE relations between successive images. Realisations of options are discussed and exemplified below and summarised in Table 3.6.

Table 3.6 Realisations of INTER-CIRCUMSTANCE options shown in Figure 3.19.

Feature/s				Realisation
vary degree:				Degree of detail in circumstantiation varies from previous depiction
	decontextualise			Circumstantial setting removed or reduced from that of previous depiction
	recontextualise			Circumstantial setting increased from that of previous depiction
sustain degree:				Degree of detail in circumstantiation at same level as previous depiction
	maintain context:			Setting depicted as the same as in previous image…
		same perspective		Same setting viewed from same perspective
		new perspective		Same setting viewed from new perspective through zooming (in or out), cropping/ expanding frame, change of angle, etc
	change context:			Setting depicted as different from that of previous image
		home:		Setting shifts over two images between interior and exterior (or vice versa) of home
			in	Setting shifts from outside to inside home with portal shown in one or both images
			out	Setting shifts from inside to outside home with portal shown in one or both images
		relocate		Setting shifts to new location from previous image

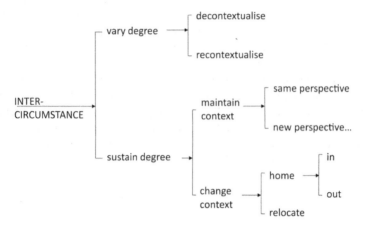

Figure 3.19 Network of INTER-CIRCUMSTANCE relations.

3.4.2.1   *Varying the degree of circumstantiation between images*

It is not uncommon to have a movement from more to less circumstantiation (or vice versa) over the course of a book depending on the moment in the story: this is the choice of [vary degree] shown in Figure 3.19. In the case of variation, a shift to decontextualise by removing any background setting brings any depicted participant into focus, highlighting and provoking appraisal,[8] while a shift to recontextualise returns our attention from the depicted participant to the story as a distinct imagined world and affords tone-setting ambience. For a discussion of the [decontextualise] choices in *Piggybook* (Browne, [1986] 1996) in terms of their relevance for generic staging and the inscription and invoking of attitude, see Painter (2008).

3.4.2.2   *Maintaining or changing of context between images*

When there is a comparable degree of circumstantiation in sequential images (i.e. the choice of [sustain degree]) there is then the option to maintain the same context or to change and depict a new location. Where the context is maintained and the same character re-appears, we understand that a later moment in the activity or activity sequence is being represented, as in Figure 3.1 or images on the first page of *The Snowman* (Briggs, 1978) or *Sunshine* (Ormerod, [1981] 1983), each of which depicts a child character in bed, gradually awakening.

Note that the [maintain context] option is in play if the location is recognisably the same place (e.g. the same room, street, garden, forest, etc.) even though it may be shown slightly differently as the time line proceeds, via the [new perspective] suboption. This latter choice can be realised in various ways: one is by panning across horizontally, as in the first and last pair of panels in Figure 3.4, or by 'dollying' up or down on a vertical axis (perhaps following a character who is climbing).

---

8. See discussion of *The Tin Pot Foreign General and the Old Iron Woman* (Briggs, 1984) in Chapter 2.

Figure 3.20 [maintain context: new perspective] – zooming in on the character in a location. From *Sunshine* (Ormerod, [1981] 1983: seventh spread, final two panels).

Alternatively, or in addition, there may be interpersonal changes in horizontal angle[9] as in the sequence shown in Figure 3.5. Finally, a change in perspective on the same location can also result from cropping or extending the image frame and/or zooming in on or out from a participant, reducing or extending the circumstantiation in the process, either to facilitate a focus on the character or conversely to bring into the story new aspects of the environment, now relevant, perhaps due to the initiation of a new activity sequence.[10] Figures 3.20 and 3.21 from *Sunshine* (Ormerod, [1981] 1983) illustrate these last possibilities. (See also Figure 3.17, where the zoom in the recto image achieves a focus on the unfulfilled nature of the magic trick).

Figure 3.21 [maintain context: new perspective] – extending the frame. From *Sunshine* (Ormerod, [1981] 1983: eleventh spread recto, final panel and twelfth spread verso).

---

9. See Chapter 2 for discussion of the interpersonal meanings realised through shifts in horizontal and vertical angles, as argued by Kress and van Leeuwen (2006).
10. Future work will need to network more delicate options for the [new perspective] option since the effects of different choices (panning versus change in vertical angle versus zooming in or out, etc.) vary.

The alternative to maintaining the same location over consecutive images is the [change context] option. This generally serves to help stage the story. For example, the relocations from child's bedroom to parent's room to hall to kitchen in the early part of *Sunshine* match the activity sequences of 'waking up', 'waking the parent', 'fetching the deliveries' and 'having breakfast'. And just as there can be lesser story phases within major stages, so some relocations will be on a smaller scale than others. For example in *Where the Wild Things are* (Sendak, 1963) there are shifts to different parts of the house initially, but then more significant relocations to the open sea and then to new land and back again, reflecting the overarching narrative structure. The [relocate] option could therefore be extended in delicacy to incorporate the choice of [major] versus [minor] shifts where this is useful in analysis of the narrative staging.

As Nodelman and Reimer (2003) have pointed out, a classic narrative structure within children's literature is one of 'home-away-home', where a child protagonist moves out from the safety and constraint of the home to have adventures in territory that is both more exciting and more insecure, eventually returning home to where he or she belongs. In picture books, a move in or out of the home base may be effected in a particular way that emphasises the crossing of a boundary and which we refer to as 'homing' in or out. The key feature of the [home: in] choice (as opposed to that of [relocate]) is that the viewer is moved from outside to inside, with a portal (doorway or window) between the two visible in the pictures in one or both locations. Figure 3.22 from the wordless text *The Snowman* (Briggs, 1978)

Figure 3.22 [change context: home in] shown in sixth image on page from *The Snowman* (Briggs, 1978).

shows the [home: in] choice being set up over the first five images on the page (all of which include the doorway) and taking place in the sixth picture where the location changes to the inside with the outside visible through a window. This choice of [home: in] strongly emphasises the nature of the home as a bounded territory, and where (as here) the inside is visible from the outside and then the outside from the inside (i.e. a portal between the two is shown in consecutive images) the significance of the boundary crossing is emphasised. See Gleeson and Greder (1995) for an example in a fairytale context.

Conversely, a choice of [home: out] moves the viewer from an interior location to an exterior one, again with a portal visible in one or both images, something that occurs earlier in the story in *The Snowman*. It is also a choice made in *Gorilla* (Browne, [1983] 1987), where Hannah and the gorilla are shown inside the house by the front door with the exterior visible through its glass panes and then in the following picture shown on the doorstep with the front door at their backs. In that story however, the return home is effected less dramatically, by a simple [relocate], as Hannah and the fantasy gorilla are shown face to face exchanging a kiss outside, followed by a picture of Hannah and the toy gorilla (in a configurational comparison) facing each other in her bed, with no portal visible in either case. It is not the return itself that carries most significance at this point but Hannah's transformed state.

3.5 Visual ideational meaning in *Lucy's Bay*

To further illustrate some of the ideational choices discussed in this chapter, we will close with a brief discussion of *Lucy's Bay* (Crew and Rogers, 1992), an Australian picture book with a fairly conventional layout where all but one double-page opening between the first and last contains a page of verbal text opposite a page containing a single framed image. *Lucy's Bay* is a story about Sam, a boy whose little sister, Lucy, drowned in the sea near their grandfather's beach home many years previously, while under Sam's supervision. This event has left Sam prey to night fears and unable to face returning to the bay where it happened. At the beginning of the verbal story we are told that Sam, now several years older, is holidaying at his grandfather's, where he loves to be, but still finds the sounds at night frightening. However he resolves for the first time to walk as far as the bay and revisit the scene of the tragedy. From that point the visual story is simply the unfolding sequence of that walk.

Initially, *Lucy's Bay* is striking in that it opens visually with an inter-circumstance sequence without any depiction of a character in the first few images. On the first spread we are simply shown a landscape in which some smudgy shapes are barely distinguishable in the far background. There is a sense of motion created by the vectors formed by waving grasses in the foreground and scudding clouds above, but no human participant is visible. In the next picture we see the exterior of a timber house against the same night sky, most easily read as [change context: relocate].[11] The

---

11. If the smudges in the background of the opening spread are interpreted (perhaps on subsequent readings) as houses, then the second picture may be read as [maintain context: new perspective] (i.e. as zooming in on a house in the far background).

Figure 3.23 *Lucy's Bay*, third picture.

Figure 3.24 [home: in] *Lucy's Bay*, fourth picture.

third image (shown as Figure 3.23) unambiguously takes up the option of [maintain context: new perspective] as we zoom in on an open window of the house. And in the fourth image we are inside the house, but with the portal to the outside still visible, as shown in Figure 3.24 – an emphatic choice of [home: in]. It is in this image we see the protagonist, Sam, for the first time.

The [home: in] option in *Lucy's Bay*'s fourth picture (Figure 3.24) does not accompany a participant crossing a key boundary, but simply takes the viewer into Sam's safe haven as the significant starting point for the activity sequences in which he is involved. Interestingly, the very next INTER-CIRCUMSTANCE choice is one of [change context: home: out] as we view Sam at a breakfast table on the verandah with the open window to the interior behind him (Figure 3.25). Homing out continues in the next picture, which initiates the main activity sequence of 'going for a walk' (see Figure 3.26). The extended homing out, and the single activity sequence it initiates, emphasise the symbolic significance of leaving the safe haven in this story.

Table 3.7 at the end of the chapter outlines the content of each image of *Lucy's Bay* and shows key visual ideational choices made. It shows that Sam is the only human participant depicted, and that he engages in little action apart from walking, standing and looking, the latter being either towards something out of frame (the first three appearances of Sam) or merely weakly implied from a back view of him. More of the dynamism in the images seems to come from the movement of plants, birds, clouds and ocean than from the boy, who does not even appear until the fourth picture. In this way the natural world appears for the most part more agentive than then the human protagonist.

Figure 3.25 [home: out] *Lucy's Bay*, fifth picture.

Figure 3.26 [home: out] *Lucy's Bay*, sixth picture.

Over the course of the story Sam engages in three activity sequences: those of waking, breakfasting and going for a walk. There is a swift succession between these from the fourth to the sixth picture (i.e. the first three images in which Sam is shown) and the rest of the story is taken up with the temporal unfolding of Sam's walk with repeated choices of [succession: within a sequence]. The only other INTER-EVENT relation between the pictures is that of projection when we simply infer from his back view that Sam is looking in one image and are then shown what he sees, even though in each case there is some shift of perspective also to make this a little ambiguous (a major change in vertical angle in the tenth picture and a zoom in the twelfth picture). And in fact the verbal text suggests that in the tenth picture it may well be a projection of memory that is presented. As presented visually, then, this story is not about the protagonist impacting on the world in any significant way, but about his mental processes and his movement through a sometimes animated environment.

From the beginning of Sam's journey, he begins to recede into the environment, emerging only at two points. In the first of these (*Lucy's Bay*, ninth picture, shown in Chapter 2 as Figure 2.13) he is presented from above in an 'over the shoulder shot', in which we share character focalisation (see Chapter 2) and are thus encouraged to empathise as Sam stands on the rocks, perhaps looking down at the ocean below (shown in the following picture, but from a level angle). His emergence from the background here points to this as a significant moment, something confirmed by the verbal text, which tells us (in the first instance of direct speech) that this is his arrival at the scene of his sister's death – 'Lucy's Bay'.[12] Sam then recedes into the circumstantiation again before emerging a second time in the penultimate image, where he is viewed from below, an unprecedented interpersonal choice which bestows power on him and is especially striking in contrast with the previous 'emergence'. The image is also arresting in being the only one in which the circumstantiation is effectively reduced since there is only a background of blue sky. Interpersonal and ideational choices thus combine to suggest a turning point here.

As well as offering a second emergence from circumstantiation, the penultimate image is notable for depicting Sam engaged in a transitive action and also for suggesting that this has symbolic significance. We view the boy against the clear blue background of the sky, with his arms raised and hands curved in front of his face, obscuring it as a stream of white 'grains' rises into the air like bubbles from his mouth. (The verbal text identifies these as seeds found on Lucy's memorial stone). We infer that he is blowing the seeds, which rise in vectors from his fingertips. The striking placement of the rising seeds in this otherwise empty background to the picture suggests they can be read as symbolic attributes, encouraging us to see the boy as releasing something psychological, rather than merely material, as he finally engages in agentive action. Moreover, the positioning of Sam's raised hands resembles an attitude of prayer, inviting the reader to interpret the scene as involving some kind of supplication on Sam's part. A broken-off utterance addressed by Sam to Lucy thus becomes interpretable as a request for her forgiveness as well as an acknowledgement of grief.

The following page confirms Sam's sense of release, as the verbiage explains that he is now going to embark on what might be regarded as a new activity sequence – that of exploring beyond Lucy's Bay. This constitutes the Resolution stage in the verbal story, which is given visual expression in a single image that extends across the double page in a new expansiveness. In this picture, Sam is shown walking across the sand towards the horizon, once again receding into the circumstantiation as he moves away from us. Then there is a final 'endpiece' image. This reinforces the Resolution by depicting a hermit crab emerging from its shell and crossing the edge of the frame. This clearly symbolises Sam moving on and emerging into the world, an interpretation the young reader can more easily make by comparing the 'frontispiece' image of the same shell in the centre of the frame with no crab visible. And having noticed the encapsulation of the story's theme in these framing images, we may also consider the shells in Figures 3.25 and 3.26 as symbolic attributes (along with the 'imprisoning' vertical lines of the fences), subtly drawing our attention to the story's thematic significance.

If simply paraphrased in terms of a young boy walking to the bay where his sister drowned some years previously and blowing some seeds into the air before continuing along the sand, *Lucy's Bay* would sound quite banal. But as Hasan (1985:

---

12. As well as POWER and FOCALISATION, the interpersonal system of AMBIENCE plays a part here, the [removed] option emphasising that Sam is in a world of reflection and memory.

98) points out, 'paraphrase is never sufficient to describe the meanings of a literature text' because the particular events described stand for more general 'second order' meanings. In *Lucy's Bay* the visual choices, perhaps even more than the verbal ones, guide the reader to an understanding of those second order meanings, clarifying the thematic significance of an apparently uneventful story. While this discussion has focussed on ideational meaning in *Lucy's Bay*, all metafunctions are simultaneously in play, and so reference has necessarily been made not only to simultaneous interpersonal choices from various systems but to features of the layout of images on the page or spread. These latter 'textual' matters will be considered in more detail in the following chapter.

Table 3.7 Lucy's Bay: visual ideational choices.

Image no.	Ideation in image	CHARACTER MANIFESTATION	CHARACTER APPEARANCE	PROCESS	INTER-EVENT all [within a sequence] are [maintain pace/+fulfilled]	INTER-CIRCUMSTANCE
Front	Long diagonal shell from centre to bottom left					
1	Thicket of spiky reeds across foreground, small pool, seeds dispersing into evening sky with travelling clouds, black shapes (of low buildings) in distance	–	–	Vectors formed by reeds, seeds and clouds suggest movement of wind	–	–
2	Oblique angle view of timber house with fenced garden, night sky	–	–	–	–	Change context: relocate
3	Window of house	–	–	–	–	Maintain context: new perspective (zoom in)
4	Boy sitting up in bed and looking out through window	Complete	Appear	Perception		Change context: home: in
5	Boy sitting at table on verandah, looking to left while holding long shell; empty breakfast dishes, shells, newspaper, spectacles on table	Complete	Reappear/immediate: varied: attribution: increase/garment	Perception: possibly verbal (inferred from mouth); material action (sits, holds shell)	Unfolding: succession: between sequences	Change context: home: out
6	View from house or verandah of boy opening gate to exit; shells noticeable on verandah ledge; boy turned, looking back to house; dunes and hint of sea beyond boy	Complete	Reappear/immediate: varied: attribution: decrease/descriptive detail/ increase/symbolic attribute	Perception: (looks at shells?); material action (opens/holds gate)	Unfolding: succession: between sequences	Change context: home: out
7	Trunks and limbs of slender trees with birds in foreground; one bird flying in with spread wings; sand and hint of sea in background; boy on sand.	Complete	Reappear/immediate: status: recede/ varied: attribution: decrease/symbolic attribute	Material action (birds perch, boy walks)	Unfolding: succession: within a sequence	Change context: relocate

Page	Description	Status	Reappear	Circumstance	Unfolding/Projection	Context
8 (double page)	Beach ending in rocky area; cliffs on left, rocks and sea on right; back view of boy at base of cliff	Complete	Reappear/immediate: unchanged	Perception (inferred)	Unfolding: succession: within a sequence	Change context: relocate
9	Back view of boy up on rocks looking down at sand	Complete	Reappear/immediate: varied: status: emerge	Behavioural (boy stands); possibly cognition (inferred from posture)	Unfolding: succession: within a sequence	Maintain context: new perspective
10	Waves breaking at sea and on rocks	–	–	Material action (waves break)	Projection: imagined*	Maintain context: new perspective
11	Cliff viewed from bay; boy near tree	Complete	Reappear/later: varied: status: recede	Behavioural (boy stands) perception (inferred)	Unfolding: succession: within a sequence	Maintain context: new perspective
12	Memorial stone (engraved with the name *Lucy*) at foot of cliff half-submerged in sand	–	–	–	Projection: real	Maintain context: new perspective
13	Facing and looking up to boy who blows grains or bubbles into sky from his raised hands	Complete	Reappear/later: varied: status: emerge/varied: attribution: increase: symbolic attribute	Material action – (boy raises hands, blows sand)	Unfolding: succession: within a sequence	Maintain context: new perspective
14 (double page)	Expanse of beach, sea, sky, boy and footprints leading away from viewer	Complete	Reappear/immediate: varied: status: recede/ varied attribution: decrease symbolic attribute	Material action (boy walks)	Unfolding: succession: within a sequence**	Change context: relocate
Endpiece	Shell in top right of picture frame with crab emerging					

*The change in perspective (see INTER-CIRCUMSTANCE column) suggests this image shows Sam's memory rather than what he actually sees.

** Reading the image with the verbiage clarifies that this is a new activity sequence. Not apparent from the visual sequence alone.

4 Composing Visual Space

4.1   Textual meaning

Very young pre-literate children sometimes surprise us by attending to a minor element in a picture book image rather than 'the main event', or may appear to enjoy one image or page without regard to its place as part of a continuous story. This suggests that part of the pedagogic work of a good picture book is to help train the child's attention and organise the meanings within the page, as well as to provide links between sequential images to help construct the rhythm and shape of the story. These are matters relevant to the textual metafunction, which is concerned with integrating ideational and interpersonal meanings, packaging them within textual units, and linking them across units to create an organised and coherent whole.

In a purely verbal text, there are a number of ways this 'text-forming' work is accomplished. On the one hand, there are text-wide strategies for creating cohesion, such as the use of pronominal reference, ellipsis and textual repetition. More locally, there is the possibility of orienting the reader or hearer through the wordings chosen to initiate each clause ('Theme' choice), as well as the use of patterns of intonation or unfolding 'word order', together with punctuation, to 'chunk' the text into units of information. Each information unit contains a peak of prominence, an 'information focus', which marks out as 'New' the information most significant for the hearer/reader to attend to (Halliday, 1977). In this way, a series of informational peaks or pulses is created as the text proceeds. Clearly the time-based unfolding of the linguistic semiotic is an important factor in these means of textual organisation, something which is relevant visually only in an image sequence. More generally in printed visual material, it is the spatial dimension that must be exploited when it comes to managing the viewer's attention. In a picture book, it is through the composition of the layout, the page and the image itself that meanings are 'packaged' into accessible units, information flow is managed and our attention is harnessed as we proceed through the narrative.

Extrapolating from verbal language, we shall refer to a unit of information in a visual text as a 'focus group', by which we mean material that is grouped together compositionally as some kind of unity or 'eyeful' to which we are guided to attend. As Kress and van Leeuwen (2006: 203) have pointed out, one way visual material is brought together or kept separate is through frames of various kinds. We could think of the double-page spread as a kind of 'macro' frame, within which other frames may be present. For example, the verbal text may be framed off from the image/s by being accorded a separate page or by being placed outside a defined frame for the image. Even within the image, there may be frames created by the ideational content – doorways, windows, or other structures – which create subspaces within the picture and invite us to attend to smaller scale focus groups.[1] The work of framing, then, is to suggest boundaries separating or enclosing elements and it will be described here in two ways. First, we will consider the layout and the different ways image and verbiage may be separated by boundaries or else integrated within the layout through choices of INTERMODAL INTEGRATION. Second, we will attend to the image itself within any layout and the meaningful choices of FRAMING available to it.

Within any space demarcated by a frame of any kind – whether it be the spread, the page or the image itself – there will be one or more visual units, or focus groups, that we may take in at a glance. Each focus group consists of either a single focus of attention or else two or more visual elements arranged in a compositional pattern that encourages us to hold them in view simultaneously. The FOCUS network, presented in Section 4.4 below, describes the principal compositional patterns that constitute options for focus groups of any size in the picture book corpus.[2] It is therefore relevant to 'macro' focus groups like layouts (which are additionally described in terms of INTERMODAL INTEGRATION), to entire images (which are additionally described in terms of their FRAMING choices), and to parts of the image, where leisured scrutiny or second viewings may be rewarded as additional details within 'minor' focal points become apparent.

4.2   INTERMODAL INTEGRATION

As a first step in considering the textual metafunction in picture books, we attend to the arrangement of the page or double-page spread where (in bimodal stories) both visual and verbal components are located. Note that we are interested in the verbal text here purely as a visual unit that inhabits the page or spread along with the image.[3] Many forms of arrangement are possible within the macro frame constituted by the edges of the page/s, but when considering the verbal text as a graphic phenomenon, the first question to address is whether it is literally 'part of the picture'.

---

1. We might draw an analogy here to Halliday's work on tonality, as a theory of how many tone groups, and thus how many pulses of news, are associated with a clause.
2. The analogy we are drawing here is to Halliday's work on tonicity, as a theory of how pulses of new information are foregrounded by the major pitch movement in a group.
3. The graphic expression of language also has various dimensions that carry interpersonal meaning, such as size, type and colour of font (van Leeuwen, 2005b), but we will concern ourselves here only with aspects of composition and layout.

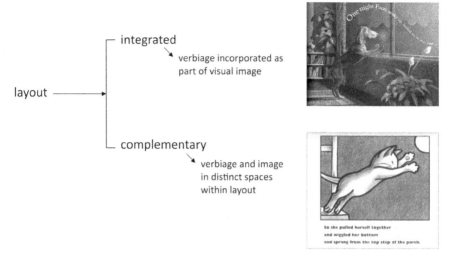

integrated
verbiage incorporated as
part of visual image

layout

complementary
verbiage and image
in distinct spaces
within layout

Figure 4.1 Basic options for INTERMODAL INTEGRATION.

In other words, is the verbiage – as a visual unit – overlaid onto the image itself or is it separated out into its own identifiable space in the layout? These basic alternative forms of INTERMODAL INTEGRATION are identified in Figure 4.1 as [integrated] and [complementary], respectively, with the single or double-page layout, rather than the image itself, as the relevant unit to which options apply.

4.2.1   Complementary layouts

The 'complementary' layout, where each semiotic resides in its own space, indicates that each has a distinct role to play in meaning-making, with different page/spread formats varying the 'weight' and perhaps the function of each. One possibility is for verbiage and image to be separated onto facing pages within a double-page layout, as on the opening pages of Sendak's (1963) *Where the Wild Things Are,* or to take up equal space side by side on the page as in Figure 4.2. In either case, by apportioning text and image the same amount of visual space, each modality can be regarded as carrying equal semantic 'weight' or importance. Thus when an image spreads across the gutter of a double page layout, or occupies most of the page in a single page layout, as in Figure 4.3, it is being privileged in relation to the verbal text. In sum, Figures 4.2 and 4.3 are similar in having complementary layouts where verbiage and image are adjacent and facing each other horizontally, but they differ in the weight accorded the image (see Figure 4.4 for the network displaying these options).

In their analysis of page layouts that are polarised in this way as left/right oppositions, Kress and van Leeuwen (2006) argue that material on the left-hand side of a layout has a different 'information value' from material on the right-hand side. Their account of visual composition claims that whichever semiotic appears on the

Figure 4.2 [facing/adjacent]/[equal].

Figure 4.3 [facing/adjacent]/[image privileged].

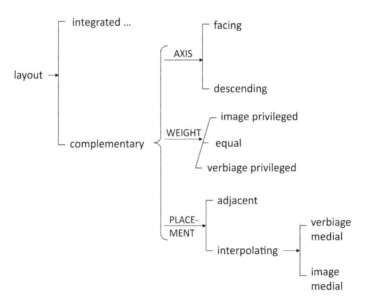

Figure 4.4 INTERMODAL INTEGRATION options for complementary layouts.

recto page of a spread constitutes the 'New', which is the information we are invited to attend to most closely. By contrast, the verso is the domain of the 'Given' – that which is already familiar or available in some way. As 'verbiage left' is the most common way for a layout divided on the horizontal axis to be organised in picture books, this analysis would argue that in these narratives, the verbiage most commonly provides some kind of given or accepted material while the less familiar aspects of the meaning are to be found in the image. We cannot, however, justify such an interpretation for picture books and it remains an open question as to what consistent significance, if any, can be assigned to this variable.

It is equally common for a complementary layout to be organised with the visual and verbal components adjacent to one another vertically in descending 'layers', either with image above verbiage or verbiage above image. Once again, the semiotic given the greatest amount of visual space has most impact and semantic weight. Most frequently, it is the image that is privileged in this way, whether it appears above or below the verbiage. The examples in Figures 4.5 and 4.6 illustrate this arrangement.

Figures 4.5 and 4.6 differ in terms of whether verbiage is placed above image or image above verbiage. According to Arnheim (1982), the upper part of a composition always has greater weight than the lower part, an argument supported by Kress and van Leeuwen's (2006) interpretation, which states that the material in the upper portion of a vertically organised layout has the function of 'Ideal' as opposed to the lower portion realising the 'Real'. In their words:

> For something to be ideal means that it is presented as the idealized or generalized essence of the information, hence also as its ostensibly,

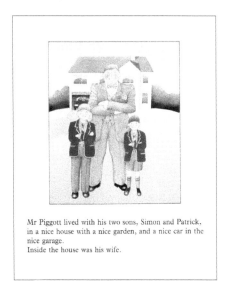

Mr Piggott lived with his two sons, Simon and Patrick, in a nice house with a nice garden, and a nice car in the nice garage.
Inside the house was his wife.

Figure 4.5 From *Piggybook* (Browne, [1986] 1996).

Figure 4.6 From *Rose Blanche* (Gallaz and Innocenti, 1985).

most salient part. The Real is then opposed to this in that it presents more specific information (e.g. details), more 'down to earth' information (e.g. photographs as documentary evidence, or maps or charts), or more practical information (e.g. practical consequences, directions for action).   (Kress and van Leeuwen, 2006: 186–7)

If the upper part of a page is occupied by the text and the lower part by one or more pictures ... the text plays, ideologically, the lead role, and the pictures a subservient role (which, however, is important in its own way, as specification, evidence, practical consequence, and so on.) If the roles are reversed, so that one or more pictures occupy the top section, then the Ideal, the ideologically foregrounded part of the message, is communicated visually, and the text serves to elaborate on it.
                                    (Kress and van Leeuwen, 2006: 187)

The more frequent choice for a complementary vertical layout in a picture book is for the verbiage to come below the picture, as in Figure 4.5, and it is undoubtedly the image that most strongly claims our attention in that case. By contrast, where the verbiage appears above the picture in Figure 4.6, it seems less easy to ignore the words, which might be taken as support for Kress and van Leeuwen's analysis. However since this layout is not frequent enough in our data to test and justify the interpretation, we prefer to take the amount of space taken up in the layout as an indicator of dominance regardless of the orientation of the axis.

So far in this discussion, it has been assumed that the complementary layout will comprise a single illustrated section and a single chunk of verbiage. However, there is a further possibility for both facing and descending layouts, which is a sandwich arrangement whereby an image interrupts two chunks of verbiage as we read down or across the page, or else a single piece of verbiage separates two images. See Figures 4.7

When Maureen had finished the story it was time for Alfie to go to bed. She came upstairs to tuck him up. They had to be very quiet and talk in whispers in case they woke up Annie Rose.

Maureen gave Alfie a good-night hug and went off downstairs, leaving the door a little bit open.

Figure 4.7 [complementary: descending/interpolating] layout from Hughes (1984).

They built
a splendid,
fat, white
snowman
in the field.

When they
had finished,
it was time
to go back
to the farm.

Figure 4.8 [complementary:
facing/ interpolating] layout.

and 4.8. This 'interpolation' of text by image or image by text is more likely in a descending layout and with the image in the centre as in Figure 4.7.

Whereas Kress and van Leeuwen interpret this kind of layout in news texts and elsewhere as a 'triptych', where the central element provides a link between an outer pair, this does not seem to be its function in narrative picture books. Instead the [complementary: interpolating] option serves to punctuate the story, staging the visual and verbal material to provide the desired rhythm for the telling. For example, the interpolating layout shown in Figure 4.7 from *An Evening at Alfie's* (Hughes, 1984) has the initial piece of verbiage describing Alfie being put to bed, an event illustrated in the centrally placed image. Then the second chunk of verbiage describes the next action, which is the carer leaving the room. The interpolated picture thus separates 'being put to bed' from 'being left alone', while illustrating only former.

In a similar way, an interpolating layout in Browne's (1998) *Voices in the Park*, begins with the narrator telling us, 'I settled on a bench and looked through the paper for a job. I know it's a waste of time really but you've gotta have a bit of hope haven't you?' Below this there is an image of the speaker with his head buried in the paper and below this again the text resumes: 'Then it was time to go ...'. On this page, the image of the narrator reading his newspaper separates the initial action + reflection utterances from the statement announcing the transition to the next activity sequence, allowing us to assume the passing of time and so guiding the pacing of the verbal text by separating it into two halves. This function of staging the story rather than linking two outer elements means that the image is often more strongly connected to one piece of verbiage than the other.

This is also the case where image interpolates text on a horizontal axis. In *The Baby Who Wouldn't Go to Bed* (Cooper, 1996), for example, there is an interpolating layout with four brief paragraphs of verbiage on the left describing the Baby's encounter with some soldiers. It quotes their conversation, which concludes with the soldier saying, 'We're going to back to our castle. And so should you.' The centrally placed image depicts the baby and the captain addressing each other, while to the right of the image, the text resumes, 'But the Baby didn't want to'. The 'pause' provided by the interpolated image effectively emphasises the *But* that signals the character's contrariness at the conclusion of this episode, predicting further adventures to come. Interpolation, then, whether image and verbiage are descending or facing, is a means to assist in staging the verbal story, helping to pace relevant linguistic or generic patterns as they unfold.

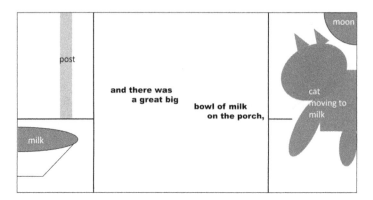

Figure 4.9 [facing/interpolating: verbiage medial]: layout of Henkes ([2004] 2006: thirteenth spread).

Accordingly we can expect that it should nearly always be the verbal text that is interrupted to achieve an appropriate textual flow. But an interesting [verbiage medial] example can be found in *Kitten's First Full Moon* (Henkes, [2004] 2006), a story of a kitten's unfortunate exploits attempting to reach the moon, which it mistakes for a bowl of milk. At the Resolution stage, the story is slowed down by interpolated verbiage as the kitten finally returns home to approach a genuine bowl of milk. See Figure 4.9 for a schematic representation of the layout.

4.2.2   Integrated layouts

Having described subtypes of the complementary organisation of image and verbiage, we can now consider the alternative kind of layout, where the [integrated] option is taken up. Here, instead of having image and verbiage on separate pages or in demarcated parts of the single page, the two come together so that the printed words feature within the image or its background in a more unified arrangement. The various subchoices within the integrated type of layout are shown in Figure 4.10 and will be discussed in turn.

As shown in Figure 4.10, verbiage and image can be integrated to form a visual unity in two distinct ways: either by utilising the choice of [projected] or that of [expanded]. Where the verbiage is presented in a speech or thought 'bubble', as in Figures 4.11 and 4.12 from *Don't Forget the Bacon* (Hutchins, 1976), a bimodal figure is created, which in terms of ideational meaning comprises a depicted projector and a verbal projection. This form of integration is therefore referred to as [integrated: projected]. The examples in Figures 4.11 and 4.12 both involve the projection of meaning – of a locution (speech) in the first case and an idea (thoughts) in the second. An alternative possibility can be found in super-hero comics or other cases of cartoon-like action, as in *The Tin Pot Foreign General and the Old Iron Woman* (Briggs, 1984), where non-speech sounds are projected, such as 'Bang!' or 'Pow!',

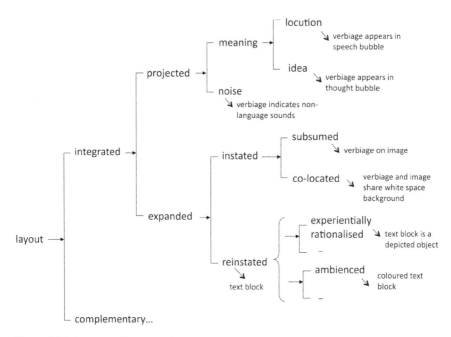

Figure 4.10 Integrated layout options.

Figure 4.11 Integrated layout [projected: meaning: locution] from Hutchins (1976).

identified in Figure 4.10 as the choice of [projected: sound]. The projecting relation is a very particular way of integrating verbiage and pictorial character so that both must be 'read' together as a unity to gain the full meaning; and it is one so familiar to us that we barely recognise the pedagogic work done to demonstrate this by a text like *Don't Forget the Bacon.*

Figure 4.12 Integrated layout [projected: meaning: idea] from Hutchins (1976).

The second major type of integrated layout, exploiting the [expanded] choice, has two subtypes, with [instated] being easily the most common. One way the instating of the two modalities may occur is by having the verbiage actually overlaid onto the image, so that it most clearly becomes part of the image itself. This is the option of [instated: subsumed], the feature name suggesting that the verbiage is subsumed into the depiction. This choice creates the strongest fusion between words and picture, guiding the reader to view the two as an integral whole (see Figure 4.1 for an example from Ottley, 1995, shown on the network).

In picture books, an equally common way of instating verbiage with image occurs where the depicted character or action is entirely or partly decontextualised and both words and image are placed on the common background of the (usually) white page. This utilises the choice of [instated: co-located], which seems to give the verbiage a little more status than the [subsumed] option – see Figure 4.13. A choice of [co-located] applies where the verbiage would be subsumed into the image if there were full circumstantiation provided in that image.

In principle a layout with the features [integrated: instated: co-located] differs from the complementary ones discussed earlier in that the image is not clearly framed off from the verbiage either by a drawn frame or by white space, so that it would generally not be possible to draw a line across the page to separate the two.[4] (Compare complementary examples in Figures 4.5–4.9 with integrated examples shown as Figures 4.13 and 4.14.) A further characteristic of integrated layouts is that the position of the verbal text is more likely to vary from page to page since the verbiage forms part of one or more focal groups within the composition. In the integrated layout, whatever suboption is involved, the reader is guided from the start to view the two modalities as forming an integrated whole. In fact, elements of the image may 'point to' or frame the verbiage to guide the novice reader to this

---

4. There may be indeterminate cases; see Section 4.5.

I saw a yellow dog
Looking at me.

Figure 4.13 Integrated layout [expanded: instated: co-located] from Machin and Vivas (1989).

understanding, as is often done in *Possum Magic* (Fox and Vivas, [1983] 2004; see Figure 4.14).

The remaining option for the [integrated: expanded] layout is one that has begun to appear more frequently, perhaps due to influences from electronic texts. This utilises the [reinstated] option (see Figure 4.10), where the verbiage is presented on the picture but instead of being subsumed into the image, it appears on its own distinct background strip or panel, as in Figure 4.15. The effect is that the verbiage has to be considered as a visual element within the image but by being framed or blocked off, it is then 'reinstated as verbiage' to be attended to in its own right.

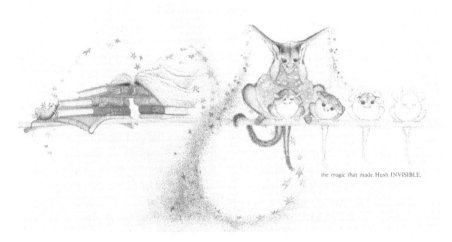

the magic that made Hush INVISIBLE.

Figure 4.14 Integrated layout [expanded: instated: co-located] from *Possum Magic* (Fox and Vivas, 1983 [2004]).

Figure 4.15 Integrated layout [expanded: reinstated] from *Hyram and B* (Caswell and Ottley, 2003).

The [reinstated] option may give rise to two further simultaneous choices. The strip or block on which the text appears may simply be the default choice of white, or (as in Figure 4.15, where in the book the panel is a warm orange colour) it may carry ambience due to the colour of the strip – instantiating the feature [ambienced]. The final possibility – one not taken up in Figure 4.15 – is for the text panel, as a visual item, to play a role in the experiential meaning of the image. This occurs, for example, in *Fox* (Wild and Brooks, 2000), which includes a layout where a text panel separating the two characters of fox and bird not only forms the central element in the composition, but its presence has experiential justification as some kind of solid object on which the fox's paws rest and at which the bird appears to have pecked. Thompson's (2004) postmodern text, *The Violin Man*, provides further examples of text panels that form part of the content of the image, such as where the frame of the text block is part of a chest depicted in the scene. The suboption of [experientially rationalised] integrates the verbiage more closely into the picture while still requiring the reader to accord it its own status as a distinct strand of meaning, a complex manoeuvring of reader attention in what is a complex text in many other respects.

Obviously the relations between words and images in any bimodal text are complex ones and no attempt is being made at this point to offer a multimodal analysis of the picture books which takes account of the specific linguistic meanings realised by the verbiage. The INTERMODAL INTEGRATION network described here suggests only that the manner in which the verbiage is visually integrated into the page or spread, or alternatively visually presented as a complementary region of meaning, indicates some very general kinds of relations between the two modalities. And because written language has a visual realisation, the verbiage needs to be brought into any account of purely visual textual choices.

4.3   FRAMING

Moving from the layout of page or double page to the image itself, we can first consider how and whether the image is framed. Options here are presented as the system of FRAMING in Figure 4.16.

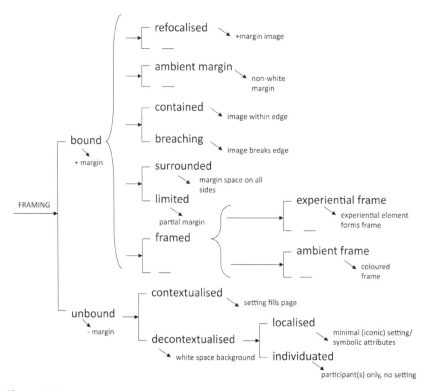

Figure 4.16 FRAMING.

4.3.1   Unbound images

The most basic choice is whether the image extends right to the page edge as an 'unbound' image or whether there is a margin of space fully or partly enclosing it, rendering it 'bound'. All the examples of complementary layouts we have given are of bound images, while the integrated layouts shown involve unbound ones. Where an image is unbound, there is in effect no boundary (other than the page edge) between the world of the child reader and the depicted story world. In Figure 4.13, the choice of [unbound] is coupled interpersonally with a generic drawing style making it easy for the reader to identify with the child character. In other books, the reader is 'invited into' the story world at selected moments, a striking example being the final spread of Browne's (2004) *Into the Forest*, where a series of bound images gives way to an unbound image of a smiling mother with welcoming open arms, who makes eye contact with the reader. This format encourages us to share the surge of positive affect inscribed in the image and also the positive feeling of security invoked in the child protagonist.

In *Piggybook*, Browne ([1986] 1996) again uses the contrast between bound and unbound images effectively, this time exploiting another aspect of the meaning. On the recto of one spread, there are four bound images of the faceless mother doing chores and then, on turning the page, we see the rest of the family relaxing in front of the television. This double-page spread is a large unbound image where the details of the setting extend to the edges of the spread. The removal of the margin not only brings us into the room with them, but chimes with the experiential content to suggest their sense of expansive ease and lack of confinement. Later in the story, there is another unbound image of the three males, but this time no setting is depicted. This is the [unbound: decontextualised] option and in this instance the image shows the three 'piggy' males kneeling disconsolately and pleadingly before us (see recto image in Figure 2.12). While Kress and Van Leeuwen (2006) regard the degree of contextualisation as a matter of the relative 'realism' of the image, the strongest effect of removing the setting in picture book stories is one of highlighting behaviour and/or affect of the character and of provoking attitude in the reader.

Sometimes of course an entire story is depicted with unbound decontextualised images, in which case the character/s rather than the imaginative story world become/s the focus of attention throughout. An example is *I Went Walking* (Machin and Vivas, 1989), where the toddler character is joined by a succession of different animals (see Figure 4.13) and the reader can enjoy the gradually increasing length of the depicted parade of participants. Each new animal participant is introduced metonymically, often by being partly obscured by some circumstantial prop – a basket of logs, a water trough, an apple tree, a flurry of straw, and so on, which gives the reader the fun of predicting each new participant before it is fully revealed. These contextual props constitute a very minimal context – the [decontextualised: localised] option, as opposed to the [decontextualised: individuated] choice, where there is no depicted context at all. In the case of *I Went Walking*, the [localised] option allows for some object to obscure the animal's head at first in order to encourage prediction and page turning, at other times achieved by showing part of the body at the edge of the page. By contrast, in Falconer's (2000) *Olivia*, minimal elements of setting are sometimes provided to clarify the action depicted; for example a basin and mirror are depicted when Olivia is shown brushing teeth. In neither text is the creation of a fully realised imaginative social world at issue. As well as clarifying the action, the chosen 'props' standing in for a completely realised setting may also provide symbolic attributes associated with the character. This can be seen in Figure 4.14 from *Possum Magic*, where a shelf of magic books is the only contextual element depicted and serves as a symbol to emphasise that Grandma Poss has wisdom and magical powers.

In sum, then, the most general option for framing a picture book image involves the presence or absence of a margin to 'hold' the image within the page. Where the margin is absent and the page edge is the only limit to the image, it is [unbound] in two senses. The depicted characters are less constrained by their circumstances (e.g. the males watching television in *Piggybook*, Max during the wild rumpus of *Where the Wild Things Are*) and the story world is more opened up to the reader. Where such an unbound image of the characters is decontextualised, attention is focussed on the behaviour or nature of the depicted character/s, which when used selectively, has the potential to trigger appraisal at particular moments in the story or, where just a few iconic elements of the setting are provided, to assist the symbolic interpretation of the character.

4.3.2   Bound images

Bound images, those set within a page margin or border, demarcate the story world as more distinctly separated from the reader's world than unbound ones and may also serve to 'contain' or confine the character. However, before elaborating on these aspects, we will refer to Figure 4.16 and note that there are in fact five different 'simultaneous' systems available for bound images, two of which relate to the way the margin of a bound image may afford interpersonal meaning. The first way this can occur is through colour. While the default choice of colour for the margin (as for any page) is white, there are picture books that make a different choice and thus enable a particular background ambience to prevail. In our corpus, the most striking example is *Lucy's Bay* (Crew and Rogers, 1992), where a light, warm ambience carried by the margin (as well as often within the image) counterbalances the dark memories of the protagonist.

Another story that makes use of the potential of the margin to afford interpersonal meaning is Caswell and Ottley's (2003) *Hyram and B*, a story of two discarded teddy bears, narrated by one of them, who is introduced as 'B'. Not only does the margin (where present) often afford ambience, but at certain points it enables a shift in point of view by containing a depiction of a character outside the main image. When this occurs, it allows for a past and present representation of a character simultaneously and signals a refocalisation, reinforcing the fact that the depicted 'flashback' in the main image constitutes the memory of the character shown in the margin. At one point, for example, the margin on the left has a picture of the young girl, Catherine, who now owns B, the teddy bear narrator. In this margin image Catherine sits shaking, cuddling B tightly, while in the main image (lower right corner), she is depicted in a corresponding posture, as a small figure in a war zone with fire, helicopter, bombed vehicles and weapons centre stage (elaborating the verbal text, which simply says 'She understands what it means to be lonely'; Figure 4.17). The use of the image in the margin – the [bound: refocalised] option – economically

Catherine
loves me.

Catherine
understands
the secret
language
of bears.

She understands
what it
means

to be lonely.

Figure 4.17 [bound: limited/refocalised] from *Hyram and B* (Caswell and Ottley, 2003).

signals that the present day Catherine is recalling her traumatic past, something carried entirely by the visual text.

Figure 4.17 introduces another aspect of the bound image, which concerns the extent of the margin. In this example the margin extends only from a single picture edge, thus limiting the area contained by the main picture but not enclosing it entirely as it does in Figure 4.5, which shows the [surrounded] option. In examples like 4.17, the image is much less tightly bound, and (especially when the margin is absent at the bottom of the page) the story world is less differentiated from the reader's world. Examples of both surrounded and limited bound layouts, as well as unbound images, can be found in Sendak's (1963) *Where the Wild Things Are* and Cleirigh (2010) offers an interpretation of the meaning of the logogenetic succession in this text, arguing that Sendak's innovations in 1963 expanded the systemic meaning potential of picture books in the culture by exploiting possible variations in the margin/ image relation.

Whether or not the margin surrounds or merely limits the extent of the image, it may be intruded upon by part of the image, as in Figure 2.12 (in Chapter 2) from *Piggybook* (Browne, [1986] 1996) showing the newly powerful mother. This choice of 'breaching' the margin provides an iconic way of suggesting that the depicted character has too much energy or presence to be entirely contained by the boundaries of the image. Sometimes though, it is an element of the setting that breaches the margin in this way as occurs in *Where the Wild Things Are* (Sendak, 1963) or in Figure 4.6 from *Rose Blanche* (Gallaz and Innocenti, 1985). The [breaching] option

Figure 4.18 Bound images without and with a frame.

thus signifies breaking out of confinement and also closer connection between reader world and story world, underlining the basic meanings of the [bound] option.

In addition to being surrounded by a margin, a bound image can of course also be distinctly framed within that margin, usually by a defined black or coloured line, as in Figure 4.5 and Figure 4.8. Figure 4.18 shows an unframed and framed example of the same image for comparison. We would argue that the effect of the frame in the right hand image is to add another boundary between the reader's world and the semiotic one, which requires us to view the depicted world more emphatically from the 'outside'. In other words, with the inclusion of a frame to the bound image, the story world is set up overtly as a picture.

One book that exploits the meaning potential of the frame is *Zoo* (Browne, 1992), a humorous account of a family's day out, which makes a serious moral point about the inhumanity of caging and objectifying animals. The book uses bound images throughout and is laid out with a small unframed picture of members of the family on each verso (together with the verbal text), and a large, beautifully rendered, clearly framed picture of the animals on each recto, a contrast which quietly emphasises the way the animals are 'a sight' displayed for human enjoyment. In the book, the reader/viewer is gradually moved to take on the animals' perspective, and as part of this process there comes a point where the left hand image of the family as part of an unpleasant crowd of zoo patrons is enclosed in a thick frame, emphasising how they appear as an ugly sight from the animal's point of view.

Frames in picture book stories can vary in at least two respects, indicated by further options shown in the Figure 4.16 network. For one thing, the frame, like the margin, may or may not be coloured. While the default option for the margin is white, for the frame it is black, but other colours may be used, in which case the frame can contribute to the ambience of the image. Regardless of colour, however, there is the further choice of a simple line frame to demarcate the image as against a frame provided by the experiential content of the image. An example of the latter can be found in *Voices in the Park* (Browne, 1998), where the children are shown playing on a climbing frame, which also constitutes the frame for the picture (see Figure 4.19). Another instance is in *My Dad* (Browne, 2000), where the edge of the blackboard on the wall behind Dad, when shown in his role as teacher, creates an

The girl took off her
coat and swung on
the climbing frame,
so I did the same.

Figure 4.19 [framed: experiential frame] from *Voices in the Park* (Browne, 1998).

experiential frame within the black line one. In each case the experiential frame serves as a symbolic attribute, conferring qualities on the participant (playfulness on the children and authority on Dad).

One particular case of the experiential frame is where the depicted participant is shown within a framed picture. This happens in Margaret Wise Brown's famous bedtime book *Goodnight Moon* (1947), where various objects in the room, including two pictures on the wall, are mentioned and displayed in turn. In the story, the pictures are at times part of the circumstantial setting of the bedroom, but also emerge to appear centre stage on successive pages as the nursery rhyme characters within each are named. Each picture – one of the cow jumping over the moon and one of the three bears – has an ornate picture frame to emphasise that it is at one remove from the world of the baby's bedroom and also that it has an iconic status as a valued aspect of childhood (Figure 4.20).

Another way of achieving an experiential frame is to use part of the circumstantial setting to mimic the appearance of a picture frame, with the depicted character or setting appearing as a mounted picture within it. Both Browne's ([1986] 1996) *Piggybook* and Baker's (1991) *Window* use elaborate timber window frames to do this. In *Piggybook* we see, 'picture-framed' in the kitchen window, the reformed male chauvinist pig of a father happily washing up, valorised as the ideal model domestic man. In *Window*, depicted characters are shown gazing through the win-

The cow jumping over the moon

And there were three little bears sitting on chairs

Figure 4.20 [framed: experiential frame] from *Goodnight Moon* (Brown and Hurd, 1947).

dow at the scene outside, which changes over the years, and it is the garden that is given iconic status.

In general, then, bound images separate the reader from the semiotic world of the story and where there is both a frame and a margin, there is a more emphatic demarcation of the two. The story world is contained as well as demarcated by the surrounding or limiting margin so that when that edge is breached by depicted characters or other depicted elements, the effect is to make greater connection with the reader's world and often to construe the breaching element as breaking through constraints. Either margin or frame, or both, afford the possibility of contributing to the ambience of the image and the margin may also allow for interpersonal refocalisation by means of additional character depiction. A defined frame marks out the image as a representation to be viewed from the outside but can also afford additional meaning when constituted by an ideational element, rather than a simple line. When this happens, it can either provoke positive reader attitude by means of a literal or invoked 'picture frame' or it can confer a symbolic attribute on the depicted character.

4.4 FOCUS

In this chapter, we have given some consideration to spreads, pages, margins and frames as boundary-forming devices. Now it is time to explore in more detail what it is that is contained within these boundaries. One of their functions is to enclose and delimit focus groups – visual elements placed in a compositional relation so as to be apprehended at a glance, with each such 'eyeful' constituting a pulse of information. Any picture book layout, framed by the page edges, constitutes a major focus group with a particular compositional pattern, but if it is a complementary layout, we will attend to its parts separately and respond to any image within the layout as an additional focus group in its own right. In turn, the major focus group constituted by the overall composition of the image may itself encompass further focus groups of varying prominence.

The organisation of meaning within a layout or image – its 'composition' – involves the weighting and placement of different visual elements within the space so as to manage the viewer's attention. In considering this aspect of visual meaning, we have drawn on scholarly work in the fields of fine arts and perception, such as Arnheim (1982) and Dondis (1973), and also on Caple's (2009) recent semiotic account of composition in news photographs, which in turn is informed by art and photography education (e.g. Präkel, 2006). The FOCUS network shown in Figure 4.21 outlines some of the principal choices found relevant for the picture book corpus in relation to spatial organisation, with realisations listed in Table 4.1. It should

Table 4.1 Realisations of FOCUS.

Feature/s				Realisation
centrifocal:				Composed on or around a centre
	centred:			Central focus
		simple		Centre filled
		extended:		Central focus includes more than one visual element
			circular	Elements ranged around central space
			triptych	Centre filled + two outer elements
	polarised:			Dual focus
		diagonal		Visual elements on diagonal axis
		orthogonal:		Visual elements on orthogonal axis
			vertical	Top/bottom composition
			horizontal	Left/right composition
		+ deictic vector		Eyeline or other vectors link polarised elements
		mirroring		Compositional poles mirror one another
		balanced		Both poles of composition filled
		unbalanced		One pole 'empty'
iterating:				Composed as a repetition of elements
	aligned			Elements iterate on any axis
	scattered			Repeated elements in random scatter

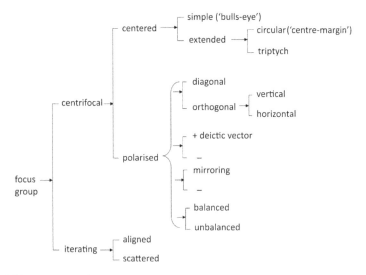

Figure 4.21 FOCUS network.

be noted at the outset, though, that picture book illustrations are more varied and often more complex than is accounted for by this figure, which is limited to the most general and repeated prototypical choices found.

4.4.1   Iterating focus groups

As shown in Figure 4.21, there are two basic and contrasting FOCUS options. Either a focus group can be placed in or balanced around a centre in various ways – the [centrifocal] option, or else it may consist of same/ similar ideational elements repeated in a series across the image – the choice of [iterating]. In the latter case, the elements are nearly always organised in fairly regular 'lines', whether vertical, slanted or horizontal, as when a row of child or animal characters is depicted. See Figure 4.22, where the character Olivia is displayed in multiple outfits.

This is the [iterating: aligned] option as opposed to that of [iterating: scattered], which occurs only infrequently in the picture book corpus. One example is on the endpapers of *The Rabbits* (Marsden and Tan, 1998), where a representation of nature in the form of a scattering of birds, leaves, twigs and so on suggests the unregimented random nature of the wilderness. Another is shown as Figure 4.23, indicating the composition of a spread from *Wolves* (Gravett, 2005), showing the scatter of mail on the doormat. In each case, lack of organisation and intervention is the point.

The alternative [iterating: aligned] choice shown in Figure 4.22 is favoured for displaying a series of characters, such as the monsters who greet or farewell Max in *Where the Wild Things Are*, or the animal companions following the child narrator in some spreads of *I Went Walking* (Machin and Vivas, 1989).

Figure 4.22 [iterating: aligned] From *Olivia* (Falconer, 2000).

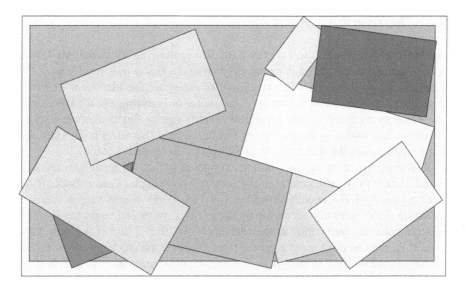

Figure 4.23 [iterating: scattered] focus group.

4.4.2   Centrifocal focus groups

A centrifocal focus group is one whose compositional elements are balanced on or around a centre. It can take a number of forms, with the principal contrast being between the features [centred] and [polarised], as shown in Figure 4.24, where the crosses indicate elements of the focus group. These basic centrifocal options are available to focus groups constituted by the layout as well as by the picture image. A [complementary: adjacent] layout for example is a polarised focus group, such as h or i in Figure 4.24, while a [complementary: interpolating] one is centred like c or d. Integrated layouts, like images, may deploy any of the patterns shown.

4.4.2.1   Centrifocal: centred
The most straightforward form for a centred image to take is for the centre of the space to be filled, perhaps by a single character, drawing the viewer's gaze to that participant in an unambiguous way. This is the option of [centred: simple] – a kind of bullseye composition that may be used to create a moment of stasis in the momentum of the narrative. Figure 3.3 in the previous chapter (from *Possum Magic*) exemplifies this, as does the dramatic image of the stepmother staring out at the viewer in Browne's (1981) version of *Hansel and Gretel*, or the mother and baby hugging when the baby is finally reconciled to bedtime in *The Baby Who Wouldn't Go to Bed* (Cooper, 1996). A simple centred image can also serve as an effective way to introduce a character – as is done on the first page of *I Went Walking* (Machin and Vivas, 1989) and *Drac and the Gremlin* (Baillie and Tanner, [1988] 1991) – or to make an effective closure, as on the final page of *Not Now, Bernard* (McKee, [1980] 2004) and *Grandpa* (Norman and Young, 1988). Wherever they occur in the story, these images allow us to attend exclusively to the single depicted participant or group without any potential distraction.

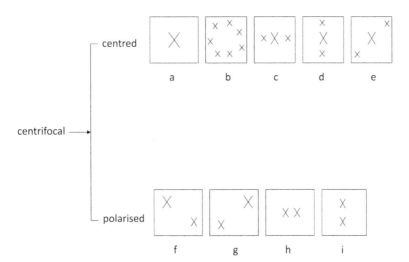

Figure 4.24 Centrifocal options, with examples a–i.

While a simple centred image has a focus group consisting of a single visual focus, other centred compositions involve additional elements. The [extended: circular] option describes what Kress and van Leeuwen refer to as a 'centre-margin' composition. Here a central element or space has additional elements ranged around it in a circular fashion. Figure 4.15 from *Hyram and B* provides an example, where the protagonists' placement on the edge of composition suits their status at this point in the story as disregarded observers of the arena that is the shop. The cover of Lunn and Pignataro's (2002) *Waiting for Mum*, about an over-anxious child, provides a rather different example. This cover shows the protagonist firmly in the centre but very closely encircled by ghostlike manifestations of her worries, using a [extended: circular] focus group to organise the experiential meaning so as to encapsulate the story's theme.

The centre of a circular focus group is not always filled, however, as can be seen in Figure 4.25, which represents the sixteenth image from *Not Now, Bernard* (McKee, [1980] 2004), the story of a boy repeatedly and unsuccessfully seeking his parents' attention. Ranged around the empty space on the patterned and bordered rug (indicated by the lines in Figure 4.25) are a television showing sport ('babysitting' entertainment for Bernard), a tray of dinner (material nourishment for Bernard) and the disappearing figure of mother on the right (emotional unavailability for Bernard). The emotional hole at the centre of Bernard's world, despite comfortable circumstances, is neatly symbolised by this compositional arrangement.

In an example from another of McKee's books, *I Hate My Teddy Bear* (1982: fourth image) represented by Figure 4.26, there are numerous participants around the edges of the image. This is in keeping with the book's visual presentation of

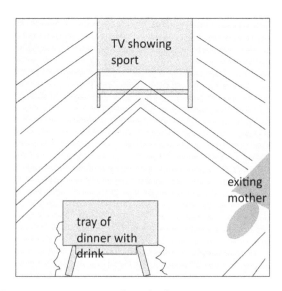

Figure 4.25 Schematic representation of circular focus in *Not Now, Bernard* (McKee, [1980] 2004: sixteenth image).

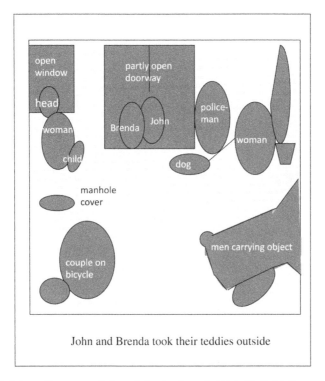

John and Brenda took their teddies outside

Figure 4.26 Schematic representation of circular focus in *I Hate My Teddy Bear* (McKee, 1982: fourth image).

Note: This circular focus group contains within it many other focal groups, which can individually engage our attention with longer or repeated 'looks'.

a variety of simultaneous (but unverbalised) 'stories' and is one example of how the book emphasises the constructedness of fiction by countering our expectations about it – such as that the narrated characters should be centre-stage visually, that everything made known to us is relevant to their story, and so on.

The circular type is not the only kind of extended centred focus group. There is also the possibility of the central element being accompanied by additional elements on either side to create a 'triptych' (Kress and van Leeuwen, 2006: 197ff.). Figures 2.12 and 4.5 show the three male members of the Piggott family organised as a close triptych – suggesting three of a kind acting in unison. A more widely spaced triptych forms several of the integrated layouts in *Kitten's First Full Moon* (Henkes, [2004] 2006), where the emphasis is on the distance between the outer elements. In these spreads a central piece of verbiage separates an image of the moon in an upper corner and another of the kitten diagonally opposite in a lower corner (see Figure 4.27). In this example the triptych lies on a diagonal axis, but any orientation is possible, and indeed the same book has a complementary triptych on a horizontal axis (see Figure 4.9).

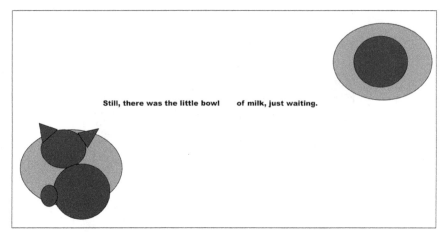

Figure 4.27 Schematic representation of [centred: triptych] focus group from *Kitten's First Full Moon* (Henkes, [2004] 2006).

4.4.2.2   Centrifocal: polarised

The second group of [centrifocal] compositions indicated in Figure 4.24 are those taking up the [polarised] option and balancing or opposing different depicted elements on a diagonal, vertical or horizontal axis. The diagonal axis is recommended to budding photographers, who are advised to place elements of their composition at particular points on the axis to create a sense of balance without filling the centre (Präkel, 2006). Figure 4.28 indicates with black dots the points favoured for creating a balanced composition around a vacant centre in this way (Dondis, 1973).

Where this is done, the polarisation is [diagonal] and [balanced] (i.e. achieving a balanced composition by having both 'poles' of the group filled), which is a very common choice for picture book images, often with characters as the opposed pictorial elements. For an example, see the images in Figure 3.16. A focus group of this kind may be further enhanced by one-way or mutual gaze between the depicted characters, which strongly guides the reader to 'take in' the focus group at a single glance as a cohering unity. Character gaze is one kind of deictic vector, an additional option helping to link elements within a focus group. (In other cases the deictic

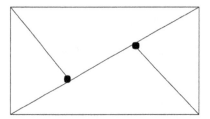 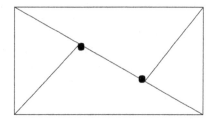

Figure 4.28 Recommended placement of pictorial elements (indicated by black dots) for a [polarised: diagonal] composition.

vector may be a pictorial element, like a drawn limb or plant, that points, for example, to verbiage.)

On occasions of course it is preferable not to resolve the polarisation, but rather to create an *unbalanced* effect in order to encourage page-turning or to foreground narrative complication. While this option is not taken up as often as might be predicted for narratives, *Not Now, Bernard* (McKee, [1980] 2004) is a text with more than one example. Figure 4.29 shows the beginning of the Complication stage, where the seventh image in the book depicts the character on the steps in the left middle and lower half of the picture space and nothing at all in the opposing corner, an absence accentuated by the vector of Bernard's upward gaze.

Polarisation in picture book focus groups occurs not only on a diagonal axis but also on a vertical or horizontal one: [polarised: orthogonal], shown on Figure 4.24 as examples h and i, and in Figure 2.1 from Chapter 2, showing a double-page spread from *Granpa* (Burningham, [1984] 1988).

Regardless of the orientation, if the polarised focus group is constituted by two human or anthropomorphised participants, as in Figures 2.1 or 3.16, it will have an important function in organising interpersonal meanings of proximity and orientation (see Chapter 2). Interpersonal relationships between characters are the fundamental concern of all kinds of stories and these relationships are readily signalled by the placement of characters on the page and their physical orientation to one another. If the characters are face to face, they are in contact, possibly in dialogue, with proximity, stance and expression indicating the intimacy and affect of the contact. If face to back, as in the first image of Figure 3.16, the relationship is more ambiguous, an approach by one character may be being initiated or denied, or one character may be observing or following another. On the other hand, if back to back with another character, disconnection or conflict is signalled, a meaning enhanced in Figure 2.1 by the lack of close proximity.

Bernard went into the garden.

Figure 4.29 [polarised: diagonal/unbalanced] seventh image of *Not Now, Bernard.*

A polarised focus group has one further option, where the depicted elements in a polarised relation 'mirror' one another. This is most likely when a character looks at their reflection, a choice that signals that issues of identity and self-worth are at stake in one way or another. A clever example is provided in *Possum Magic* (Fox and Vivas, [1983] 2004) where Grandma Poss peers into a pool and sees her own reflection but grandchild Hush fails to see his, hinting at the problem for him of being invisible as he grows up. Another instance is found in *Voices in the Park* (Browne, 1998) when the browbeaten child, Charles, has his first taste of independence and adventure by playing with another child at the park. As he sits at the top of the playground slide (or 'slippery dip'), his lack of self-confidence is neatly captured by his tiny mirrored facial reflection represented as a version of Munch's famous painting *The Scream* (Figure 4.30).

This image demonstrates that it would be a considerable over-simplification to suggest that most picture book images do in fact have only one compositional principle. The picture is essentially a [centred: simple] composition with the playground slide with children aloft filling the centre. But closer inspection reveals that Charles and his reflection are in a [mirroring] relation. Thus while there is an overall [centred] 'gestalt', the image incorporates an additional view or focus of attention. It is important to remember, then, that while some picture book images comprise a single focus group arranged in one of the basic idealised compositions described by the network, very many images incorporate additional focus groups of different kinds.

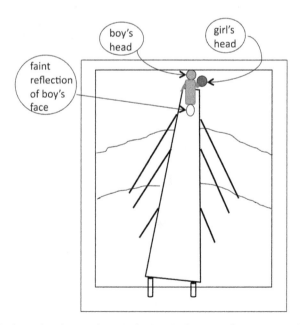

Figure 4.30 [polarised: orthogonal: vertical: mirroring] – minor focus group within a centred image. Schematic representation of fifteenth image in *Voices in the Park* (Browne, 1998).

This fact brings up the question of whether the visual semiotic has structure comparable to the linguistic 'hierarchy of periodicity' (Martin, 1996b; Martin and Rose, 2007: 186) found in verbal text. This term refers to the fact that because language unfolds in time, the dynamics of sequence and major pitch movement[5] allow information to be packaged according to the speaker/writer's chosen point of departure (Theme) and chosen focus of hearer/reader attention (New), which creates 'periodic' or 'wave-like' textual structures in a verbal text (Halliday, 1979). As well as choices of Theme and New made clause by clause, a written text may also set up higher level structures for the paragraph or whole text. Thus a topic sentence, or 'hyper-Theme' may predict the course of a paragraph, while an introductory paragraph, or 'macro-Theme', may predict the course of an entire text. Correspondingly, hyper- and macro-New elements may retrospectively contribute to the higher level structuring of a verbal text. Clearly a spatially organised image has to package information quite differently from this, but the fact that a whole picture can be 'taken in' in an instant does not mean that closer inspections or re-viewings do not reveal additional meanings. Even where there is one prominent focus group capturing our attention, there may be in fact be an array of different focus groups available, which are revealed almost immediately, or as we remain looking, or when we re-read, or simply when we are attuned to notice them for intra- or extra-textual reasons. Whether visual focus groups constitute a hierarchy within an image is questionable given that all are in view simultaneously, but it can be argued that there is often an array of focal groups with varying degrees of prominence, one of which may have the greatest salience.

In organising a complex composition, different artists may prefer different means of training and guiding the viewer's attention. Vivas in *Possum Magic* (Fox and Vivas, [1983] 2004) tends to create salience through the use of size and subtle colour choices in order to offer a number of potential foci within an overall view. By contrast, Browne is an artist who makes heavier use of internal frames to provide an array of focus groups. For example, in one image from *Gorilla* ([1983] 1987), the protagonist Hannah is in the centre of the page in a [centred: extended: triptych] composition where she stands between two large male father figures (on the left a gorilla in coat and hat and on the right the father's outdoor clothes hanging on a hook over his boots). Within this overall composition, a door jamb provides an internal frame which allows us to notice the gorilla and Hannah as a distinct face-to-face pair in a polarised diagonal focus group with a deictic gaze vector. The six panes of the window set in the door offer further frames for additional foci of attention though these will not necessarily be attended to at first. Indeed Browne famously includes visual elements on the page that are not highly salient on the viewer's first 'eyeful', so that they are revealed only on closer scrutiny or subsequent readings. The possibility of doing this depends on managing the viewer's attention so that particular depicted elements have prominence for the viewer on the first 'take'.

While most images offer an overall compositional principle 'at first glance', McKee's (1982) *I Hate My Teddy Bear* is interesting for its distracting and somewhat

---

5. More technically, tonic placement.

confusing images in which the two child protagonists are rarely centre stage or made particularly salient in any way. This is in keeping with the book's metafictive nature, which frustrates our expectations of a simple narrative line with main characters, offering instead a myriad of potential, but incomplete visual stories. Thus there are on most pages several competing focus groups, without necessarily any single overarching compositional principle to guide the reader. By disturbing our expectations in this way McKee makes clearer what is going on in the more typical case, and also offers the reader the freedom to imagine fuller stories from the fragments depicted.

A picture book spread affords considerable complexity in composition, having fewer restrictions in layout than some other visual-verbal media (such as newspapers) and few limits on constructedness (compared with news photos for example). Consequently there is enormous variety in the way pages and spreads are laid out and in the way images themselves are framed and composed. The three networks we have proposed describe a large number of options, yet are unlikely to have captured the variety and complexity of the compositional dimension. Nonetheless, the aim has been to set out some of the principal significant recurring oppositions found in the corpus, while recognising that not every option will be relevant to a particular individual book and that some books may offer patterns that we have not included in our description.

4.5   Visual textual meaning in *Possum Magic*

To illustrate how some of the options described in this chapter can contribute to understanding the visual meaning of a picture book text, we will conclude here with a brief discussion of visual textual meaning in the prizewinning Australian picture book, *Possum Magic*. This book, with a verbal text by Mem Fox and illustrations by Julie Vivas, has proved enduringly popular within and beyond Australia since its first publication in 1983, and many different editions are available, ranging from a 'big book' for the classroom to a board book version for babies. Here we will use the standard 2004 Omnibus Books paperback edition and refer also to minor differences in the earlier 1989 Omnibus paperback version. The story of *Possum Magic* is generally viewed as a celebration of Australian identity, naming and depicting the country's unique animals and birds, its capital cities and its iconic foods. The partly rhyming verbal text constitutes a classic narrative structure with the stages of Orientation, Complication, Evaluation, Resolution and Coda.

The story begins with Grandma Poss, the possum, using her powers of 'bush magic' to play various tricks, including that of making her grandchild, Hush, invisible. This at first provides Hush with opportunities for fun as well as protection from snakes, but the Complication stage of the narrative arises when Hush suddenly wishes to know what she looks like and Grandma Poss fails to find the appropriate magic to restore her visibility. Eventually Grandma Poss remembers it is something to do with food: 'people food – not possum food.' They travel from the bush to each of the four major capital cities of Australia eating various (European) Australian foods, such as Anzac biscuits and pumpkin scones. Eventually the Resolution is attained when they visit the more remote capitals of Darwin, Perth and Hobart and eat in turn a Vegemite sandwich, a portion of pavlova and finally a lamington cake. In the Coda, these three iconic Aussie foods are eaten once a year on Hush's birthday to ensure Hush's continuing visibility.

With respect to FRAMING, with few exceptions the images in the book are unbound, giving a sense of freedom and space to the possums' adventures and perhaps symbolising the 'boundless' Australian outback. The images are also decon-textualised, offering only occasional limited localised elements of the spatial setting, either to clarify the activity sequence (a pool for reflecting Grandma's reflection but not Hush's) or to depict symbolic attributes. For example, the opening spread shows a delicate pink awning and a tiny washing line suspended among branches near the hollow in the tree where the possums live. These symbolic attributes of domesticity attached to the tree are just enough context to make it clear that the tree is home to the possums. (The fact that this home is 'deep in the Australian bush', however, is only made clear in the verbiage. No attempt has been made to render a typically Australian landscape or rural setting in a fully contextualised image.) The dominance of unbound de-contextualised images throughout the book draws our attention to the playful and dynamic behaviour of the possum characters and to their affect, which is expressed facially and through body movement.

The exceptions in the book are occasional bound images when the material action comes to a halt – images within the Evaluation section (discussed further below) and later in a city scene where the possums watch a show in a picture theatre. The first bound image is at the opening of the Evaluation stage; it is a [bound: limited] picture extending over the top half of the page only. It shows Grandma sitting with her magic books unable to find a solution to the problem of Hush's invisibility. By being partly bound, there is some sense of containment in this image as she sits there stumped. The more strongly bound examples are the only two interior scenes: one where the possums are snugly inside the nest in the tree trunk (with the nest creating a circular experiential frame) and the other a city scene where the possums are shown watching a show inside a theatre. In the 1989 edition, this picture is bound on all sides by a narrow margin, while in the 2004 edition it is [bound: limited], taking up the upper part of the page. In each case the fact of the characters being physically inactive and in an enclosed space is emphasised by the bound nature of the image – a stronger emphasis in the earlier edition.

In terms of layout, the book comprises fifteen double-page openings, which in the Orientation create intermodal integration through the choice of [integrated: expanded: co-located/balanced]. That is to say, image and verbal text share the white space of the page, with the verbiage positioned in a way that contributes to the harmonious organisation of the layout. This means that elements in the image often frame or point to the words, as shown in Figure 4.14 (page 101). Beginning with integrated co-located layouts of this kind encourages the young reader to 'read' the words and pictures as a unity, even though the images in the Orientation convey sufficient meaning in themselves to indicate the events taking place.

With the start of the Complication stage, the pattern of intermodal integration begins to shift to a complementary arrangement (where image and verbiage have distinct and separate spatial domains). The first spread of the Complication has text on the verso and image on the recto, as in a complementary layout, but circumstantial elements of the image continue across the gutter into the verso to create a partial framing for the verbiage in a way similar to previous integrated spreads (see Figure 4.31). This intermodally transitional spread is also transitional in terms of the narrative structure. It potentially opens the Complication stage (signalled in the verbiage by *But …*) but then appears to resolve it immediately with Grandma asserting that there is no problem. In the next spread, however, (Figure 4.32) we learn that the Complication continues and at this point the layout shifts more decisively to one that is [complementary: facing/adjacent/equal weight].

What is of interest here is not whether the illustrator or editor consciously thought about integrated versus complementary layouts, but whether the change from one to the other at this point makes any contribution to meaning. In *Possum Magic*, the movement from integrated to complementary layouts is in synchrony with the generic staging of the text and emphasises the interruption to the fun caused by Grandma's inability to find a solution. The [complementary: facing] layout asks for verbiage and image to be attended to in turn and helps to slow the pace as the Complication emerges. The verbiage outlining the crisis (that none of the many magic books contains the right magic) has an entire page to itself and faces the first fully contextualised image of the book. Since the narrative Complication rests on an absence – what is not in the magic books – which cannot be made explicit in an image, the verbal text has a more distinct role at this point, symbolised by the new layout. At the same time, the shift in framing from decontextualised images in the Orientation to a contextualised one here allows for the introduction of a cool, relatively dark ambience appropriate to the negative feelings being expressed by the characters. The change to a contextualised image also supports a shift from the focus on character action (magic tricks) to one on mental processes (peering at books).

The complementary layouts continue over the next two pages, which comprise an Evaluation section, further pausing the action. This time each individual page contains an image and a line or two of verbiage, with both images having an enveloping

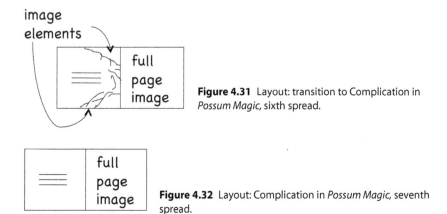

Figure 4.31 Layout: transition to Complication in *Possum Magic,* sixth spread.

Figure 4.32 Layout: Complication in *Possum Magic,* seventh spread.

cool ambience, linking them with the previous full page image representing the nub of the Complication. Then after this section, with the beginning of the Resolution, the cool ambience disappears and in the 1989 edition, the layout changes again. In that version, the spreads have a complementary [descending/interpolating] layout on one page and a large image or images only on the other. In the interpolating layout, a 'medial' image of the possums separates the account of Grandma's Eureka moment – 'She shouted, "It's something to do with food"' – from the beginning of a new activity sequence – 'So later that day, they left the bush'. The recto has no verbiage and shows the possums heading off on a bicycle (see Figure 4.33). This pattern is reversed when the page is turned. Now the left page has images only and the recto has another [descending/interpolating] layout with the medial image separating the description of their eating activities from its result: 'Hush remained invisible'. The interpolated layouts in this earlier version thus facilitate the rhythm of the verbal story-telling, something achieved in the 2004 edition by having verbiage and image in complementary layouts on each successive page (see Figure 4.34).

With the advent of the successful Resolution ('It was there in the far north of Australia …'), the layout shifts once more to an interesting combination of complementary and integrated. In the upper part of the spread, we see a series of nine participants sitting on a bench that extends across the whole double page. Below that there is verbiage on the left hand page and the two possums in the foreground on the lower recto – see Figure 4.35. Because of the extent of the upper image, we must read the double-page spread as a single integrated layout, instantiating the feature [co-located]. However, since the layout affords an array of focus groups (see

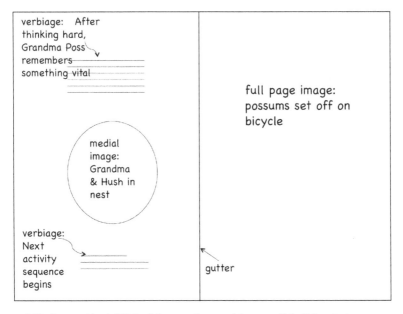

Figure 4.33 *Possum Magic* 1989 edition: tenth spread: Intro. to (failed) Resolution stage.

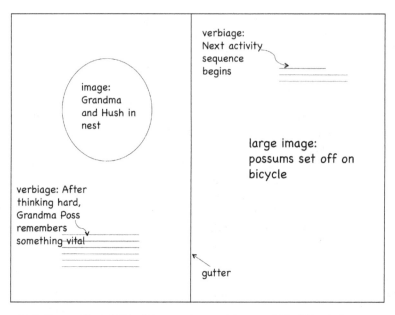

Figure 4.34 *Possum Magic* 2004 edition: tenth spread: Intro. to (failed) Resolution stage.

further below) we may also wish to read the verso as a page in its own right, consisting of a [polarised: orthogonal: vertical] focus group arising from a descending complementary layout, and/or read the lower part of the whole spread separately, as a [complementary: facing/adjacent] layout. The effects are to slow the story (while we take in all this), to suggest a new stage in the narrative (since the layout choice has changed) and to accord the verbiage some prominence (since it enters into all three views).

The Resolution continues with more clearly complementary layouts, which seems appropriate as the verbiage in this section has to play a truly complementary role in

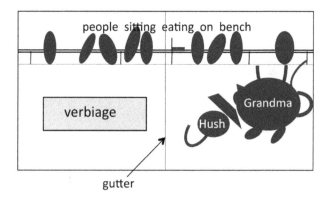

Figure 4.35 Layout of Resolution stage in *Possum Magic* (twelfth spread).

supplying the proper names of the places visited (not all of which can be imaged) as well as identifying by name the 'magic' Australian foods. Finally, after a whole page image of Grandma Poss and Hush dancing in celebration, the Coda returns us to an integrated double-page layout of the [co-located] type found in the Orientation section, underlining the function of the Coda in signalling a renewed equilibrium.

So far, the discussion has considered the instantiation of choices from FRAMING and INTERMODAL INTEGRATION. In relation to framing, we have suggested that the relative consistency of the [unbound: decontextualised] choice throughout the book places the emphasis on the appearance and expansive movements of the animal protagonists; it is interrupted only where depiction of setting is needed to afford enveloping ambience or where a bound image is useful to emphasise mental or physical containment. In relation to layout choices, there is interesting variation that supports the staging and pacing of the narrative, and also some complexity – as in the example shown as Figure 4.35 – arising from the presence of more than one prominent focus group within the layout.

When it comes to FOCUS choices in the book, in relation to both layouts and images within them, it is striking how varied these are and how frequently several focus groups call for our attention, despite the uncluttered nature of the designs. The choices made work very effectively to highlight experiential meaning and the array of focus groups in many cases rewards longer or repeated looking. As an example we can consider the focus group choices in the image shown as Figure 4.14 (introduced briefly in Section 4.2.2 above), which has been schematically represented in Figure 4.36. In this spread, there is most obviously a [polarised: orthogonal: horizontal] relationship between the magic books on the left and the possums on the right, with both resting on the branch that spans the spread. The source of the magic and those participating in it are thus a principal focal point of meaning, with Grandma and the books linked as the source of the magic by the trails of stars emanating from

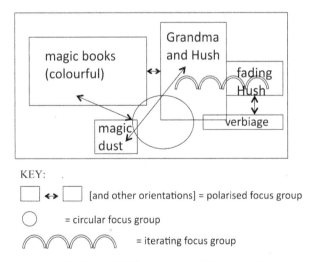

Figure 4.36 Focus groups in Figure 4.14, *Possum Magic* (third spread).

each. At the same time, the ongoing process of the magic spell (not explicitly stated in the verbiage) is emphasised by two [polarised: diagonal] relationships: Grandma and Hush (as participants) in relation to the bulk of the magic dust (as process), and conversely the books of spells (as source of magic) and the 'magic ring' formed by the dust and stars (as process). This magic ring is itself a circular focus group and the fact that the possums' tails intrude into it also reinforces their involvement in the spell.

Ideational meaning is further supported by the composition in relation to the result of the spell, which is brought to the viewer's notice by additional focus groups. The various versions of Hush form an [iterating: aligned] arrangement on the recto page, indicating (as the verbiage does not) that the spell involves a gradual move-ment from partial to total invisibility (something relevant to the narrative's later Resolution stage). This group also forms one pole of a [polarised: orthogonal: verti-cal] focus group comprising the fading Hushes and the verbiage. The relationship is reinforced by deictic vectors formed by the tails, with the tail of the fully 'invisible' Hush pointing directly at the capitalised word 'INVISIBLE'; in this way the decoding of the written word is clarified for a young reader as is correspondingly the decoding of the faint broken outline to represent invisibility.

Laborious though it is to write or read about the instantiation of multiple focus groups in this way, the effect of viewing them in an image is of course quite different. While some focus groups within an array may only be attended to by careful viewers or on subsequent readings, others will be taken in by the eye very rapidly. Because of this, and because the images are so skilfully composed to bring out experiential and interpersonal meanings, the images in *Possum Magic* are very accessible. They are, however, less 'simple' than they may appear, as can be seen from Table 4.2 at the end of the chapter, which provides a summary of key choices in FOCUS instantiated on each spread.

From this summary it can be seen that the FOCUS choices in *Possum Magic* serve the narrative in various ways. In particular, the key ideational meanings of the story are always brought to the viewer's attention, as already exemplified for the third layout (Figures 4.14, 4.36). Building on this spread, Hush's invisibility is repeatedly made prominent through choices in subsequent spreads (e.g. 4, 5 and 7), and the variety of uniquely Australian animals is also brought to prominence at different places in the story (e.g. in spreads 2, 4, 5, 6, 8 and 15). As well as these experiential aspects of the story, choices in FOCUS keep attention on the close interpersonal relationship between Grandma and Hush and also establish themes of fellowship and solidarity, between animals, between humans, and – during the adventure – between the animals and humans. This is done through [iterating: aligned] choices (e.g. in spreads 5, 12, 15) and polarised ones, where characters are face to face (e.g. spread 14). Iteration is also used to draw attention to a process in this book, as in spread 3 (Hush's gradual change to invisibility), the recto of 5 (looking for Hush) and spread 12 (eating; see Figure 4.35).

Often in *Possum Magic*, the array of focus groups on any spread allows particular visual elements to gain prominence by participating in more than one focus group in the way described earlier for both characters and verbiage in spreads 3 and 12.

Other examples of such elements are Grandma's reflection (pointing up Hush's invisibility) in spread 7 or the verbiage in spreads 1 and 12. In this way, key characters, events and stages of the narrative are highlighted. Choices in FOCUS are also important in pacing the reading. For example, the use of [centred: simple] for the images in spread 9 (which lacks a complex array of foci on either page) creates a stillness and allows the viewer space to pause and empathise at this Evaluation stage. Later, in spread 12 (see Figure 4.35), an array of polarised focus groups holds our attention as we attend to the spread and to the different groups on each page. The very final image also encourages us to linger, offering an integrated layout formed by a [polarised: orthogonal: vertical] focus group reinforced by deictic vectors and an [iterating: aligned] image, with minor pulses of information within that.

This discussion suggests some of the ways in which the textual metafunction is brought into play in *Possum Magic* when we consider the book primarily as a visual narrative. Only a few different options are instantiated from FRAMING, with the great majority of the images being unbound and decontextualised. This sets up a default 'tone' of expansiveness and freedom and makes the behaviour and affective postures of the characters highly salient. It also means that any shift in this default pattern (as in the Evaluation stage) becomes marked. Similarly, the way the integrated layouts of the Orientation shift to ambiguous and complementary ones before bringing us back to the integrated Coda, assists the reading of the generic structure of the narrative. As we have seen, the greatest complexity in the instantiation of textual choices in this book lies in the region of FOCUS, which is used to integrate ideational and interpersonal meanings and to manage our attention so that the events and themes of the story are clarified. The rich array of focus groups provided also means that sustained and repeated viewing is rewarded and the pacing of the story is well managed. In addition, the way the verbiage participates in many of the compositions maintains our awareness of the book as a truly bimodal one and not just a story in pictures. To do justice to the bimodal nature of such books, however, requires two further steps: the verbiage needs to be analysed for linguistic meaning (rather than seen only as a visual element within a composition) and the way the visual and linguistic meanings work together to create new meaning must be explored. These tasks will be undertaken in the following chapter on intermodality.

Table 4.2 Analysis of main FOCUS choices in *Possum Magic* (2004 edition). Focal elements in the focus group are indicated in brackets following feature description; all polarised groups are [balanced] unless otherwise stated; in a polarised focus group the 'polar' elements are linked with &. Spreads 9, 10 and 11 vary in the 1989 edition.

Spread		Focus	Contribution to meaning
1	whole	centrifocal: polarised: diagonal (possums & lower tree trunk);	Characters linked to their bush home
		centrifocal: polarised: diagonal (story verbiage & home)	Visual and verbal representations of home linked
	verso	centrifocal: polarised: diagonal (×2) (nest & awning), (nest & washing)	Tree hole and sticks symbolised as domestic space: 'home'
	recto	centrifocal: polarised: orthogonal: vertical (possums & verbiage)	Possums as central characters; visual and verbal identity linked
2	whole	centrifocal: polarised: diagonal/+deictic vector (×2) (bush creatures)	Varied participants in actions; variety of Australian animals
	verso	centrifocal: polarised: orthogonal: vertical/+deictic vector (Grandma+verbiage & wombat)	Grandma Poss above wombat reinforcing her agency visual and verbal wombat linked
	recto	centrifocal: centred: extended: triptych (image–verbiage–image)	Repetition of Grandma Poss graduates her actions
		Other groups within this include:	
	upper image	centrifocal: centred: extended: triptych (kookaburras)	Note: the posture of the central bird may draw the eye to see a triptych (and ignore the fourth leftmost bird) rather than iteration
	lower image	centrifocal: polarised: diagonal (×3) (dingo head & tail) (Grandma arm & tail) (Grandma & emu: + deictic vectors)	Focus on smile of dingo invokes jollity; tail draws attention to emu; vectors emphasise Grandma's agency over emu
3	whole	centrifocal: polarised: orthogonal: horizontal (magic books & possums)	Attention to source of magic: Grandma linked to her symbolic attributes (magic books)
		Other focus groups within this include:	
		centrifocal: polarised: diagonal (Gma+Hush & magic dust)	Magic prominent: participants and process linked
		centrifocal: polarised: diagonal (magic books & magic ring of dust)	Magic prominent: participant and process linked

Spread		Focus	Contribution to meaning
	lower spread	centrifocal: centred: extended: circular (magic ring of dust)	Attention drawn to magic
		centrifocal: polarised: diagonal: unbalanced ('fading' Hush & blank space)	Reinforcement of Hush as invisible
		centrifocal: polarised: orthogonal: unbalanced (verbiage & white blank space)	Reinforcement of notion of invisible
	recto	centrifocal: polarised: orthogonal: vertical/+deictic vector (Hushes & verbiage)	Visual and verbal representations of 'invisible' linked
		iterating: aligned (4 Hushes)	Attention to result of magic: iteration to suggest time passing (becoming invisible gradually)
4	whole	centrifocal: polarised: diagonal: (koala & blossom+verbiage)	Attention to iconic Australian animal and plant
		centrifocal: polarised: diagonal: (koala & verso white space)	Koala's 'weight' emphasised, relevant to squashing action
	recto	centrifocal: polarised: diagonal (koala & Hush)	Size and solidity difference emphasised – Hush ignorable, as in story
5	whole	centrifocal: polarised diagonal/ +deictic vector (kangaroo & animals+verbiage)	Attention drawn to kangaroo (Australian icon) in particular
	recto	iterating: aligned (searching animals)	Attention to Hush's near absence and to taxonomy of marsupials
6	whole	centrifocal: polarised: diagonal (snake head & tail end+verbiage)	Linking verbal *safe from* and visual danger
		note: layout of spread 6 deploys the variable of depth, not accounted for in the current focus network	
	recto	centrifocal: polarised: orthogonal: vertical (snake head & Hush)	Attention to vulnerability of suspended Hush
7	whole	centrifocal: polarised: orthogonal: horizontal (verbiage & image)	Attention to verbiage of Complication attention to recto image
	recto	centralised: polarised: orthogonal: vertical/mirroring (Grandma & reflection)	Attention to Grandma having a reflection
		centralised: polarised: diagonal (Hush & Grandma's reflection)	Attention to Grandma's as the sole reflection Hush sees, suggesting identity problem

Table 4.2 *(Continued)*

Spread		Focus	Contribution to meaning
8	whole	centrifocal: polarised: orthogonal: horizontal (verbiage & image)	Attention to ambienced image; attention to verbalisation of problem
	recto	centrifocal: polarised: orthogonal: vertical (Hush with Grandma reading & other animals)	Contrast of the anxious and the resting; Grandma's difference and wisdom emphasised
		Within this focus group:	
		centrifocal: centred: extended: triptych (possum–koala–possum)	Solidarity of bush animals
9	whole	centrifocal: polarised: orthogonal: vertical (×2) (image & verbiage)	Affect and ambience in image linked to appraisal in verbiage
	verso	centrifocal: centred: simple (Grandma with books)	Focus on Grandma's dejected stance (closed books symbolic of failure of magic)
	recto	centrifocal: centred: simple (Hush)	Focus on Hush's downcast stance
10	whole	centrifocal: polarised: diagonal (×2) (opposing verbiage, opposing images)	Images: contrast of confinement/thought and openness/ action verbiage: thought and speech choppy versus jaunty fluency of narrated action
	verso	centrifocal: polarised: orthogonal: vertical (image & verbiage)	Complementary roles for image and verbiage
	image	centrifocal: centred: simple	Interior of tree (home) reinforces interiority of (mental) activity
	recto	centrifocal: polarised: orthogonal: vertical (verbiage & image)	Complementary roles for image and verbiage
	image	centrifocal: centred: simple	Focus on ideation – getting going; expansiveness of image references release of action
11	verso	centrifocal: polarised: orthogonal: vertical (image & image +verbiage)	Staging of journey indicated
		centrifocal: polarised: diagonal/+deictic vector (minties & verbiage)	Attention to names of iconic foods and place names, linking visual minties to verbal *minties*
	upper image	centrifocal: centred: extended: triptych (boy–possums–boy)	Fellowship and solidarity between possums and humans
	lower	centrifocal: polarised: orthogonal: horizontal (verbiage & image of possums on bike)	Attention to names of iconic foods and place names; linking places with travel

Spread		Focus	Contribution to meaning
	recto	centrifocal: polarised: orthogonal: vertical/+deictic vector (image & verbiage)	Invisible Hush linked to verbiage: *invisible*
	image	centrifocal: polarised: orthogonal: horizontal/(partly) unbalanced	Contrast of visible Grandma and invisible Hush; invisibility emphasised
12	whole	centrifocal: polarised: orthogonal: vertical (seated people & verbiage + possums)	Similarity and contrast of possums and people, attention to possums in story
	upper spread	*Within this:*	
		iterating: aligned (seated people)	Fellowship; eating emphasised
	lower spread	centrifocal: polarised: orthogonal: horizontal	Complementarity of verbiage and image
	verso	centrifocal: polarised: orthogonal: vertical (image & verbiage)	Attention to verbiage
	recto	centrifocal: polarised: orthogonal: vertical (people & possums)	Similarity and contrast of possums and people; eating emphasised
		Within this:	
		centrifocal: centred: extended: triptych (Hush–sandwich–Grandma)	Centrality of vegemite sandwich, displayed as symbolic attribute
		Within this:	
		centrifocal: polarised: diagonal/ +deictic vector (Grandma & Hush tail)	Attention to visibility of Hush's tail
13	whole	if viewed as integrated spread (due to minor 'spillage' of recto image onto verso) centrifocal: polarised: diagonal (×2) (small umbrellas & large umbrella; verbiage & Hush aloft on mast)	Grandma's lolling posture doubled giving emphasis to repletion and relaxation; repeated warm ambience emphasising joy; Hush's depicted body and verbiage on reappearance of body linked
	verso	centrifocal: polarised: orthogonal: vertical (umbrellas & verbiage)	Complementarity of image and verbiage
	verso image	centralised: polarised: orthogonal: horizontal (left & right umbrellas with possums on each)	Emphasis on action (possums on left umbrella) and result (possums on right)

Table 4.2 *(Continued)*

Spread		Focus	Contribution to meaning
		Within this:	
		e.g. centrifocal: polarised: diagonal (×2) (Grandma eating & Grandma in chair; empty chair & hanging Hush)	Various contrasts made: busy versus resting Grandma absence (empty chair) versus visible presence (Hush)
	recto	centrifocal: centred: simple (sailing in umbrella)	Emphasis on Resolution – wind in their sails – towards finishing line
14	verso	centrifocal: centred: extended: triptych (verbiage–image–verbiage)	Story phased to make eating a lamington the central and extended moment
	verso image	centrifocal: polarised: diagonal: /+deictic vector (Hush eating & Grandma watching)	Focus on Hush eating lamington
	recto	centrifocal: centred: polarised: diagonal/ + deictic vector (Grandma & Hush)	Emphasis on mutual joy
15	whole	integrated: co-located	Restoration of wholeness
	upper spread	*Within that:*	
		iterating: aligned (animals)	Different indigenous Australian animals and (European) Australian foods – Australia's heritage
		And/or centrifocal: centred: extended: triptych (koala–wombat–Grandma)	
	lower spread	centrifocal: polarised: orthogonal: horizontal (verbiage & verbiage)	Phasing of story – attention to separated recto verbiage providing closure

5 Intermodality: Image and Verbiage

5.1 Instantiation of meaning

Up to this point our focus has been on the analysis of images within picture book stories. To this end we have built on Kress and van Leeuwen's (2006) visual grammar and extended it in ways that are relevant for the interpretation of picture book images. But of course the pictures are only 'half the story' when it comes to most picture books. To do justice to any picture book that includes words, our analysis must recognise the book's bimodal nature and come to grips with the way it makes meaning through both image and language. This chapter will sketch out the way image analysis can be implemented alongside linguistic analysis to bring out the interplay between the two semiotic systems in examples of bimodal stories. To do this we will draw on the descriptions of visual meaning systems described in earlier chapters and the descriptions of linguistic meaning systems provided in Halliday and Matthiessen (2004) and Martin and Rose (2007).

Differences between the two semiotics in the way they afford meaning have often been noted in the literature (e.g. Nodelman, 1988; Schwarcz and Schwarcz, 1991; Lemke 1998; Nikolajeva and Scott 2001; O'Halloran, 2008). Most obvious is the fact that a verbal text unfolds over time in a dynamic, sequential way and language has a rich potential for the construal of temporal deixis, sequencing, location, phasing and aspect. This is in contrast with the 'instantaneous' holistic apprehension of an individual image and the corresponding potential of the visual semiotic for non-sequential spatial and comparative relationships. Recognition of such differences (elaborated in O'Halloran, 2008) suggests some of the more obvious ways meanings might be expected to be 'shared out' in a bimodal text. But complementarities in affordances are also to be found in areas where language and image are equally well-suited, as for example in the construal of human emotion. Here, each semiotic can create a similar kind of meaning while drawing on its own distinct range or configuration of options. In such areas, a bimodal text may make use of either or both semiotics depending on whether sharing the semantic load, amplifying a common meaning or some more complex kind of counterpointing is being managed.

Other SFL approaches to the analysis of bimodal texts have tended to analogise from the text-forming resources of language to explain intermodality. Such resources as cohesion (Royce, 1998), logico-semantics (Martinec and Salway, 2005), rhetorical structure theory and conjunctive relations (Bateman, 2008), information structure (Kress and Van Leeuwen, 2006) and relational transitivity (Unsworth and Cleirigh, 2009; Chan, 2011) have all been used to theorise the linking of verbal and visual components within a multimodal text. Our approach, however, is to treat intermodality as different in kind from intramodal texturing and to capture this difference by focusing instead on the SFL dimension of instantiation.

Instantiation is the relation between the potential for meaning that inheres in the system of language (and/or another semiotic) and the specific, actual text which incorporates limited choices and realisations from the overall system/s (Halliday and Matthiessen, 2004: 27). While realisation is the relation between any option in the system and its associated form of expression, instantiation is the relation between the meaning potential as a whole and the particular selections and realisations from that system that are actualised in an individual text. It is thus a relation between language or image in general – as a totality of systems – and a linguistic and/or visual text as a particular instance of that totality, one whose meaning resides in the specific options selected and realised in relation to the totality of possibilities. The complexity of a bimodal text arises from the fact that there is more than one meaning system at play. To understand such a text, we must map out two complementary sets of meaning systems and track the way each is instantiated in the text so as to compare their relative contributions to overall meaning.

5.1.1   Commitment

To facilitate this comparison, we draw on Martin's recently articulated notions of 'commitment' and 'coupling' in relation to instantiation (Martin, 2008a, 2008c, 2010), focussing initially on the former. The idea of 'commitment' can be illustrated by reconsidering the system of CHARACTER MANIFESTATION introduced in Chapter 3. There, a choice is set up between a depiction of a character that is complete (realised by inclusion of the head, which is so important for recognition) and a depiction that is metonymic (realised by depiction of only a body part, silhouette or shadow). These two possibilities are set up as an opposition in the meaning potential so that any specific image in a book will be described as instantiating one or other choice (and its associated realisation). An alternative way to describe this particular variation, however, would be to say that different instances of character depiction simply 'commit' more or less meaning. In other words, a depiction of a character showing recognisable facial features would be described as instantiating more meaning than a depiction solely of the character's arm. Similarly a verbal description of a character as *an attractive young Australian girl with a healthy tan* commits more meaning than one describing her simply as *a girl*.

In the context of discourse analysis, the term commitment refers to the amount of meaning potential that is taken up from any particular meaning system in the

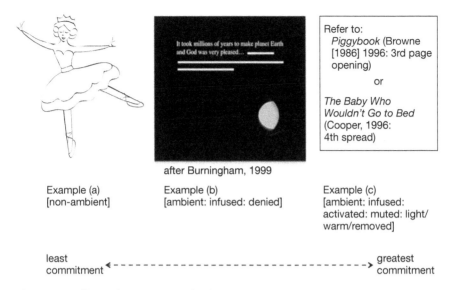

after Burningham, 1999

Example (a)	Example (b)	Example (c)
[non-ambient]	[ambient: infused: denied]	[ambient: infused: activated: muted: light/ warm/removed]

least commitment ←--→ greatest commitment

Figure 5.1 Differential commitment of ambience.

process of instantiation (Hood, 2008). What determines this is both whether the meaning system is deployed at all, and if it is, how extensively[1] and to what degree of delicacy. Figure 5.1 gives examples of images that vary in terms of the commitment of ambience. Example (a) in Figure 5.1 commits no ambience, while example (b) commits only the minimal meanings of [ambient: infused: denied]. Images referred to in example (c), on the other hand, commit the most meaning in this area, instantiating options from each of the [ambient: infused: activated] subsystems of VIBRANCY, WARMTH and FAMILIARITY.

Linguistically, we can again exemplify in relation to the construal of a participant in a clause. This may be done using a minimal nominal group structure such as *the spiders,* taking up only options from the system of DETERMINATION and that taxonomising living creatures. More meaning can be committed if the latter is more delicately classified, as in *the funnelweb spiders*; more again if the optional system of NUMERATION is brought into play with *the two funnelweb spiders* or if that of EPITHESIS is taken up, as in *the two large hairy funnelweb spiders,* or if an attitudinal dimension is committed, as in *the two terrifying funnelweb spiders,* and so on. Different monomodal texts on the same topic can therefore vary in terms of which aspects of meaning are more or less fully committed (see Hood, 2008; Martin, 2008a), while a bimodal text has the potential to commit greater or lesser amounts of any kind of meaning from either semiotic system.

Children's picture books deploy considerable variation in commitment as one of their literary and pedagogic strategies. For example, the classic story of *Rosie's Walk* by Pat Hutchins (1968), written for the very young, consists verbally of a single

---

1.   Extent in this context refers to how many optional systems are taken up.

sentence, its phrases distributed across some of the thirteen double-page spreads and the final closing page. That sentence has only one participant, 'Rosie the hen', a single process and a series of circumstantial locations to create a very flat and minimal verbal recount. The images commit these same meanings but a great deal more besides. Not only is the circumstantiation of the farmyard setting much more fully presented in the pictures, but an entire additional narrative is imaged. With every second turn of the page, we view a fox in the process of leaping for Rosie and on the following page, we see the fox coming to comic grief through some mishap or misjudgement while Rosie walks on apparently unawares. While the verbal text makes sense on its own and the visual text would still be entertaining without any words, the juxtaposition of the two with their contrasting levels of commitment adds a great deal. It contributes a layer of irony, raises ambiguities about Rosie's role in the fox's downfall and also apprentices the child reader into an agentive reading stance to negotiate the gap between the verbal and visual components of the text. Thus the variation in commitment creates interdependence not simply by sharing the semantic load between the visual and verbal systems (so that a novice reader is not daunted by too much verbiage) but serves in addition to multiply meaning and draw the reader into the text.

To look in more detail at the interplay of commitment in a bimodal picture book, it is useful to map out the complementarities between systems of meaning across image and language within each of the three metafunctions. We provide an outline of complementary systems in Tables 5.1–5.3. These are organised by metafunction and within that into broad areas relevant for the consideration of any narrative.

Two points should be made about these tables at the outset. The first is that they serve only as a schematic summary, indicating the general name or characterisation of the visual or linguistic meaning potential involved and the general nature of its realisations. Each cell of meaning potential should, however, be understood as a system of meaning choices, each of which has identifiable realisations (or a set of such systems). Chapters 2–4 of this book, together with Kress and van Leeuwen (2006), provide details of the visual systems summarised here, while Halliday and Matthiessen (2004) and Martin and Rose (2007) provide details of the linguistic systems referred to. A second issue is that since each semiotic system has its own affordances, there is not always a tidy complementarity between the two in respect of particular domains. In the tables, the visual systems have been listed first and areas of linguistic meaning potential have been identified which complement these, rather than the other way about. This means that some areas of linguistic potential need to be repeated at different points. For example verbal attitude complements both visual affect and (in part) visual ambience; similarly relational transitivity is relevant for character attribution and character relations, while visual pathos and inter-circumstance relations are not in an obvious complementary relationship with any specific verbal system. Despite these limitations, the tables can be useful as a general map of complementarities between the two semiotic systems to guide analysis of individual texts.

To exemplify the notion of commitment more fully, let us now briefly consider the story of *Not Now, Bernard* (McKee, [1980], 2004) in terms of the commitment

Table 5.1 Complementary interpersonal meaning systems across image and language.

	Visual meaning potential	Visual realisations	Verbal meaning potential	Verbal realisations
Affiliation	Visual focalisation	Direction of gaze of character; reader's gaze aligned or not with character's	Verbal focalisation	Sourcing of perceptions as internal or external to story
	Pathos	Drawing style: minimalist, generic, naturalistic	Characterisation	Various descriptive and attitudinal linguistic resources
	Power	Vertical angle of viewing (high, mid or low) by viewer; by depicted characters in relation to another	Power	Reciprocities of linguistic choices between characters (e.g. in naming, speech function, tagging, interpersonal metaphor,…)
	Social distance/ proximity	Shot size; proximity/touch of depicted participants	Social distance	Nature of naming choices, endearments, etc.
	Involvement/ orientation	Horizontal angle of viewer; horizontal angle of character to other depiction; +/– mutuality of character gaze	Solidarity	Proliferation of linguistic choice[1] (e.g. in attitude, naming, specialised lexis, slang, topics); contraction of realisations
Feeling	Ambience	Colour choices in relation to vibrancy, warmth and familiarity	'Tone'	Elaboration of circumstantiation in service of 'tone'
			Attitude	Evaluative language
	Visual affect	Emotion depicted in facial features and bodily stance	Verbal affect	Emotion language
	(Judgement) no system, but meaning may be invoked in reader		Attitude	Evaluative language
	Graduation: force	'Exaggerated' size, angle, proportion of frame filled, etc.; repetition of elements …	Graduation: force	Intensification, quantification, repetition …

1.   Originally proposed by Poynton (1985) as the realisation of the tenor variable of 'contact'.

Table 5.2 Complementary ideational meaning systems across image and language.

		Visual meaning potential	Visual realisations	Verbal meaning potential	Verbal realisations
Action		Visual 'action'[1]	Depicted action with:	Actional figures	Tense, phase, etc with transitivity structures:
		Action	Vectors		Material, behavioural processes
		Perception	Gaze vectors		Mental perception processes
		Cognition	Thought bubbles, face/hand gestures		Mental cognition processes
		Talking	Speech bubbles, face/ hand gestures		Verbal, behavioural processes
		Inter-event relations	Juxtaposition of images (+/– change of setting or participant)	Conjunction, projection	Logico-semantic relations of expansion and quoting/reporting
Character		Character attribution[2]	Depiction of physical attributes	Participant description, classification, identification	Relational transitivity nominal group structures, deixis
		Character manifestation and appearance	Character depiction		
		Character relations	Adjacent/symmetrical arrangement of different participants	Participant classification, description	Comparative epithets (*fatter*, *livelier*); classifying clauses (*they are soldiers*), etc.
Setting		Circumstantiation	Depiction of place, time (e.g. clock, moon), manner (e.g. lines indicating speed, trembling, etc.)	Circumstantiation	Specification of time, place, cause, manner, matter, contingency, role, etc.
		Inter-circumstance	Shifts, contrasts continuities in locations		Logico-semantic relations of enhancement

1. 'Narrative processes' for Kress and van Leeuwen (2006).
2. Through 'conceptual: analytical' processes in Kress and van Leeuwen's (2006) account.

of meaning across systems and metafunctions for each modality. Every page in the book has a complementary descending layout, alerting us to the likelihood of somewhat distinct roles for the two semiotics. The story opens with a set of scenes in which Bernard attempts to tell his father and mother of a monster in the garden about to eat him up. Each attempt to engage his busy, preoccupied parents is brushed off with the routine response 'Not now, Bernard'. Bernard then goes into

Table 5.3 Complementary textual meaning systems across image and language.

	Visual meaning potential	Visual realisations	Verbal meaning potential	Verbal realisations
Prominence	Framing	Binding of visual elements into units, separation of units via frames, margins, page edges	Tonality	Tone groups per clause
	Intermodal integration	Image and verbiage placement within layout	–	–
	Focus	Compositional arrangement	Information flow	Tonic prominence/ order of elements, hierarchy of New
Phasing	Genre stages and phases	Visual dis/ continuity	Genre stages and phases	Verbal texture (via internal conjunction, text reference, periodicity

the garden and greets an angry-looking monster, who promptly consumes him. The monster then enters the house and attempts to engage each of the (still preoccupied) adults in turn, by roaring at the mother and biting the father, who respond to these aggressive approaches with 'Not now, Bernard' exactly as before. The routines of the day continue with the monster misbehaving through a solitary dinner (left for him in front of the TV) and playtime. The final page shows the bewildered monster tucked up in bed with a teddy bear and a glass of milk, protesting to Mum 'But I'm a monster', only to meet her standard refusal to negotiate: 'Not now, Bernard'.

Turning first to the opening spread of the story, displayed in Figure 3.16, we can see some similarities with *Rosie's Walk*. Once again, the visual text is much 'bigger' than the verbal – not only in terms of its space allocation on the page – an [image privileged] layout – but also in terms of the meanings committed. To clarify this point, we will analyse these two images, metafunction by metafunction, looking first at the visual text and then at the verbal. As interpersonal meaning is mapped on to experiential content, it will be convenient to begin the analysis with reference to Table 5.2 and to first describe the ideational meanings instantiated in these two images. (To help relate the discussion to the tables, the key narrative domains for each metafunction have been placed in bold in the discussion. For ease of reading, system names have also been kept in lower case and meaning options are only placed in square brackets where essential for clarity.)

Looking at Figure 3.16 through an ideational lens, we can observe various **actions** depicted – a man getting ready to hammer a nail into the wall, as indicated by the position of his arms and the 'invisible gaze vector' between his eye and the nail (indicating a perception process) and a small boy watching him from behind (with his mouth open, suggesting verbal action as well as perception). In the second image, alongside the first, we see the man with head back, mouth wide and tongue visible (presumably yelling), having just hammered his finger instead of the nail. At the same time, the boy is walking away from the scene, his mouth now closed. The juxtaposition of the two images indicates a temporal inter-event relation of succession between the two scenes – one that is unfulfilled, as the nail did not get hammered. It can also imply a causal relation between the child's verbal action in the first image and the 'resulting' action by the man. Then, as far as **character** depiction is concerned, materialisation is complete and each character re-appears immediately, unchanged in status or attribution, creating maximal accessibility for the reader. We can also infer the age, race and perhaps social class of the characters from their depicted attributes of size, hair and skin colour, clothing, etc. The **setting** meanwhile involves minimal commitment of circumstantiation, suggesting no more than an interior space with floor and walls. This degree of circumstantiation is maintained from first to second image as is the context itself – the same room seen from the same perspective.

Interpersonally we need to consider both our **affiliation** with the characters and theirs with each other. In terms of visual focalisation, we viewers have no eye-contact with the characters and thus remain outside the story world as unmediated observers, but in a neutral relation of power, as we neither look up to nor down on the scene. In terms of involvement, we are 'detached' from the scene by having it presented to our gaze sideways-on and we are also kept at a far social distance by the long shot (Kress and van Leeuwen, 2006) as well as by the cartoonlike or 'minimalist' drawing style, which creates an 'appreciative' rather than empathetic or personalising pathos. Turning to affiliation between the characters, the systems of power, proximity and orientation are all important. The fact that the child is looking upwards at the man initially indicates the latter's power or authority in that image, a relation that has been equalised in the second picture. While the characters are in quite close proximity to one another, the child's posture in the first picture, leaning back with arms behind his back ensures no actual physical touch between the two, increasing the interpersonal distance. Choices from orientation reinforce this separation. In the first image, the adult is intent on the nail and the child faces the man's back, precluding any mutual eye contact. In the second image, the back-to-back orientation of the two characters makes a strong statement of interpersonal disengagement.

When it comes to the expression of **feeling**, the choice of a full palette of warm, bright shades creates an ambience that is both vibrant and familiar and that keeps the readers in an upbeat mood. The emotion or affect of each character meanwhile is provided through facial expression and bodily stance and gesture. Notably, the man's facial expression shifts from neutral in the first image to agonised in the second, while the child's postural stance shifts from tentative in the first to assumed nonchalance in the second (eyes raised, head tilted, hands in pockets). Graduation is not committed in terms of quantification but the salience of the colour of the man's face and finger may be taken as upscaling or intensifying the affect depicted.

Finally, in terms of textual organisation, **prominence** is achieved through framing and focus groups. The [bound: surrounded/contained] choices in framing facilitate some of the interpersonal meanings by providing a window into a distinct story world, thus distancing the reader who engages as an observer. Both pictures have a polarised and balanced focus group, facilitating our immediate apprehension of the two participants as a pair and encouraging comparison between the two. A deictic vector formed by the child's gaze strengthens the polarised focus in the first image and is notably absent in the second, underlining the interpersonal disen-gagement here (since the polarised composition also facilitates the interpersonal orientation choices). The two images are linked as a single **phase** in the story by recurrence of the same characters contextualised with a common ambience and circumstantiation (distinct from the following two spreads, where there is a shift of character and location). Thus visual textual choices help to organise the ideational and interpersonal realisations and all three metafunctions are co-present in the visual text, with some commitment of meaning from most systems.

The linguistic text by comparison is much smaller, construing ideationally only the verbal action and projections of direct speech. The characters are not described verbally at all but they are identified in terms of their familial roles as father and son, Bernard. There is no verbalisation of any other kind of action, nor of the expansion relations committed visually. Interpersonally, focalisation is external to the story (as in the visual) and otherwise the only meaning systems in play are those of power and proximity between the characters, realised by choices in exchange structure and naming. The exchange structure consists of an unreciprocated Greeting by Bernard followed by a non-compliant parental response, hinting at possible conflict, while the elliptical nature of the response ('*Not now*') reduces social distance. This degree of proximity is matched by Bernard's Vocative, '*Dad*', suggesting ordinary family intimacy, while the narrator's more formal reference to *his father* keeps the reader at a greater distance (in keeping with the visual long shot). Textually, just as the visual ambience links the two pictures as a unity distinct from the following scene, so the verbal exchange creates a mini text structure distinct from a new exchange initiated on the following page.

If we consider the issue of how the modalities contribute to meaning in terms of commitment, it is clear that there is more ideational meaning committed in the image than in the verbiage (in terms of action, inter-event relations, circumstantia-tion and participant attribution) but also that the verbiage commits a few meanings unavailable to the image, resulting in a(n uneven) degree of sharing of the semantic load (see Table 5.4). With respect to interpersonal meaning, there is a contrast between affiliation and feeling. As we discuss below, both image and verbiage com-mit very similar meanings with respect to affiliation but in the realm of feeling, there is no such sharing. While there is some degree of commitment of every visual meaning system for feeling, there is no commitment at all of any complementary verbal one. The differing commitment of image and verbiage in Figure 3.16 with respect to ideational choices and choices in feeling is summarised in Table 5.4.

If we were to continue the analysis of commitment through the rest of the book, we would find similar patterns throughout. Although after the first three double page spreads, the verbiage does on occasion commit material as well as verbal action, it only commits temporal relations between actions. The humour of the

Table 5.4 Degrees of commitment of ideational meaning and interpersonal meanings related to feeling in Figure 3.16. Shading in the cells is used to facilitate an overview of areas of commitment. Dark shading signifies no commitment, light shading indicates minor degree of commitment only.

	Image	Commitment	Verbiage	Commitment
Action	Action	Full: action depicted with vectors	Material/ behavioural process	
	Perception cognition?	Full: gaze vectors (image 1) via facial expression	Mental	
	Verbal	Partial: mouth open	Verbal	Full: *said Bernard*
	Inter-event (across pages)	Succession: within sequence/ unfulfilled implied cause	Expansion	
			projection	full: projected speech
Character	Attribution	Full (Father and Bernard) size, weight, age, hairstyle, dress …	Attribution	
	Family role	Partial: implied only	Role specification	Full: *his father*
	Manifestation & reappearance	Full (Father and Bernard)	Identification	Full: *Bernard – his*
Setting	Circumstantiation	Minimal location (interior, walls, floor) Manner of processes	Circumstantiation	
	Inter-circ	Full: same location		
Feeling	Visual affect	Full: (Father) 'absorbed' to 'upset' (Bernard) 'cheerful' to 'nonchalant'/ 'guilty'	Verbal affect	
	Ambience	Full: warm, light, familiar	Attitude, tone	
	(Evoked judgement)	(Father) 'unlucky'/ 'clumsy' (Bernard) 'responsible'/ 'pesky'	Attitude	
	Graduation	Colour of father's finger, face upscales affect	Graduation	

counter-expectation in the opening scenes (the [unfulfilled] visual inter-event option) and the implications of causality are only ever present in the visual story. Even more noticeably, the verbiage never inscribes attitude while the great majority of the images depict emotion via facial expressions and stance (and also invoke judgement via depicted affect and action). We see the father engrossed, shocked and outraged; Bernard cheerful, nonchalant and pensive; his mother preoccupied, irritated and longsuffering; and the monster hostile, satisfied (having consumed Bernard), angry, taken aback and bewildered by turns. And in the phases where the monster roars at mother and bites father, there is an additional strand of humour created by the disjunction between the monster's behaviour on the verso and his depicted facial affect at the result on the recto (since he appears taken aback rather than gleeful at what he has done). The verbal narration, however, commits none of this at any point. Indeed the parents' depicted negative emotions are always coupled with the same understated verbal routine '*Not now*' addressed with the same neutral Vocative, '*Bernard*'. Verbally, then, repetition upscales the parental refusal to engage rather than any overt expression of feeling. The incongruity in commitment between the visual and verbal is both a source of fun in the book and a means of underlining both the self-absorption of the adults and the provocativeness of the monstrous child.

5.1.2   Coupling

Where *Not Now, Bernard* differs substantially from *Rosie's Walk*, however, is in the fact that there are more semantic areas where both visual and verbal components commit some meaning. Here we can bring in the notion of 'coupling', which refers to the repeated co-patterning within a text of realisations from two or more systems. In principle, this can be within or across metafunctions[2] – either with respect to a mono-modal text or across different semiotic modalities. For example, intramodally, one might find a consistent coupling of linguistic choices from two interpersonal systems such as graduation: force (e.g. by intensifying) and attitude: affect/negative, evidenced by group structures such as *very sad*, *highly distressed*, *angrier and angrier* (see Figure 5.2). Across metafunctions, an example would be the consistent coupling of such interpersonal affect with a particular character (as for Amanda in the text shown in Figure 5.2). In a bimodal text a hypothetical example of coupling might be a consistent co-patterning of particular ambience choices in the visual, such as vibrant, warm and light, with complementary choices of positive attitude in the verbal.

This is not to suggest, however, that choices made within the two semiotics will always amplify one another, multiplying corresponding kinds of meaning by means

2. The key theoretical point here is that the realisation hierarchy radically underspecifies the ways in which systems from different strata, metafunctions and ranks combine with one another; it is the responsibility of instantiation to account for the way in which cultures enact patterns of interacting meaning.

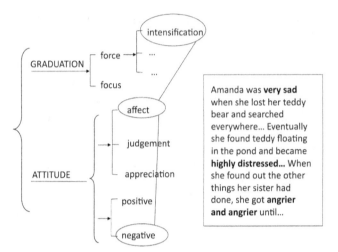

Figure 5.2 Example of coupling within a metafunction for a linguistic text.

of 'convergent' coupling. Apparently simple picture books are often rich in meaning precisely because couplings between choices from the different modalities may be more or less 'divergent'. For example, it is quite possible in a picture book to have character focalisation in the verbiage through a first person narrator coupled with a 'third person' visual focalisation by means of the 'observe' option, where we neither make eye contact with the character nor share their line of regard. In such a case there is a divergence that adds to the meaning potential by allowing us two points of view simultaneously. For any pair of complementary meaning systems in Tables 5.1–5.3, then, the couplings can be considered in terms of convergence or divergence, with converging ideational couplings creating 'concurrence', converging interpersonal couplings creating 'resonance' and converging textual couplings creating 'synchrony' across all or part of the text.[3]

5.1.2.1   Intermodal couplings in *Not Now, Bernard*

Let us now briefly consider McKee's *Not Now, Bernard* in terms of the main couplings evident. To begin, we can note that there is ideational concurrence in the fact that all the characters are identified in the verbiage on each visual appearance. (A minor exception is that the monster is announced verbally in the third spread ahead of a verbal and visual coupling on the recto of the fourth, adding the zest of anticipation to the story's major incident). The characters' acts of speaking are also both depicted and verbalised. And as the story continues, there is frequently concurrence between actions depicted and those narrated (e.g. picture of Bernard descending steps into garden + 'Bernard went into the garden'; picture of monster throwing toy across room + 'the monster broke one of Bernard's toys'; picture of Bernard's mother

---

3. Note that these terms are used here to describe convergent couplings within a particular metafunction, but coupling may also occur across metafunctions.

holding a plate of dinner, speaking and looking sideways out of frame + '"Your dinner's ready" said Bernard's mother'). In general, while by no means all the ideational meanings found in one modality are committed in the other, the only apparently divergent couplings are in the parents' naming of the depicted monster as *Bernard* during the second half of the story. This divergence is a means of creating humour and of invoking negative judgment of the inattentive parents, but at the same time it is not actually a divergent coupling for anyone reading the monster metaphorically as a transformed version of Bernard.

The transformation occurs in the ninth image, verbalised as 'The monster ate Bernard up, every bit'. The image is a largely conceptual one of the monster licking its chops and displaying Bernard's shoe in the manner of a symbolic attribute. In this way 'Bernardness' is visually conferred on the monster. Again there is concurrence in the intermodal coupling since the verbal text can correspond to both the literal aspect of the image – every bit of Bernard has been eaten – and the metaphorical aspect: Bernard (as will be seen) is utterly 'eaten up' or 'taken over' by something monstrous. Since all following images and narrative verbiage concur in presenting the monster as the protagonist, taking over Bernard's role in the story, we are also guided to read this ninth image as signalling the attribution of monstrous qualities to Bernard as much as the reverse.

Interpersonally, there is intermodal resonance in the couplings between several complementary affiliation systems. Firstly, both visual and verbal focalisation choices result in observation from outside the story. That is, visually we do not make eye contact with the characters, nor do we visually adopt or align with any character's point of view, and verbally we have only the external narrator's point of view. (The exception is on the final page where the monster faces out, possibly making eye contact with us, a visual choice that nonetheless resonates with the accompanying shift to first person declaration: '*I'm a monster*'.[4]). The general lack of verbal character focalisation also resonates with the appreciative stance we are invited to take by the minimalist drawing style and the repeated visual long shots creating 'far' social distance between viewer and character. Over the course of the book, too, interpersonal separation of the characters becomes evident. This is underlined by a resonance resulting from the absence of verbal intimacy markers converging with visual choices in proximity: the characters never touch, lean towards, make eye-contact with or gesture in the direction of the other except on the occasion when the monster bites the father's leg – and even here the father's upheld newspaper maintains a separation between the two. Finally there is further resonance in the visual choices of bodily orientation between the characters – never face to face – and the restricted nature of the verbal conversations, which do not create solidarity.

In the realm of affiliation, then, there is considerable intermodal resonance in the story, serving to keep the reader relatively detached, amused and observing (rather than involved and participating) and building an unambiguous picture

---

4. The shift allows the reader either to accept the implied role of Mum-as-addressee, or simply to align in the end with Bernard/monster.

of dysfunction in the depicted family relationships. At the same time, there is a striking absence of resonance to be found in the domain of feeling, resulting from differences in commitment, since the visuals depict and foreground affect while the verbiage is devoid of attitude or graduation. (Compare the visual depiction in Figure 3.16 of the father's facial expression and stance which show him yelling in pain, with the verbal text which instantiates no affect and no graduation of the verbal process, simply using *said.*)

Finally, it can be noted that textually, in this story, complementary systems tend to converge to create synchrony rather than the reverse, something that may be expected in a book for very young children. The alternating warm and cool ambience of successive double pages is used to mark the story into episodes in a way that corresponds neatly with the verbal structuring, and within any page or spread our attention is similarly focused by visual focus groups and the verbal information flow. Table 5.5 shows that, with only three exceptions, every element of verbal news is also a visual focus on the same page. Where this does not occur is with Bernard's previewing speech on spread 3 of the 'monster in the garden', which only becomes visual focus on spread 4, and mother's mention of bed and milk on spread 11, which are in the centred focus group on the following page. Apart from these, there are the humorous cases where *Bernard* is verbal New and the monster is the visual focus, or – in the final image – where neither is committed visually. With these exceptions, the verbal News are always picked up in the main focus group of the image, adding synchrony in prominence to that found in the phasing of the story. Overall then, it can be argued that in terms of couplings between the meanings committed from image and language there is generally convergence between the choices made within each metafunction, resulting in a general amplification of any meaning committed, with affiliation foregrounded as the most significant semantic domain.

To consider the text as a whole, both commitment and coupling need to be explored. *Not Now, Bernard* is a story for preschool or very young children and it is not unexpected that it would leave much of the ideational meaning – including the humour of 'unfulfilled' adult activity sequences – to be presented via the visual modality. It also caters for its young audience, as we have seen, by ensuring that its meanings are made accessible through textual synchrony and its themes through amplification of choices of (dis)affiliation, created by the intermodal resonance here. At the same time, the incongruity of the differential commitment of appraisal by the two modalities is equally important. It provides an additional source of humour to that available purely from the visuals through the 'slapstick' misadventures of the characters – humour which depends absolutely on the bimodality of the text. The incongruity also requires readers to make their own ethical judgements of the characters according to their own standpoint and experience, something that caters nicely to the dual address (Wall, 1991) of successful children's books. Taken together, the emphasis given to affiliation through resonating intermodal couplings and the 'gap' created by the disjunction between the action and feeling committed in the images and the dialogue committed in the verbiage work together to mobilise the book's implicit commentary on dysfunctional nuclear family roles and relationships.

Table 5.5 Correspondence between linguistic news and visual focus in *Not Now, Bernard*.

Spread		Verbal New		Elements in major Focus group		
1	verso	Dad	Bernard	Dad		Bernard
				Dad		nail
	recto	Bernard	his father	Dad		Bernard
2	verso	Mum	Bernard	Bernard		mother
	recto	Bernard	his mother	Bernard	(stool)	mother
3	verso	a monster	in the garden	Bernard		mother
		eat me	Bernard	Mother		water plant
	recto	Bernard	mother	Bernard		mother
				plant		mother
4	verso	into the garden		Bernard on steps		(unbalanced)
	recto	monster		Bernard	monster	tree
		the monster				
5	verso	(ate) up, … bit		monster	palm	
				lick		
				chops		
				monster	shoe	
	recto	indoors		monster at door		
6	verso	the monster	Bernard's mother	monster		mother
	recto	Bernard	Bernard's mother	monster		mother
7	verso	Bernard's father		monster	newspaper	father
	recto	Bernard	Bernard's father	newspaper		father
				monster		father
8	verso	'ready'	Bernard's mother	table		mother+dinner
	recto	dinner	television	TV	dinner	Mother's leg
9	verso	the dinner		monster eating		(unbalanced)
	recto	the television		monster	TV	(unbalanced)
10	verso	one of Bernard's comics		monster reading comic on bookcase		
	recto	one of his toys		toys		monster
11	verso	to bed		mother		setting
		your milk	Bernard's mother			
	recto	upstairs		setting		monster/stairs
12	verso	monster	the monster	monster in bed with milk		
	recto	Bernard	Bernard's mother	mother		

Texts like *Rosie's Walk* and *Not Now, Bernard* have considerable pedagogic power as they use intermodal complementarity to scaffold literary ways of reading, which involve going beyond the mere events of the story to appreciating that these symbolise something beyond themselves – some theme serving a moral or ethical goal.

A very young child may be unable to read much (or any) verbal text independently or to understand a literary style of language, but the way the resources of the two semiotics are skewed in terms of commitment not only invites initial access to the story, but provides experience in recognising what is involved in valued ways of taking meaning from a story. In *Not Now, Bernard,* neither the visual nor the verbal sequence of actions on its own carries the full meaning nor provides the full enjoyment and fun of the text – this requires negotiating the gap between the two modalities and thus arriving at a new meaning that results from the co-patterning of semiotic resources. Even if the child does not reach an interpretation such as 'busy, self-absorbed, individualistic parents create monstrous children' – one possible reading of the text – he or she is still being scaffolded into appropriate reading strategies by being positioned to respond to thematically relevant meaning patterns made highly salient through intermodal convergence (e.g. in the domain of affiliation) and by the need to actively negotiate the commitment gap to gain meaning not available from the 'face value' of either words or pictures. Such 'simple' and entertaining picture books are therefore potentially significant in terms of providing an educationally worthwhile experience for the child.

5.2   Visual–verbal instantiation in *Way Home*

Of course, as children's language develops they are able to negotiate more sophisticated verbal material; but this does not mean that the picture book is no longer an appropriate vehicle for literary learning. In contrast to stories like *Rosie's Walk* and *Not Now, Bernard*, which have very little verbiage and are designed for beginning readers, let us now consider an Australian text for older children in which much more meaning is committed by means of the verbiage but which still depends crucially on intermodal complementarities to construct its theme (Painter and Martin, 2011). *Way Home* (1994), written by Libby Hathorn and illustrated by Gregory Rogers,[5] tells the story of a young boy's evening journey home through the city and comprises fourteen double-page openings, plus a final page.

Apart from the final page, the layout of each spread is a complementary one, with a single large unframed image extending over the gutter and separated from the accompanying verbiage by a single jagged 'torn paper' edge in a [bound: limited] form of framing. The 'torn' edge to the margin (see Figure 5.3), effectively hints at the socially disvalued nature of the depicted experiences. The verbiage is in white type on a black page background and varies from a few sentences to a few paragraphs on each spread. The complementarity of the layout points to the distinct roles played by image and verbiage in the unfolding of the story, especially in relation to ideational meaning.

The story opens one evening when the barking of a dog frightens a stray kitten, which is adopted by 'a boy called Shane', the protagonist. After this, Shane proceeds on his way home with the kitten, pausing at various points to gaze in at a lighted

---

5.   Rogers was awarded the Kate Greenaway medal for his illustrations in *Way Home.*

A dog barks and this cat with no name scrambles up a fence. This boy called Shane sees the little cat and yells, 'Hey, you! Scaredycat!'

The cat with no name hears the loud voice of the boy. And way up there on the top of the fence, this clever baby thing rolls itself up. Such a tight little ball of fierce cat. It growls and then it spits right at the boy called Shane. Mad as anything!

Figure 5.3 Opening spread of *Way Home* (Hathorn and Rogers, 1994).

house or shop window, but running scared at other times to escape the danger of a threatening gang or a fierce dog. Finally Shane negotiates the final steps and alleys of his journey to bring the kitten to 'my place'. On the final page turn, this place is revealed to be a makeshift shelter for a boy we now understand to be homeless. The book's thematic concerns with bonding (being part of a community) and belonging (having a place) are established in the Orientation and carried by Shane's journey with the kitten through the city – a journey during which the interplay of commitment and coupling across the metafunctions keeps the readers slightly off balance, as we are invited to empathise with Shane's situation while simultaneously kept at a distance from it.

Table 5.6 shows the sequence of episodes in the story and how they are distributed visually. The opening two spreads constitute an Orientation that sets up homelessness as a theme and 'going home' as the predictable activity sequence, which is then interrupted a number of times. Two of the ensuing episodes (summarised in the table as 'chased by the gang' and 'the fierce dog') constitute embedded narratives with Complications resolved through a quick and resourceful reaction to danger. The other episodes are evaluative rather than dramatic: Shane is distracted by sights of the social world from which he and the kitten are excluded, and he comments on these sights to the kitten.

The episodic structure of the story is created ideationally through inter-image relations coupled with verbal conjunctive relations. Visually the story is structured through inter-circumstance and inter-event relations. Inter-circumstance relations

Table 5.6 Summary of *Way Home* story structure.

Spread	Image content	Verbal episode	Structuring signal
1	Shane running, kitten on fence	'setting off home with	
2	Shane looks at cradled kitten	kitten'	
3	Shane looks at a pampered cat	'the pampered cat'	*But*
4	Shane spots hostile gang	'chased by the gang'	*But*
5	Shane chased by gang		
6	Shane escapes to freeway		
7	Shane looks at car showroom	'the well lit street'	*But*
8	Shane chats to girl in street		
9	Snarling dog	'the fierce dog'	*But*
10	Shane reaches to kitten up tree		
11	Shane's view over city	'up in the tree'	Visual projection
12	Shane up the tree		
13	Shane goes up alleyway steps	'getting home'	
14	Shane crawls through wire fence		
15 (verso only)	Shane is home		

contribute by means of changes in context or new perspectives on a context, concluding with a [home: in] sequence to emphasise the significance of the final arrival (see Table 5.7 at the end of this chapter). At the same time, the temporal unfolding of the journey is carried by the way all but one image links to the previous one through [unfolding: succession] relations, sometimes between different sequences (different interruptions to Shane's journey home) and sometimes within the same sequence, when more text time is devoted to a single episode, such as Shane's flight from the gang. Similarly, the verbal text also commits (mainly implicit) conjunctive relations of temporal succession throughout. In other respects, however, the two modalities play complementary roles in structuring the story. Visually, the journey is laid out with at least one image devoted to each episode, while verbally each of four delays to the journey is signalled with an explicit counter-expectation conjunctive *But*, a relation absent from the visual inter-event sequence (see Table 5.6). The fifth delaying episode is not verbally signalled like the others but is created by a visual shift to a projection link between spreads 10 and 11. In these ways, the 'non-dramatic' episodes (which are thematically very important) gain intermodal or visual salience along with the chases. See Table 5.8 at the end of this section for a more detailed summary of the commitment of (visual) inter-event and (verbal) conjunctive relations.

The complementary layout is one giving greater semantic weight to the images since they always take up more than half the space, but in comparison with *Not Now, Bernard*, the verbiage, comprising third person narration and one-way dialogue (from the boy to the kitten), provides much more of the ideational meaning. Not only are there many more actions and locations narrated in the verbiage than are depicted, but these meanings in the verbiage are graduated to foreground two ideational motifs not readily imaged: the sounds of the city (*a thud, thud, thud; a screaming of tongues and tires; a blare of horns*) and more especially the sense of motion, which is construed on every page through both action (*scrambled, go and go, leaps, crawls quickly*, etc.) and circumstantiation (*over the bins and garbage bags, up the lane, all the way down the other side, past the sharp smell of food shops, up and up and up*, etc.). The verbal text is in fact notable for its repeated use of locative circumstances to construe movement (see Table 5.9 for further exemplification).

The images play a supporting role here, depicting only a small selection of the narrated actions and only four of them having diagonal vectors. Rather than construing movement, the main ideational function of the images is to commit additional circumstantial details (e.g. broken fences, drains, doorways, posters, barred windows and graffiti) to the many already committed in the verbiage. This is especially important in the final sequence where there is no verbal description of 'home' at all. The images also serve to make available the physical attributes of the characters, which (with the exception of the kitten) are committed verbally only in very general terms as *a boy called Shane, that lot, they, a girl*. But even here the role of the images is relatively minor: the first dog and the gang appear and reappear only metonymically (as shadow or outline) while the kitten is not only described verbally as a personality but is much more consistently present in the story through verbal identity chains than through its four visual reappearances. Overall then, verbiage and image both construe temporal succession and spatial circumstantiation but otherwise make very unequal contributions in terms of the commitment of ideational meaning. Apart from some additional details of setting and character attribution, the verbiage does the lion's share of the ideational work, especially in committing counter-expectancy and in creating the action and momentum of the journey.

As well as these differences in commitment, *Way Home* makes thematic use of some key divergences in the coupling of visual and verbal ideational meaning. First, there is the fact that Shane recedes into the circumstantiation in more than one image (see Table 5.10), while being constantly to the fore verbally, a divergence which allows him to be the centre of the story, while simultaneously construed as an insignificant circumstantial element in the cityscape. Secondly, the punch-line of the story is facilitated by two key divergences between image and verbiage at particular points. Close to the end of the book we see the boy atop a tree (where he followed the kitten) and our eyes are drawn to a lighted upper window in an adjacent house, the only visible building (see Figure 5.4). The adjacent verbiage comprises speech by the boy to the kitten in which he comments on a very different scene – the whole city at night full of empty office blocks where no one lives, something actually imaged on the previous page. The second paragraph then begins 'Guess what? I can see our place' and closes 'we're going right on home.' Readers will tend to assume textual synchrony between the verbal News (*our place, home*) and the visual focus (the lighted upper window) and so expect that the boy will simply enter the occupied house. They therefore remain unprepared for the final page where the image of the boy crawling into a pathetic windowless shelter is coupled with 'Here we are. We're home!' This final ideational coupling (of visual hovel and verbal *home*) – highly divergent in terms of the experience of the typical reader – provides a surprise and problematises the meaning of 'home'. The divergent

'Get that stack of big buildings.
Nobody lives in them — no way.
They're all mostly empty — specially nights.
I've been there once.
They're to look at I guess.
So why don't you look, Kittycat?
Hey, get those people down there.
Talk about crazy.
There's our Jag too.
It's cool up here, I reckon.'

'Guess what? I can see our place, Catseyes.
And we gotta go down right now.'
Hand over hand, branch over branch, down the slippery trunk
to the tindery fence. It's an easy jump to the ground.
The boy called Shane takes the cat with no name back down.

'No more pussyfooting, Cat Number One. This time, we're
going right on home.'

Figure 5.4 Twelfth spread of *Way Home* (Hathorn and Rogers, 1994).

intermodal couplings are thus very significant in achieving effects that highlight the theme concerning the importance for everyone of 'belonging' somewhere.

The discussion of ideational meaning has already indicated that the imaged story and the linguistic one are not necessarily synchronised textually, and divergences here create an unsettling effect at times. Table 5.11 shows how the phases of the verbal narrative are not always in comfortable synchrony with the visual pagination. On occasion (e.g. spreads 2 and 7) several distinct phases in the story are committed verbally while a single moment is imaged, and at other times an important verbal stage is not committed visually at all (Evaluations on spreads 7 and 10). On spread 4, a new narrative stage begins verbally mid-page, while on spread 8, a minor phase (chatting to the girl) gains visual prominence, rather than the moment of delay that is given verbal prominence (with *but* ...). At several points (spreads 2, 4, 9 and 13) the verbiage runs ahead of the following image, while on spread 12 (shown in Figure 5.4) the reverse occurs and the verbiage (about *the stack of big buildings*) proves relevant to the previous, rather than the adjacent image. These textual divergences that keep the reader slightly off balance appear to act as a metaphor for a somewhat ambiguous reading position created by interpersonal choices, which paradoxically both invite and prevent ready alignment with the central character.

As always in children's picture book stories, the interpersonal domain is central and in *Way Home*, both image and language commit meaning across a range of systems. One of the most obvious features of the verbiage, for example, is the very extensive commitment of graduation in the form of upscaled force, with intensification by means of repetition (*up and up and up*; *turning and turning*, etc.), infused manner (*scrambles, screaming, blare*, etc.), and modification (*fast as anything, crawls quickly, quickly, real light*) as well as upscaled quantification (*lots and lots, all the way down, stack of big buildings*), all making a contribution to the drama and flagging invoked attitude throughout. While the ideational meanings being graduated may not be committed in the images, graduation itself is also committed visually, though to a lesser degree. There are, for example, two 'excessively' low-angled images making an impact at key points: the first when Shane spots the gang, adding visual drama to the initiation of that Complication and the second when Shane is high in the tree (see Figure 5.4). In addition, the high number of some circumstantial elements, particularly lighted windows, is an upscaled quantification choice in many images that clues us in to their role as a 'motif' contributing thematic meaning.

In other systems related to feeling there are divergences in commitment and coupling that tend to complicate the reader's response to this story. Unlike *Not Now, Bernard, Way Home* does not rely on visual facial expressions here. The only unequivocal depiction of facial affect occurs in a tattered poster on the wall in the first image (see Figure 5.3), alerting us from the outset to the fact that all is not well in this urban environment. In the course of the book, however, there are surprisingly few images where we have any clear view of Shane's face, and only one where he is responding to a moment of drama (on escaping from the gang). This means that the power of the image to create instant alignment with a character through an empathetic response to his/her depicted feeling is barely taken up at all. Instead it is the verbiage which plays a bigger role in committing affect, both positive and negative. For example, after Shane escapes from the gang, the verbiage commits a strong surge of positive affect (the boy is *laughing and laughing*) while the image shows only a long shot back view of him looking into the showroom. The consistent choice not to amplify verbal affect through intermodal resonance with visual affect works to prevent too close an identification with the protagonist.

Rather than through facial expression, attitudinal work is done by the images in *Way Home* through the system of ambience, which invokes a general emotional tone. In fact, the most immediately striking feature of *Way Home* is the [denied] ambience of the black page margins and the enveloping [muted: dark] ambience created by the dull browns and greys of most of the night scenes. This is relieved by contrasting splashes of warmth and light emanating chiefly from the windows of a comfortable domestic property or prosperous commercial world into which Shane gazes as an excluded outsider. Thus while the verbal attitude alternates between negative (*the scared fur*, '*they don't like me*') and positive (*the boy ... laughs*, '*I like you, Spitfire*') inscriptions and invocations (see Table 5.12), the visual ambience is more consistently negative – especially when coupled with circumstantial details of litter, graffiti and dilapidated buildings and fences). The effect is subtle – a generally negative situation is tempered by regular verbal expressions of positive attitude, but these latter are not amplified by intersemiotic resonance. Positive verbal attitude may be considered to resonate with the 'positive' visual splashes of warmth and light but since these are visually coupled with ideational spaces forbidden to Shane, the effect is poignant rather than reinforcing.

In the realm of affiliation, there is also complexity in the intermodal relations and in the resultant alignment of readers. This arises in part from minor divergences between image and verbiage, but more significantly from the patterned interplay of different systems: those of social distance (visual and verbal) on the one hand and involvement/orientation (visual) complemented by solidarity (verbal) on the other. With respect to social distance, the choices partly resonate between the two semiotic systems: in the images Shane is often depicted at a far social distance, while the narrator even more consistently does this by referring to him throughout only as *the boy called Shane* or *the boy*, constructing him as someone we are not in a social relation with. On the other hand, there is some disturbance of this intermodal resonance in that it is often while Shane is visually very distant from us that the verbiage commits his speech to the kitten he is carrying, as though we were close up and able to hear. And there are also a few occasions when we are permitted a closer view of the boy. Overall, we are inconsistently invited to get close while simultaneously being kept at arm's length. By contrast, distance between the characters themselves is unambiguously a close one. In his speech Shane ascribes endearing pet names to the cat (*Kitten number one, Bestcat, Whiskettes*, etc.), inscribing and invoking his positive feelings for his newly adopted charge and so constructing intimacy between the two (see Table 5.13). This resonates with the close visual proximity between them in those images where the kitten is shown tucked inside Shane's jacket.

Visual involvement/orientation choices work in a similar way to inhibit involvement of the reader with Shane and promote it between the kitten and Shane. Involvement options keep us detached by repeatedly showing Shane at oblique angles and in rear views that function to 'other' him. At the same time two key close or mid-shot images show the boy and the cat facing and gazing at each other, an orientation choice resonating with the amount of naming of the cat by Shane in the verbal text (26 Vocatives, as shown in Table 5.13), a highly marked proliferation constructing solidarity between them and invoking positive appraisal by the reader.[6] This proliferation is in a sense highlighted for a young reader by the irony of the narrator referring to the kitten simply as *the cat with no name*. The effect of the intermodal resonances in both social distance and involvement/solidarity choices is therefore to keep the reader at some distance and detachment from Shane most of the time, even while we are privy to his private conversation with the kitten and feel positively towards that relationship. At the same time, they underline the close, involved relation between Shane and the kitten, constructing the need for community as a significant theme – one explicitly articulated for the reader on the penultimate spread when Shane says 'Yeah. It's spooky right here. But we got each other, right?'

The other major area of interpersonal meaning relevant to affiliation is that of focalisation. It is handled carefully in *Way Home* so as to keep the reader aligned with Shane but not sharing his experience too closely. The third person verbal narration commits Shane's behaviour (*laughs, runs, leaps…*) and speech ('*You're with me now, Cat*'), but does not overtly inform us of his sensations and has no direct

---

6. See Poynton (1985) for discussion of proliferation as a realisation of solidarity.

access to his interior world. All this resonates with the observer stance we maintain visually in the absence of any eye contact with him. On the other hand, this visual observer stance is mediated at times, allowing us to view the world 'along with' the character by being positioned behind him, seeing what he sees. Up until the final image, however, the occasions of mediated focalisation all involve long shots so that we have much more of 'our' view than the shared view. We seem to be following Shane from a distance rather than living his experience. It is only with the final page turn that there is a clear 'over the shoulder' view where we are 'with' Shane as he enters his home. This adds to the impact of this image where the nature of his relation to society is revealed, at which point we may with hindsight guess at unexpressed feelings behind the bravado of some of his upbeat comments to the kitten along the way.

Another aspect of focalisation in the book concerns the kitten's role, since, by contrast with Shane, we do verbally experience the journey from the kitten's point of view on more than one occasion (*the cat with no name hears the loud voice of the boy*; *the cat … is cosy*; *the cat feels safe*; *it's very black down there for the cat*; *in a panic …*). The cat may not be imaged at each such point, creating divergence at particular moments, but in one notable instance we are intermodally positioned to adopt its visual point of view. This occurs when the verbal text focalises the cat with 'And the cat with no name sees a flash of cruel teeth, hears the angry loud bark of the monster dog, smells the blood and the thunder and danger', while a visual, uncircumstantiated close-up of a snarling slavering dog stares straight out at us from the page. Coupled with the verbal text, this visual choice of [contact] positions us to empathise with the kitten by viewing the dog through its eyes. The reader is thus invited to share the experience of danger in the story as the kitten rather than the boy, whose own insecurities must be inferred (there are 12 verbal invocations of Shane's negative security presented in Table 5.12 compared with just two inscriptions). Together with the other interpersonal choices discussed, the intermittent use of the kitten as focaliser would seem to be a way of drawing the readers into Shane's world while simultaneously allowing them to remain at an emotionally safe distance from his experience.

The fact that *Way Home* has a darker content than is typical in picture books and is attempting to raise the awareness of its (probably) middle-class readership about the experience of children in their urban environment but not 'of their world' explains the complexity of some of the semantic choices made in this picture book. The reader needs to be engaged in the drama of the story (achieved by the graduated ideational choices of verbiage) and 'with' Shane, as is achieved by hearing his speech, 'following' him through the streets and observing and appraising his relation with the kitten; but the reader is positioned not to identify with him or treat him as an individual whose psychological make-up is the focus of concern. Because of this, the book uses 'unsettling' strategies and passes up on many opportunities for aligning the reader more closely with the protagonist, thus avoiding the dangers of being either too negative (and taking the child reader into an emotionally insecure space), or of encouraging a purely emotive response to Shane's plight. The book's strategies for constructing the boy as other to the reader/viewer make salient the status of such children as outsiders in the community in a way that may leave us somewhat uncomfortable, while simultaneously underlining the positive values of companionship and security symbolised by Shane's relationship with the kitten and the visual and verbal emphasis on 'home'. Through interpersonal resonances between many systems as well as unexpected divergences and incomplete convergences in the coupling of visual and verbal meaning, the book manages to negotiate a tricky relationship between the reader and the world depicted, scaffolding the reader into the values and themes being made salient rather than encouraging a purely affectual response.

5.3   Coda

In this chapter we have focused on the analysis of discourse rather than the building of systems, which has been the concern of earlier chapters. To this end we have introduced and taken up the notions of commitment and coupling in relation to the instantiation of meaning. While these concepts are relevant for considering mono-modal texts (such as a picture or a purely verbal story), our concern here has been to mobilise them in the interpretation of bimodal stories. This has been enabled by a framework where complementary systems of image and language are laid out according to metafunction so as to facilitate the consideration of contributions made by each semiotic individually and in concert. Those contributions have been discussed partly in terms of commonalities or variations in the degree of commitment of different areas of meaning in a particular picture book – for example, whether and how much affect or circumstantiation is committed by each modality. Meaning contributions have also been considered in terms of the multiple coupling relationships (across complementary systems) simultaneously in play in the text – both convergent and divergent ones. In this way, rather than applying a limited taxonomy of possible image-verbiage relations to a text, we can do better justice to the way instantiation of meaning from two semiotic systems may 'multiply' meaning.

When we apply this framework to the analysis of high quality picture books such as *Rosie's Walk*, *Not Now, Bernard* and *Way Home*, we can also better appreciate the pedagogic role of such texts in apprenticing young readers into the understanding of literature. Unlike the innumerable, unmemorable picture books marketed with groceries in supermarkets and newsagents, such books constitute important texts for literary training, using the two modalities with great skill to help readers to perceive that the events of the story 'stand for' something beyond themselves. In a 'literary' picture book, amplification of semantic domains through multiple intermodal convergences helps to signal the thematic concerns of a story, but is far from the only strategy used. As we have seen, gaps created by differential commitment, shifts in established intermodal patterns and incongruities created by divergent couplings all create anomalies that require symbolic interpretation of the story events if they are to be resolved. Books like these are not only enjoyable and engaging for young readers, but offer a very important 'training' in becoming sensitised in how to read narrative texts (including monomodal ones) in ways that are educationally valued.

Table 5.7 INTER-CIRCUMSTANCE relations in *Way Home*.

Spread	Image content	(Visual) INTER-CIRCUMSTANCE RELATIONS	Note on analysis [sustain degree] throughout except for spreads 9 and 10
1	Dog shadow, Shane, kitten, details of backstreet location		
2	Shane gazes at kitten tucked into jacket	sustain degree/ maintain context: new perspective	Context ambiguous but dog shadow and background and lighting suggest some movement within same location
3	Shane looks at a pampered cat	sustain degree/ maintain context: new perspective	The context is taken to be 'back lanes with dilapidated fencing', but if construed more narrowly as a particular lane, this can be taken as [change context: relocate]
4	Shane turns from gang	sustain degree/ maintain context : new perspective	As above
5	Shane runs from gang shadow	sustain degree/ maintain context : new perspective	A transitional image with back street and main street both visible, so could equally be taken as [change context: relocate] even if spreads 3 and 4 are not
6	Shane in traffic	sustain degree/change context: relocate	Relocation to a 'main street'
7	Shane looks in at car showroom window	sustain degree/ maintain context: new perspective	
8	Shane talks to girl in street	sustain degree/ maintain context : new perspective	
9	Dog menacing	vary degree: decontextualise	Context unrecognisable in the dark so effect is to decontextualise
10	Shane reaches across to kitten up tree	vary degree: recontextualise/change context: relocate	
11	City view from treetop	sustain degree/ maintain context: new perspective	Change of horizontal angle, so this 'slows' the pace
12	Shane up tree near house with lighted window	sustain degree/ maintain context: new perspective	As above

Table 5.7 *(Continued)*

Spread	Image content	(Visual) INTER-CIRCUMSTANCE RELATIONS	Note on analysis [sustain degree] throughout except for spreads 9 and 10
13	Shane going up alley steps in background	sustain degree/change context: relocate	The end of the alley in front of Shane resembles a doorway
14	Shane crawls through wire fence	sustain degree/change context: home: in	A variation on the classic [home: in] since we have not seen the fence gap from the outside. Justified by the rear view of Shane in spread 13 and his position 'in-between' the outside and inside here (and deeper inside in the following image).
15 (verso only)	Shane inside shelter	sustain degree/maintain context: new perspective	

Note: Both [change context: relocate] and [maintain context: new perspective] – where the latter involves panning or tracking rather than change in horizontal/vertical angle or extending/shrinking frame – present the character as moving. In *Way Home*, the inter-circumstance analysis here suggests three key sections to the journey: the 'back street' section, the 'lit-up' street section and the 'home alleyways' section, with a reflective pause before the last. Alternative analyses offered for the 'back street' section link the spatial location more closely to the different activity sequences.

Table 5.8 INTER-EVENT and CONJUNCTION relations in *Way Home*.

Spread	Image content	INTER-EVENT (image)	CONJUNCTION (verbiage)	Verbiage realisation, in bold; implied links in brackets
1	Shane, kitten, city lanes, etc.		implicit succession	
2	Shane gazes at kitten tucked into jacket	unfolding: succession: within sequence	implicit succession	**(then)** *he lifts* … **(then)** *he puts it*
3	Shane looks at a pampered cat	unfolding: succession: between sequences	explicit counter-expectation	**But…** *the boy stops*
4	Shane turns from gang	unfolding: succession: between sequences	explicit counter-expectation	**But** … *the boy stops dead*
			implicit cause	**(So)** *He pushes the little catface* …
			explicit addition	**And** *he runs hard*
			explicit counter-expectation	**But** *they run hard too*
5	Shane runs from gang shadow	unfolding: succession: within sequence	implicit succession explicit simultaneous	(Between minor clauses) *Hold tight* **while** *I scare*
6	Shane in traffic	unfolding: succession	implicit succession	**(Then)** *The boy leaps*
		within sequences	explicit counter-expectation	**But** *the cat feels safe*
7	Shane looks at car showroom	unfolding: succession: between sequences	explicit addition, implicit succession	**And** *all the way down the other side* …
			explicit: counter-expectation	**but** *they've only got red*
8	Shane talks to girl in street	unfolding: succession: between sequences	explicit counter-expectation	**But** *the boy… stops*
			explicit counter-expectation	'… **but** *don't get ideas*'
			implicit succession	(between minor clauses)

Table 5.8 *(Continued)*

Spread	Image content	INTER-EVENT (image)	CONJUNCTION (verbiage)	Verbiage realisation, in bold; implied links in brackets
9	Menacing dog	unfolding: succession: between sequences	explicit counter-expectation	**But** *a dark shape comes bounding....*
			implicit succession	**(then)** *onto the fence and into...*
			explicit succession	**Then** *up and up and up*
10	Shane reaches across to kitten in tree	unfolding: succession: within sequence	implicit succession	*(then) a steady brown hand reaches out*
11	City view from treetop	projection: real	implicit succession	**(Then)** *the soft zippered jacket again*
12	Shane up tree near lit window	unfolding: succession: within sequence	implicit cause implicit succession	**(So then)** *hand over hand*
13	Shane goes up	unfolding: succession:	implicit succession	**(Then** *they go and go ...)*
	Alley steps	between sequences	explicit succession	**Then** *he crawls...*
14	Shane crawls through wire	unfolding: succession: within sequence		
15 (verso only)	Shane inside shelter	unfolding: succession: within sequence		

Table 5.9 Distribution of action and circumstantiation in *Way Home.*

Spread	Image: depicted action and circumstantiation (Motion vectors on spread 1 (very minor), 4, 5 and 6 only)	Verbiage: verbs of motion (in **bold**) and circumstantial locations of movement	Verbiage: other actional processes (material: **bold**; behavioural: roman; mental: SMALL CAPS; verbal: *italics*)
1	largely conceptual image incorporating action, perception, talking dog shadow; boy running (v. minor vectors) with open mouth possibly eyeing kitten on corrugated iron fence; tattered posters on wall, lean-tos, backs of houses, tall buildings in background, dilapidated fences and gates	way up there on the top of the fence [kitten] **scrambles** up a fence.	dog barks (S) SEES and yells the cat ... HEARS baby thing **rolls up** it growls it spits
2	largely conceptual image incorporating perception boy looks down at cat tucked into jacket	you**'re coming** home to my place. 'Shane**'s taking** ...home' Over the bins and garbage bags, past a row of seamed-up houses. 'we**'re going** way away home ...'	S laughs 'I LIKE you' ('2) He **reaches** out 'you LIKE me' (S) **strokes**... He talks and talks growls **slide** he **lifts** the cat he **puts** it ...
3	largely conceptual image incorporating perception boy looks at 'Fatcat' in window from behind iron railing; garbage bins and bags, fencing	the boy **stops**. 'let's **shove off**.'	'Take a look... I'm *telling* you...**eats** fancy mince...'
4	action legs of boy in motion (exaggerated angle) three shadowy boys, one pointing at S backstreet setting	'we**'re going** home' the boy **stops** dead. 'they**'re coming**. **Gotta get** out of here. Away from them.' he **runs** hard. they **run** hard	the boy sings the cat peers out... purrs.. 'BELIEVE me they DON'T LIKE me DON'T PANIC **act** kinda cool' glances back he **pushes** the little catface right down

Table 5.9 *(Continued)*

Spread	Image: depicted action and circumstantiation (Motion vectors on spread 1 (very minor), 4, 5 and 6 only)	Verbiage: verbs of motion (in **bold**) and circumstantial locations of movement	Verbiage: other actional processes (material: **bold**; behavioural: roman; mental: SMALL CAPS; verbal: *italics*)
5	action boy running down lane to main street – vectors of body shadows of gang loom; foreground of litter, drains and stray cat in lane	the boy **runs** fast. They **follow**. **Go!** **Go!** Up the lane, all the way they follow. **Go!** **Get away!** **Go!** To a large lit up street **going** every which way. Right to an edge of a wide shiny river of cars.	'Hold tight... I SCARE this lot'
6	action, perception and talking vectors of cars; S's body; (S with wide eyes and open mouth looking back; kitten in jacket looking out)	**leaps** out on the freeway. as he **dives** through. '**won't follow**... here'	the cat FEELS safe (S) yells
7	conceptual image, no action lit up windows of grand car showroom; far rear view of boy in front of windows	all the way down the other side of the lit up road Past a showroom. **can come** out Past busy windows and clean steps. Past a crumbling dark church. Past the sharp smell of food shops.	the boy is laughing and laughing 'take a look' the cat in the coat **sits** tight
8	largely conceptual image incorporating perception street girl and Shane (looking at each other, inferrably talking); window of restaurant, fronts of buildings, lamp post with signage, people on pavement, office block in distance	**I'm taking** it home to my place' 'Non stop, express!' But the boy called Shane **stops** again. Past the light-and-stripe of the slatted shop blinds. Past houses all lit up. Past a thin forlorn park. '**to go** home.' 'we'**re going** this way. This way home.'	a girl *asks* 'SEE they **cook** stuff right on the table in front of you... **don't get** ideas' The boy... peers

Spread	Image: depicted action and circumstantiation (Motion vectors on spread 1 (very minor), 4, 5 and 6 only)	Verbiage: verbs of motion (in **bold**) and circumstantial locations of movement	Verbiage: other actional processes (material: **bold**; behavioural: roman; mental: SMALL CAPS; verbal: *italics*)
9	conceptual image close up of snarling dog	[dog] **comes bounding** out of the long lane. out of the coat onto the fence into the tree. up and up and up. **scritches** and **scratches** to the topmost, thinnest branches.	the cat… SEES a flash HEARS the…bark, SMELLS the blood… it's **hanging** high
10	largely conceptual image incorporating perception boy up tree reaching horizontally to kitten (mutual gaze) buildings in background	'where… **gone** to…?' hand over hand, **goes** up and up towards the topmost, thinnest branches. '**come** here'	'FORGOT to *tell* you' a steady brown hand **reaches** out 'I'**d break** my neck.. you KNOW that? I'**d break** my stupid neck'
11	conceptual image view of city		'you can purr' (S) stares
12	conceptual image exaggerated angle garbage bin, boxes of empties by broken fence, high tree with boy just visible in branches, tall house with lighted upper window, sky with stars	'**gotta go** down' Hand over hand, branch over branch, down the slippery trunk To the tindery fence. (an easy jump) to the ground **takes** (the cat with no name) back down. 'we'**re going** right on home.'	'GET that… nobody **lives** in them.. why don't you look?' 'GET those people' 'I CAN SEE our place'
13	largely conceptual image wire fencing, graffiti on wall, litter, upended bins, boy ascending alleyway steps (v. minor vector)	They **go** and **go** by buildings lit up and buildings in the dark, until there's a path. 'Not far now.' '**Tread** light, … Real light.' **crawls** quickly, quickly through a hole in a fence.	the boy looks up and looks down
14	action and perception boy crawling through wire fence into gloom	'From here on…' 'we're nearly home.' 'Down there and round here … through here'	'I *promise*… like I *told* you… **hold** on real tight'

Table 5.9 *(Continued)*

Spread	Image: depicted action and circumstantiation (Motion vectors on spread 1 (very minor), 4, 5 and 6 only)	Verbiage: verbs of motion (in **bold**) and circumstantial locations of movement	Verbiage: other actional processes (material: **bold**; behavioural: roman; mental: SMALL CAPS; verbal: *italics*)
15 verso	conceptual image 'over shoulder' view of boy's shelter containing blanket, mug, milk carton, lamp, bowl, carrier bag, posters, newspapers		

Table 5.10 CHARACTER MANIFESTATION and APPEARANCE in *Way Home* images.

Spread	Shane	Kitten	Others
1	complete/appear	complete/appear	**dog** metonymic/appear
2	complete/reappear: unchanged/immediate	complete/reappear: unchanged/immediate	metonymic/reappear: unchanged/immediate
3	complete/reappear: unchanged/immediate	–	
4	metonymic/reappear: unchanged/immediate	–	**gang** metonymic/appear
5	complete/reappear: unchanged/immediate	–	metonymic/reappear
6	complete/reappear: unchanged/immediate	complete/reappear: unchanged/later	
7 car showroom	complete/reappear: varied: status: recede/immediate		
8 talks to girl	complete/reappear: varied: status: emerge/immediate		**girl** complete/appear
9	–		**dog** complete/appear (or re-appear: later)
10	complete/reappear: unchanged/later	complete/reappear: unchanged/later	
11	–		
12 lit window	metonymic/reappear: varied: status: recede		
13 up alley	complete/ reappear: unchanged/immediate		
14	complete/reappear: varied: status: emerge	complete/reappear: unchanged/later	
15 (verso only)	complete?/reappear: unchanged/immediate	–	

Table 5.11 Textual asynchrony in *Way Home*.

Spread	Stage/phase	Image content	Verbiage content	Lack of synchrony
1	Orientation/ Abstract Shane befriends homeless kitten;	dog shadow, kitten on fence, Shane yelling	dog scares kitten, Shane calls out; kitten reacts to Shane	
2	they set off home	Shane communes with cat in jacket	Shane soothes kitten Shane adopts kitten	
		–	They set off home... **over the bins and garbage bags**	verbiage runs ahead
3		**bins and garbage bags**		
	pause (reflection)	Shane gazes at Fatcat	Shane appraises Fatcat	
4	journey resumes	–	journey resumes kitten happy, Shane sings	
	Complication	Shane near gang	Shane appraises gang, **chase begins**	new stage mid page verbiage runs ahead
5		**chase**	chase	
6	Resolution	Shane and traffic	Shane dives into traffic	
7	Evaluation	–	Shane laughs at escape	genre stage not imaged
	journey resumes delay (reflection)	car showroom –	journey resumes Shane comments on cars	
	journey resumes	–	journey resumes	
8		girl talks to Shane	brief dialogue	no major phase
	delay (reflection)	–	But Shane distracted by restaurant	counter-expectant delay not imaged
9	Complication	snarling dog	dog scares cat	
		–	cat climbs to top of tree	verbiage runs ahead

Spread	Stage/phase	Image content	Verbiage content	Lack of synchrony
10	Resolution	–	Shane climbs tree	
		Shane reaches for cat	Shane reaches for cat	
11	Evaluation	–	rescued cat is happy	genre stage not imaged
		view of city	Shane looks at city	
12	pause (reflection)	low angle view of Shane in tree	**Shane appraises city buildings…**	verbiage runs behind
		lighted upper window in house	Shane sees home	image/verbiage divergence
		–	Shane climbs down tree	
13	journey resumes	Shane in alley	go past buildings **Shane crawls through fence**	verbiage runs ahead
14	arrival	**Shane crawls through fence**	Shane reassures cat Shane feels insecure	
15 (verso only)	Coda	shelter	home	

Note: Bold indicates asynchronous coupling of visual and verbal content.

Table 5.12 Verbal attitude in *Way Home*.

Spread	Verbiage	Attitude		Appraised	Source
		inscribed	invoked		
1	scrambles		−ve security	cat	Narrator
	Scaredycat!	−ve security		cat	Shane
	clever	+ve esteem		cat	Narrator
	fierce	−ve satisfaction		cat	Narrator
	growls	−ve satisfaction		cat	Narrator
	spits	−ve satisfaction		cat	Narrator
	Mad as anything!	−ve satisfaction		cat	Narrator
2	wild cat!	+ve esteem	+ve affect	cat	Shane
	Wildcat!	+ve esteem	+ve affect	cat	Shane
	laughs	+ve happiness		Shane	Narrator
	like	+ve happiness		cat	Shane
	Spitfire	+ve esteem	+ve affect	cat	Shane
	Kitten Number 1	+ve esteem	+ve affect	cat	Shane
	spiked fur	−ve security		cat	Narrator
	do; like	+ve happiness ×2		boy	Shane
	you like me	+ve happiness		cat	Shane
	strokes	+ve happiness		boy	Narrator
	scared	−ve security		cat	Narrator
	growls slide into silence		+ve security	cat	Narrator
	Bestcat	+ve esteem		cat	Shane
	he puts it deep inside his coat		+ve affect	Shane	Narrator
3	Fatcat	−ve appreciation	−ve esteem ×2	Fatcat	Shane
	loser	−ve esteem		Fatcat	Shane
	eats fancy mince		−ve esteem	Fatcat	Shane
	Disgusting	−ve sanction		Fatcat	Shane
	a joke	−ve esteem		Fatcat	Shane
4	cosy	+ve security		cat	Narrator
	sings	+ve happiness		Shane	Narrator
	purrs	+ve happiness		cat	Narrator
	nasty	−ve sanction		gang	Shane
	don't like	−ve affect		gang	Shane
	panic	−ve security		cat and Shane	Shane
	act cool; Cool		−ve security ×2	cat and Shane	Shane
	gotta get out of here		−ve security	Shane	Shane
	runs		−ve security	Shane	Narrator

Spread	Verbiage	Attitude		Appraised	Source
		inscribed	invoked		
5	*runs fast*		−ve security	Shane	Narrator
	Go! Go!		−ve security	Shane	Narrator
	Fast		+ve esteem	Shane	Narrator
	scared as anything	−ve security		Shane	Narrator
	Go! get away! Go!		−ve security ×3	Shane	Narrator
	scare this lot	−ve security		gang	Shane
6	*leaps out on the freeway*		−ve security +ve esteem	Shane	Narrator
	they won't follow		+ve security	Shane	Narrator
7	*feels safe*	+ve security		cat	Narrator
	laughing and laughing	+ve happiness		Shane	Narrator
	shiny	+ve appreciation		sportscars	Narrator
	No worries	+ve security		Shane and cat	Shane
	only red	−ve appreciation		cars	Shane
	want green		−ve satisfaction	Shane and cat	Shane
	clean	+ve appreciation		steps	Narrator
	crumbling, dark	−ve appreciation		church	Narrator
8	*cook ... stacks of meat*		+ve apprec	restaurant	Shane
	Hungry		−ve satisfaction	cat	Shane
	light and stripe	+ve appreciation		blinds	Narrator
	lit up	+ve appreciation		houses	Narrator
	thin forlorn		−ve appreciation	park	Narrator
	No worries	+ve security	−ve security	Shane and cat	Shane
9	*cruel*	−ve sanction		dog	Narrator
	angry	−ve satisfaction		dog	Narrator
	monster	−ve sanction		dog	Narrator
	hunger	−ve satisfaction		dog	Narrator
	danger	−ve appreciation		situation	Narrator
	smells the blood and the hunger and the danger		−ve security	cat	Narrator
	in a panic	−ve security		cat	Narrator
	out of the coat...into the tree...up and up		−ve security	cat	Narrator

Table 5.12 *(Continued)*

Spread	Verbiage	Attitude		Appraised	Source
		inscribed	invoked		
10	*stupid*	−ve esteem		cat	Shane
	goes up and up	+ve esteem		Shane	Narrator
	friends	+ve happiness		Shane and cat	Shane
	break my neck for you	−ve security	+ve affect	Shane	Shane
	break my stupid neck	−ve esteem	+ve affect	Shane	Shane
11	*soft ... jacket ... warmth against the chest*	+ve appreciation	+ve security, +ve satisfaction	jacket, cat	Narrator
	purr	+ve happiness	+ve happiness	cat	Shane
	Crazycat	−ve esteem	+ve affect	cat, Shane	Shane
12	*stack of big buildings*		+ve appreciation	buildings	Shane
	nobody lives in them		−ve sanction	buildings	Shane/ Narrator
	... mostly empty	−ve appreciation			
	crazy	−ve esteem		people	Shane
	cool	+ve appreciation		up in tree	Shane
	Cat Number One	+ve esteem		cat	Shane
13	*spooky*	−ve appreciation	−ve security	place; Shane	Shane
	we got each other		+ve security; +ve happiness	Shane and cat	Shane
	Tread light		−ve security	Shane	Shane
	looks up and looks down		−ve security	Shane	Shane
	quickly, quickly		−ve security	Shane	Shane
14	*okay as anything*	+ve appreciation		situation	Shane
			+ve security	Shane	
	No dogs. No fights.	+ve appreciation		situation	Shane
			+ve security	Shane and cat	
	safe	+ve security		cat	Shane
15 (verso only)	*home*		+ve security	Shane and cat	Shane

Table 5.13 Naming choices in *Way Home*. (Italics used to indicate Shane's speech)

Spread	Naming of Shane	Naming of cat
1	this boy called Shane the boy the boy called Shane	this cat with no name the little cat *Hey, you! Scaredycat!* The cat with no name this clever baby thing Such a tight little ball of fierce cat.
2	the boy called Shane the boy called Shane *Shane*	*wild cat! Wildcat!* *Spitfire.* *Kitten Number One!* the ball of spiked fur; the scared fur *Bestcat* the cat with no name *Catlegs; Cat. Cat.*
3	the boy	*Mycat*
4	the boy called Shane the boy the warm boy's (warm coat) the boy the boy called Shane	the cat with no name the cat *Animal* *Catlegs* the little catface
5	the boy	the cat in the coat *Kittycat*
6	the boy the boy's (jacket) the boy called Shane	the cat with no name

Table 5.13 *(Continued)*

Spread	Naming of Shane	Naming of cat
7	the boy	*Whiskettes* the cat in the coat
8	'...Shane?' (a girl asks) 'Bye Shane' (she calls) the boy called Shane the boy called Shane	*Hungry.* *Skinny Minny*
9		the cat with no name the cat
10	the boy called Shane	*Upcat* *stupid* *Blackeyes* *pussycat.*
11	the boy called Shane the boy called Shane	*Crazycat.*
12	the boy called Shane	*Kittycat* *Catseyes* *Cat Number One*
13	*Shane boy* the boy	
14		*Noname.* *Mycat*

Note: italicised examples are in Shane's voice.

References

Aesop ([1484] 2002) The fox and the crow. In *Aesop's Fables*. Tr. L. Gibbs. Oxford: Oxford University Press.

Agosto, D. E. (1999) One and inseparable: interdependent storytelling in picture storybooks. *Children's Literature in Education* 30.4: 267–80.

Albers, P. (2008) Theorising visual representation in children's literature. *Journal of Literacy Research* 40.2: 163–200.

Anstey, M. and Bull, G. (2000) *Reading the Visual: Written and Illustrated Children's Literature*. Sydney: Harcourt.

Anstey, M. and Bull, G. (2006) *Teaching and Learning Multiliteracies: Changing Times, Changing Literacies*. Newark, DE: International Reading Association.

Arizpe, E. and Styles, M. (2002) On a walk with Lily and Satoshi Kitamura: how children link words and pictures along the way. In G. Bull and M. Anstey (eds) *Crossing the Boundaries* 333–48. Sydney: Pearson Education Australia.

Arizpe, E. and Styles, M. (2003) *Children Reading Pictures: Interpreting Visual Texts*. With contributions from H. Bromley, K. Coulthard and K. Rabey. London and New York: Routledge Falmer.

Arnheim, R. (1974) *Art and Visual Perception: A Psychology of the Creative Eye*. Revised edition. Berkeley, CA: University of California Press.

Arnheim, R. (1982) *The Power of the Center: a Study of Composition in the Visual Arts*. Berkeley, CA: University of California Press.

Baldry, A. and Thibault, P. J. (2006). *Multimodal Transcription and Text Analysis*. London/ Oakville, CT: Equinox.

Bang, M. (1991) *Picture This: How Pictures Work*. Boston, MA: Little, Brown & Co.

Barone, D. M. (2011) *Children's Literature in the Classroom: Engaging Lifelong Readers*. New York: Guilford Press.

Barthes, R. (1977) *Image, Music, Text*. London: Fontana.

Bateman, J. A. (2007) Towards a grande paradigmatique of film: Christian Metz reloaded. *Semiotica* 167: 13–64.

Bateman, J. A. (2008) *Multimodality and Genre: a Foundation for the Systematic Analysis of Multimodal Documents*. London: Palgrave.

Bateman, J. A. (2009) Film and representation: making filmic meaning. In W. Wildgen and B. van Heusden (eds) *Metarepresentation, Self-organisation and Art* 137–62. Bern, Switzerland: Peter Lang.

Bateman, J. (2011) The decomposability of semiotic modes. In K. O'Halloran and B. Smith (eds) *Multimodal Studies: Exploring Issues and Domains* 17–32. London: Routledge.

Bednarek, M. and Martin, J. R. (eds) (2010) *New Discourse on Language: Functional Perspectives on Multimodality, Identity, and Affiliation.* London and New York: Continuum.

Bull, G. and Anstey, M. 2010 *Evolving Pedagogies: Reading and Writing in a Multimodal World.* Melbourne, Australia: Curriculum Press, Educational Services Australia.

Burnett, F. H. (1911) *The Secret Garden.* London: Heinemann.

Caple, H. (2008) Intermodal relations in image nuclear news stories. In L. Unsworth (ed.) *Multimodal Semiotics: Functional Analysis in Contexts of Education* 125–38. London and New York: Continuum.

Caple, H. (2009) *Playing with Words and Pictures: Intersemiosis in a New Genre of News Reports.* PhD thesis, University of Sydney. Available at http://hdl.handle.net/2123/7024.

Chan, E. (2011) Integrating visual and verbal meaning in multimodal text comprehension: towards a model of inter-modal relations. In S. Hood, S. Dreyfus and M. Stenglin (eds) *Semiotic Margins: Meaning in Multimodalities* 144–66. London and New York: Continuum.

Cleirigh, C. (2010) Bewildering: the stylistic deployment of layout in Maurice Sendak's *Where the Wild Things Are.* Unpublished talk given at University of Sydney SFL Research Seminar.

Coats, K. (2010) Postmodern picturebooks and the transmodern self. In L. Sipe and S. Pantaleo (eds) *Postmodern Picturebooks: Play, Parody, and Self-Referentiality* 75–88. New York and London: Routledge.

Crawford, P. A. and Hade, D. D. (2000) Inside the picture, outside the frame: semiotics and the reading of wordless picture books. *Journal of Research in Childhood Education* 15: 66–80.

Djonov, E. (2007) Website hierarchy and the interaction between content organization, webpage and navigation design: A systemic functional hypermedia discourse analysis perspective. *Information Design Journal* 15.2: 144–62.

Djonov, E., Knox, J. and Zhao, S. (forthcoming) *Tools for Critical Multimodal Analysis of Websites.* London and New York: Routledge.

Dondis, D. A. (1973) *A Primer of Visual Literacy.* Cambridge, MA: MIT Press.

Doonan, J. (1993) *Looking at Pictures in Picture Books.* Stroud, UK: Thimble Press.

Doonan, J. (1999) Drawing out ideas: a second decade of the work of Anthony Browne. *The Lion and the Unicorn* 23: 30–56.

Economou, D. (2009) *Photos in the News: Appraisal Analysis of Visual Semiosis and Verbal-visual Intersemiosis.* PhD thesis, University of Sydney. Available at http://hdl.handle.net/2123/5740.

Eggins, S. and Slade, D. (1997) *Analysing Casual Conversation.* London: Cassell.

Genette, G. (1980) *Narrative Discourse: An Essay in Method.* Tr. J. E. Lewin. Ithaca, NY: Cornell University Press.

Gill, T. (2002) *Visual and Verbal Playmates: An Exploration of Visual and Verbal Modalities in Children's Picture Books.* Honours thesis, Department of Linguistics, University of Sydney.

Golden, J. M. (1990) *The Narrative Symbol in Childhood Literature: Explorations in the Construction of Text.* Berlin and New York: Mouton de Gruyter.

Halliday, M. A. K. (1977) Text as semantic choice in social contexts. In T. A. van Dijk and J. S. Petofi (eds) *Grammars and Descriptions: Studies in Text Theory and Text Analysis* 176–226. Berlin: Walter de Gruyter.

Halliday, M. A. K. (1978) *Language as Social Semiotic.* London: Arnold.

Halliday, M.A.K. (1979) Modes of meaning and modes of expression: types of grammatical structure and their determination by different semantic functions. In D. J. Allerton,

E. Carney and D. Holdcroft (eds) *Function and Context in Linguistic Analysis: A Festschrift for William Haas* 57–79. Cambridge: Cambridge University Press.

Halliday, M. A. K. (2002) *Linguistic Studies of Text and Discourse. The Collected Works vol. 2* ed. J. Webster. London and New York: Continuum.

Halliday, M. A. K. (2003) *On Language and Linguistics. The Collected Works vol. 3* ed. J. Webster. London and New York: Continuum.

Halliday, M. A. K. (2004) *The Language of Science. The Collected Works vol. 4* ed. J. Webster. London and New York: Continuum.

Halliday, M. A. K. and Hasan, R. (1976) *Cohesion in English*. London: Longman.

Halliday, M. A. K. and Martin, J. R. (1993) *Writing Science: Literacy and Discursive Power.* London: Falmer.

Halliday, M. A. K. and Matthiessen, C. M. I. M. (2004) *Introduction to Functional Grammar.* Third edition. London: Arnold.

Halliday, M. A. K. and Matthiessen, C. M. I .M. (2009) *Systemic Functional Grammar: A First Step into Theory.* Beijing, China: Higher Education Press.

Hasan, R. (1985) *Linguistics, Language and Verbal Art.* Geelong: Deakin University Press.

Hood, S. (2008) Summary writing in academic contexts: implicating meaning in processes of change. *Linguistics and Education* 19: 351–65.

Hood, S. (2011) Body language in face-to-face teaching: a focus on textual and interpersonal meaning. In S. Dreyfus, S. Hood and M. Stenglin (eds) *Semiotic Margins: Meaning in Multimodalities* 31–52. London and New York: Continuum.

Hunt, P. (1991) *Criticism, Theory, and Children's Literature.* Oxford: Blackwell.

Iedema, R. (2003) Multimodality, resemiotization: extending the analysis of discourse as multi-semiotic practice. *Visual Communication* 2: 29–57.

Iedema, R., Feez, S. and White, P. (1994) *Media Literacy.* Write it Right Industry Research Report 2. Sydney: NSW Dept. of Education, Disadvantaged Schools Program Metropolitan East.

Jewitt, C. (ed.) (2009) *Handbook of Multimodal Analysis.* London: Routledge.

Kiefer, B. Z. (1995) *The Potential of Picturebooks: From Visual Literacy to Aesthetic Understanding.* Englewood Cliffs, NJ: Merrill.

Körner, H. (2000) *Negotiating Authority: The Logogenesis of Dialogue in Common Law Judgements.* PhD thesis, University of Sydney.

Kress and van Leeuwen, T. (1996) *Reading Images: The Grammar of Visual Design.* London: Routledge.

Kress, G. and van Leeuwen, T. (2001) *Multimodal Discourse: The Modes and Media of Contemporary Communication.* London: Arnold.

Kress, G. and van Leeuwen, T. (2002) Colour as a semiotic mode: notes for a grammar of colour. *Visual Communication* 1.3: 343–68.

Kress, G. and van Leeuwen, T. (2006) *Reading images: The Grammar of Visual Design.* Second edition. London: Routledge.

Lacey, L. E. (1986) *Art and Design in Children's Books: An Analysis of Caldecott Award Winning Illustrations.* Chicago, IL: American Library Association.

Lemke, J. (1998) Multiplying meaning: visual and verbal semiotics in scientific text. In J. R. Martin and R. Veel (eds) *Reading Science: Critical and Functional Perspectives on Discourses of Science* 87–113. London: Routledge.

Lemke, J. (2002) Travels in hypermodality. *Visual Communication* 1.3: 299–325.

Lewis, D. (1992) Looking for Julius: two children and a picture book. In K. Kimberley, M. Meek and J. Miller (eds) *New Readings: Contributions to an Understanding of Literacy* 50–63. London: A & C Black.

Lewis, D. (2001) *Reading Contemporary Picturebooks: Picturing Text*. London and New York: Routledge.

Macken-Horarick, M. (2003a) The children overboard affair. *Australian Review of Applied Linguistics* 26.2: 1–16.

Macken-Horarick, M. (2003b) Working the borders in racist discourse: the challenge of the children overboard affair in news media texts. *Social Semiotics* 13: 283–303.

Martin, J. R. (1992) *English Text: System and Structure*. Philadelphia/Amsterdam, John Benjamins.

Martin, J. R. (1996a) Evaluating disruption: symbolising theme in junior secondary narrative. In R. Hasan and G. Williams (eds) *Literacy in Society* 124–71. London and New York: Longman.

Martin, J. R. (1996b). Waves of abstraction: organising exposition. In T. Miller (ed.) *Functional Approaches to Written Text: Classroom Applications*. Paris: TESOL France and USIA.

Martin, J. R. (2006) Vernacular deconstruction: undermining spin. *DELTA (Documentação de Estudos em Linguistica Teorica e Aplicada)* 22:177–203.

Martin, J. R. (2008a) Innocence: realisation, instantiation and individuation in a Botswanan town. In A. Mahboob and N. Knight (eds) *Questioning Linguistics* 27–54. Newcastle upon Tyne, UK: Cambridge Scholars Publishing.

Martin, J. R. (2008b) Intermodal reconciliation: mates in arms. In L. Unsworth (ed.) *New Literacies and the English Curriculum: Multimodal Perspectives* 112–48. London and New York: Continuum.

Martin, J. R. (2008c) Tenderness: realisation and instantiation in a Botswanan town. In N. Nørgaard (ed.) *Systemic Functional Linguistics in Use* 30–62. Odense Working Papers in Language and Communication 29. Odense, Denmark: University of Southern Denmark, Institute of Language and Communication.

Martin, J. R. (2010) Semantic variation: modelling system, text and affiliation in social semiosis. In M. Bednarek and J. R. Martin (eds) *New Discourse on Language: Functional Perspectives on Multimodality, Identity and Affiliation* 1–34. London and New York: Continuum.

Martin, J. R. (2011) Multimodal semiotics: theoretical challenges. In S. Dreyfus, S. Hood and M. Stenglin (eds) *Semiotic Margins: Meaning in Multimodalities* 243–70. London and New York: Continuum.

Martin, J. R. and Matthiessen, C. M. I. M. (1991) Systemic typology and topology. In F. Christie (ed.) *Literacy in Social Processes: Papers from the Inaugural Australian Systemic Functional Linguistics Conference, Deakin University January 1990* 345–83. Darwin, Australia: Centre for Studies of Language in Education, Northern Territory University.

Martin, J. R. and Rose, D. (2007) *Working with Discourse: Meaning Beyond the Clause*. London and New York: Continuum.

Martin, J. R. and Rose, D. (2008) *Genre Relations: Mapping Culture*. London and Oakville, CT: Equinox.

Martin, J. R. and White, P. (2005) *The Language of Evaluation: Appraisal in English*. Basingstoke, UK: Palgrave Macmillan.

Martinec, R. (2000) Types of process in action. *Semiotica* 103.3: 243–68.

Martinec, R. (2001) Interpersonal resources in action. *Semiotica* 135.1: 117–45.

Martinec, R. and Salway, A. (2005) A system for image–text relations in new (and old) media. *Visual Communication* 4.3: 337–71.

McCloud, S. ([1993] 1994) *Understanding Comics: The Invisible Art*. New York: HarperPerennial. First published by Kitchen Sink Press.

Meek, M. (1988) *How Texts Teach What Readers Learn*. South Woodchester, UK: Thimble Press.

Michaels, W. and Walsh, M. (1990) *Up and Away: Using Picture Books*. Melbourne, Australia: Oxford University Press.

Moebius, W. (1986) Introduction to picture book codes. *Word and Image* 2:141–51.

Mullins, K. (2009) Crossing boundaries and forming identity in Beatrix Potter's *The Tale of Peter Rabbit* and *The Tale of Benjamin Bunny*. *The Looking Glass: New Perspectives on Children's Literature* 13: 1–9.

Nikolajeva, M. and Scott, C. (2001) *How Picture Books Work*. New York: Garland.

Nodelman, P. (1988) *Words about Pictures: The Narrative Art of Children's Picture Books*. Athens, GA: University of Georgia Press.

Nodelman, P. ([1999] 2005) Decoding the images: illustration and picture books. In P. Hunt (ed.) *Understanding Children's Literature: Key Essays from the International Companion Encyclopedia of Children's Literature*, 69–80. Second edition. London and New York: Routledge.

Nodelman, P. and Reimer, M. (2003) *The Pleasures of Children's Literature*. Third edition. Boston, MA: Allyn & Bacon.

O'Halloran, K. (2004) *Multimodal Discourse Analysis: Systemic–Functional Perspectives*. London: Continuum.

O'Halloran, K. (2008) Systemic-functional multimodal discourse analysis (SF-MDA): constructing ideational meaning using language and visual imagery. *Visual Communication* 7.4: 443–75.

O'Toole, M. (1994) *The Language of Displayed Art*. London: Leicester University Press.

O'Toole, M. (1995) A systemic–functional semiotics of art. In P. H. Fries and M. Gregory (eds) *Discourse in Society: Systemic Functional Perspectives. Meaning and Choice in Language: Studies for Michael Halliday*, 159–81. Norwood, NJ: Ablex.

Painter, C. (2007) Children's picture book narratives: reading sequences of images. In A. McCabe, M. O'Donnell and R. Whittaker (eds) *Advances in Language and Education* 40–59. London and New York: Continuum.

Painter, C. (2008) The role of colour in children's picture books: choices in AMBIENCE. In L. Unsworth (ed.) *New Literacies and the English Curriculum: Multimodal Perspectives* 89–111. London and New York: Continuum.

Painter, C. and Martin, J. R. (2011) Intermodal complementarity: modelling affordances across image and verbiage in children's picture books. *Studies in Systemic Functional Linguistics and Discourse Analysis (III)*, 132–58. Beijing, China: Higher Education Press.

Pantaleo, S. (2002) Grade I students meet David Wiesner's three pigs. *Journal of Children's Literature* 28.2: 72–84.

Pantaleo, S. (2004) Young children interpret the metafictive in Anthony Browne's *Voices in the Park*. *Journal of Early Childhood Literacy* 4.2: 211–33.

Pantaleo, S. (2008) *Exploring Student Response to Contemporary Picturebooks*. Toronto, Canada: University of Toronto Press.

Peim, N. (2005) The life of signs in visual history. In U. Mietzner, K. P. F. Myers, and N. A. Peim (eds) *Visualising History: Images of Education* 7–34. Frankfurt, Germany: Peter Lang.

Poynton, C. (1985) *Language and Gender: Making the Difference*. Geelong, Australia: Deakin University Press.

Präkel, D. (2006) *Composition*. London: AVA.

Rose, D. (2011) Meaning beyond the margins: learning to interact with books. In S. Dreyfus, S. Hood and M. Stenglin (eds) *Semiotic Margins: Meaning in Multimodalities* 177–209. London and New York: Continuum.

Rothery, J. (1996) *Making Changes: Developing an Educational Linguistics*. In R. Hasan and G. Williams (eds) *Literacy in Society* 86–123. London and New York: Longman.

Royce, T. D. (1998) Synergy on the page: exploring intersemiotic complementarity in page-based multimodal text. *JASFL Occasional Papers* 1: 25–50.

Royce, T. D. and Bowcher, W. L. (2007) *New Directions in the Analysis of Multimodal Discourse.* Mahwah, NJ: Lawrence Erlbaum Associates.

Schwarcz, J. (1982) *Ways of the Illustrator: Visual Communication in Children's Literature.* Chicago, IL: American Library Association.

Schwarcz, J. and Schwarcz, C. (1991) *The Picture Book Comes of Age: Looking at Childhood through the Art of Illustration.* Chicago, IL: American Library Association.

Scott, C. (1994) Clothed in nature or nature clothed: dress as metaphor in the illustrations of Beatrix Potter and C. M. Barker. *Children's Literature* 22: 70–89.

Serafini, F. (2010) Reading multimodal texts: perceptual, structural and ideiological perspectives. *Children's Literature in Education* 41: 85–104.

Sipe, L. (1998) How picture books work: a semiotically framed theory of text-picture relationships. *Children's Literature in Education* 29.2: 97–108.

Sipe, L. (2011) The art of the picturebook. In S. Wolf, P. Enciso, K. Coats and C. Jenkins (eds) *Handbook of Research in Children's and Young Adult Literature.* New York and London: Routledge: 238–51.

Sipe, L. and Pantaleo, S. (eds) (2008) *Postmodern Picturebooks: Play, Parody, and Self-Referentiality.* New York and London: Routledge.

Spitz, E. (1999) *Inside Picture Books.* New Haven, CT and London: Yale University Press.

Stenglin, M. (2004). *Packaging Curiosities: Towards a Grammar of Three-dimensional Space.* PhD thesis, University of Sydney. Available at: http://ses.library.usyd.edu.au/handle/2123/635.

Stenglin, M. (2008) Binding: a resource for exploring interpersonal meaning in 3D space. *Social Semiotics* 18.4: 425–47.

Stephens, J. (1992) *Language and Ideology in Children's Fiction.* Harlow, UK and New York: Longman.

Stephens, J. and Watson, K. (eds) (1994) *From Picture Book to Literary Theory.* Sydney: St Clair Press.

Styles, M. and Arizpe, E. (2001) 'A Gorilla with Grandpa's Eyes': How children interpret visual texts – a case study of Anthony Browne's *Zoo. Children's Literature in Education* 32.4: 261–81.

Thibault, P. J. (2000). The multimodal transcription of a television advertisement. In A. Baldry (ed.) *Multimodality and Multimediality in the Distance Learning Age* 311–85. Campobasso, Italy: Palladino Editore.

Tian, Ping (2011) *Multimodal Evaluation: Sense and Sensibility in Anthony Browne's Picture Books.* PhD thesis, University of Sydney.

Toolan, M. (2001) *Narrative: A Critical Linguistic Introduction.* Second edition. London and New York: Routledge.

Torr, J. (2004) Talking about picture books: the influence of maternal education on four-year-old children's talk with mothers and preschool teachers. *Journal of Early Childhood Literacy* 4.2: 181–210.

Torr, J. (2008) Multimodal texts and emergent literacy. In L. Unsworth (ed.) *New Literacies and the English Curriculum* 47–66. London and New York: Continuum.

Torr, J. and Clugston, L. (1999) A comparison between informational and narrative picture books as a context for reasoning between mothers and four year old children. *Early Child Development and Care* 159: 25–41.

Tseng, Chiaoi (2009*) Cohesion in Film and the Construction of Filmic Thematic Configuration: A Functional Perspective.* PhD dissertation, University of Bremen, Germany.

Unsworth, L. and Cleirigh, C. (2009). Multimodality and reading: the construction of meaning through image–text interaction. In C. Jewitt (ed.) *Handbook of Multimodal Analysis* 151–64. London: Routledge.
Unsworth, L. and Wheeler, J. (2002) Re-valuing the role of images in reviewing picture books. *Reading: Language and Literacy* 36.2: 68–74.
van Leeuwen, T. (1991) Conjunction structure in documentary film and television. *Continuum: Journal of Media and Cultural Studies* 5: 76–114.
van Leeuwen, T. (1999) *Speech, Music, Sound*. London: Macmillan.
van Leeuwen, T. (2005a) *Introducing Social Semiotics*. London: Routledge.
van Leeuwen, T. (2005b) Typographic meaning. *Visual Communication* 4.2: 137–43.
van Leeuwen, T. (2009) Parametric systems: the case of voice quality. In C. Jewitt (ed.) *The Routledge Handbook of Multimodal Analysis* 68–77. London and New York: Routledge.
van Leeuwen, T. (2011) *The Language of Colour: An Introduction*. London: Routledge.
Ventola, E., Charles, C. and Kaltenbacher, M. (eds) (2004) *Perspectives on Multimodality*. Amsterdam and Philadelphia, PA: John Benjamins.
Wall, B. (1991) *The Narrator's Voice: The Dilemma of Children's Fiction*. New York: St. Martin's Press.
Welch, A. (2005) *The Illustration of Facial Affect in Children's Literature*. Unpublished BA Hons coursework paper, University of Sydney.
Williams, G. (1998) Children entering literate worlds. In F. Christie and R. Missan (eds) *Literacy in Schooling* 18–46. London: Routledge.
Williams, G. (2001) Literacy pedagogy prior to schooling: relations between social positioning and semantic variation. In A. Morais, H. Baillie and B. Thomas (eds) *Towards a Sociology of Pedagogy: the Contribution of Basil Bernstein to Research*. New York: Peter Lang.
Yannicopoulou, A. (2010) Focalisation in children's picture books: who sees in words and pictures? In M. Cadden (ed.) *Telling Children's Stories: Narrative Theory and Children's Literature* 65–85. Lincoln, NE: University of Nebraska Press.
Zhao, Sumin (2011) *Learning through Multimedia Interaction: the Construal of Primary Social Science Knowledge in Web-Based Digital Learning Materials*. PhD thesis, University of Sydney.

Picture books

Ahlberg, J. and Ahlberg, A. ([1978] 1989) *Each Peach Pear Plum*. London: Penguin.
Ahlberg, J. and Ahlberg, A. ([1982] 1984) *The Baby's Catalogue*. Harmondsworth, UK: Picture Puffins.
Ahlberg, J. and Briggs, R. (2001) *The Adventures of Bert*. New York: Viking.
Allen, P. (1991) *Black Dog*. Ringwood, Australia: Viking.
Allen, P. (1982) *Who Sank the Boat?* Melbourne, Australia: Nelson.
Baillie, A. and Tanner, J. (illus.) ([1988] 1991) *Drac and the Gremlin*. Camberwell, Australia: Puffin Books.
Baker, Jeannie (1991) *Window*. London: Julia MacRae Books.
Briggs, R. (1978) *The Snowman*. London: Hamish Hamilton.
Briggs, R. (1984) *The Tinpot Foreign General and the Old Iron Woman*. London: Hamish Hamilton.
Briggs, R. (1994) *The Bear*. London: Red Fox.
Brown, M. W. and Hurd, C. (illus.) (1947) *Goodnight Moon*. New York: Harper.
Browne, A. (illus.) (1981). *Hansel and Gretel*. London: Julia MacRae.

Browne, A. ([1983] 1987) *Gorilla.* London: Walker Books.

Browne, A. ([1986] 1996) *Piggybook.* London: Walker Books.

Browne, A. (1989) *The Tunnel.* London: Julia MacRae Books.

Browne, A. (1990) *Changes.* London: Julia MacRae Books.

Browne, A. (1992) *Zoo.* London: Julia MacRae Books.

Browne, A. (1998) *Voices in the Park.* London: Doubleday.

Browne, A. (2000) *My Dad.* London: Doubleday.

Browne, A. (2004) *Into the Forest.* London: Walker Books.

Browne, A. (2008) *Little Beauty.* London: Walker Books.

Bunting, E. and Wiesner, D. (illus.) (1994) *Night of the Gargoyles.* New York: Clarion Books, Houghton Mifflin.

Burningham, J. (1977) *Come Away From the Water, Shirley.* London: Jonathan Cape.

Burningham, J. ([1984] 1988) *Granpa.* Harmondsworth, UK: Picture Puffins.

Burningham, J. (1999) *Whadayamean.* London: Jonathan Cape.

Caswell, B. and Ottley, M. (illus.) (2003) *Hyram and B.* Sydney: Hodder Children's Books.

Child, L. (2002) *Who's Afraid of the Big Bad Book?* London: Hodder Children's Books.

Cole, B. ([1987] 1997) *Prince Cinders.* London: Puffin Books.

Cooper, H. (1996) *The Baby Who Wouldn't Go To Bed.* London: Doubleday.

Cooke, T. and Oxenbury, H. (illus.) (1994) *So Much.* London: Walker Books.

Crew, G. and Gouldthorpe, P. (illus.) (1993) *First Light.* Melbourne, Australia: Lothian.

Crew, G. and Scott, A. (illus.) (2000) *In My Father's Room.* Sydney: Hodder Children's Books.

Crew, G. and Rogers, G. (illus.) (1992) *Lucy's Bay.* Nundah, Australia: Jam Roll Press.

Crew, G. and Woolman, S. (illus.) (1994) *The Watertower.* Flinders Park, Australia: ERA Publications.

Falconer, I. (2000) *Olivia.* London: Simon and Schuster.

Fox, M. and Vivas, J. (illus.) ([1983] 2004) *Possum Magic.* Sydney: Omnibus Books.

Gaiman, N. and McKean, D. (illus.) (2003) *The Wolves in the Walls.* London: Bloomsbury Publishing.

Gallaz, C. and Innocenti, R. (illus.) (1985) *Rose Blanche.* London, Cape.

Gleeson, L. and Greder, A (illus.) (1992) *Uncle David.* Sydney: Ashton Scholastic.

Gleeson, L. and Greder, A (illus.) (1995) *The Princess and the Perfect Dish.* Sydney: Scholastic Australia.

Gleeson, L. and Greder, A (illus.) (1999) *The Great Bear.* Sydney: Scholastic Press.

Gravett, E. (2005) *Wolves.* London: Macmillan, 2005.

Hathorn, L. and Rogers, G. (illus.) (1994) *Way Home.* Sydney: Red Fox.

Henkes, K. ([2004] 2006) *Kitten's First Full Moon.* London: Simon & Schuster.

Hughes, S. (1984) *An Evening at Alfie's.* London: Bodley Head.

Hutchins, P. (1968) *Rosie's Walk.* London: Bodley Head.

Hutchins, P. (1976) *Don't Forget the Bacon.* London: Bodley Head.

Hutchins, P. (1983) *You'll Soon Grow into Them, Titch.* London: Bodley Head.

Jennings, P. and Gouldthorpe, P. (illus.) ([1992] 1994) *Grandad's Gifts.* Ringwood, Australia: Puffin Books.

Jorgensen, N. and Harrison-Lever, B. (illus.) (2002) *In Flanders Fields.* Fremantle, Australia: Sandcastle Books.

Kitamura, S. (1997) *Lily Takes a Walk.* London: Happy Cat Books.

Lunn, H. and Pignataro, A. (illus.) (2002) *Waiting for Mum.* Sydney: Scholastic.

Machin, S. and Vivas, J. (illus.) (1989) *I Went Walking.* Norwood, SA: Omnibus Books.

McKee, D. (1982) *I Hate My Teddy Bear.* London: Andersen Press.

McKee, D. ([1980] 2004) *Not Now, Bernard.* London: Andersen Press.

Marsden, J and Tan, S. (illus.) (1998) *The Rabbits*. Melbourne, Australia: Lothian Books.

Norman, L. and Young, N. (illus.) (1988) *Grandpa*. Sydney: Margaret Hamilton Books.

Ormerod, J. ([1981] 1983) *Sunshine*. Harmondsworth, UK: Puffin Books.

Ottley, M. (1995) *What Faust Saw*. Sydney: Hodder and Stoughton.

Potter, B. (1908) *The Tale of Jemima Puddle Duck*. London: Frederick Warne.

Potter, B. (1902) *The Tale of Peter Rabbit*. London: Frederick Warne.

Rowe, J. (2006) *Whose Family?* Sydney: ABC Books.

Sendak, M. (1963) *Where the Wild Things Are*. New York: Harper & Row.

Thompson, C. (2004) *The Violin Man*. Sydney: Hodder Headline.

Van Allsburg, C. (1981) *Jumanji*. Boston, MA: Houghton Mifflin.

Van Allsburg, C. (1990) *Just a Dream*. Boston, MA: Houghton Mifflin.

Wagner, J. and Brooks, R. (illus.) (1977) *John Brown, Rose and the Midnight Cat*. Harmondsworth, UK: Penguin.

Wild, M. and Vivas, J. (illus.) (1991) *Let the Celebrations Begin*. Norwood, Australia: Omnibus.

Wild, M. and Brooks, R. (illus.) (2000) *Fox*. Sydney: Allen and Unwin.

Winton, T. and Louise, K. (1998) *The Deep*. Fremantle, Australia: Sandcastle Books.

Wolfer, D. and Harrison-Lever, B. (illus.) (2005) *Photographs in the Mud*. Fremantle, Australia: Fremantle Arts Centre Press.

Index

action   10, 55, 58, 68ff, 138, 139, 161–4
activity sequence   71–4, 80–97
Adventures of Bert, The (Ahlberg & Briggs)
   20, 31
affect   19, 24, 30, 104, 117, 137, 142
   see also AMBIENCE
affiliation   137, 140–41
affordance   5, 133
AMBIENCE   35ff, 137, 142
   system   36
   textual distribution   40–41
An Evening at Alfie's (Hughes)   33, 76, 96, 97
APPEARANCE   58ff, 165
   ATTRIBUTION variation   64ff
   realisations   65
   STATUS variation   61ff
   system   61, 64
attitude   168–70
ATTRIBUTION *see* APPEARANCE

Baby Who Wouldn't Go to Bed, The
   (Cooper)   ix, 17, 19, 33, 53, 54, 58, 60,
   63, 97, 113, 135
Baby's Catalogue, The (Ahlberg & Ahlberg)
   31
Bear, The (Briggs)   31, 73, 76
bimodal *see* intermodality, multimmodality
black and white   41ff
Black Dog (Allen)   31
bound images   105ff

caricature   34
cause and effect sequences   74–5

centrifocal focus groups   113ff
   system   113
Changes (Browne)   65, 66
CHARACTER APPEARNCE *see*
   APPEARANCE
CHARACTER MANIFESTATION *see*
   MANIFESTATION
CHARACTER RELATIONS   66–8, 138,
   140
   realisations   68
   system   67
children's literature (criticism)   4–6
circumstances   55, 78ff, 138, 161–4
cline (system)   10, 36
co-classification   66
colour *see* AMBIENCE
Come away from the Water, Shirley
   (Burningham)   19, 31
commitment   134ff, 141–2
complementary layouts   93ff
conceptual processes   56
contact (FOCALISATION)   20–21
CONTACT   17, 18–19
counter-expectation   73–4
coupling   143ff

depiction style *see* PATHOS
Deep, The (Winton & Louise)   33
Don't Forget the Bacon (Hutchins)   98, 99,
   100
double page spread   11–12
Drac and the Gremlin (Baillie & Tanner)
   17, 20, 21, 22, 33, 78, 113